Leslie Joseph = Margaret Douglas
B 12.8.1919
M 6.12.1958

David Joseph
B 28.3.1961

Robert Joseph
B 29.5.1962
M 19.5.1984

Stephen Joseph
B 13.6.1921
D 12.9.1967

Shirley Joseph = Michael Savage
B 26.9.1927
M 13.3.1948
Divorced 1968

Nicholas Savage = Janet Berry
B 27.7.1950
M 10.4.1974   B 3.5.1946

Polly Savage
B 19.10.1979

= Geoffrey Simmonds
M 6.5.1970
Divorced
Toby Simmonds
B 11.10.1970
Sophie Simmonds
B 7.2.1972

Charlotte Savage = Oliver Jameson-Till
B 5.6.1952
M 24.6.1972
Divorced 10.8.77

= Antony Rowe
M. 11.1.1985

Adam Joseph
B 13.8.1966

Richard Joseph = Elizabeth Berry
B 3.9.1940   B 10.4.1944
M 3.3.1962

Rachel Joseph
B 19.4.1969

Charlotte Joseph = Neil Primrose
B 4.6.1952   B 12.9.1950
M 29.12.1973   Divorced 29.6.1983
Michael Anthony 19.7.1985

Hugh Joseph = Juliet Ashworth
B 13.12.1954   B 9.5.1954
M 2.3.1982

Esther Joseph
B 22.7.1983

Peter Joseph = Christine Fitzgerald
B 20.9.1931   B 30.9.1949
M 4.8.1979

Michael Joseph
B 17.8.1984

Michael Joseph
26.7.1933

Anthea Chorlton
B 30.4.1962

Audrey Joseph = Christopher Chorlton
B 2.5.1935   B 25.7.1931
M 2.11.1957

Stuart Chorlton
B 12.11.1963

David Joseph
B 14.5.1957

Adam Joseph
B 19.1.1981

Jonathan Joseph = Jennifer Stone
B 2.7.1950
M 7.3.1972
Divorced 8.1977

= Carole Milton
B 5.2.1952
M 25.2.1979

Paul Joseph
B 27.10.1983

Anthony Joseph
B 7.11.1954
D 9.11.1954

Richard Joseph
B 6.6.1956

Jeremy Joseph = Jill Abrahamson
B 19.6.1958   B28.5.1959
M 11.8.1985

MICHAEL JOSEPH
MASTER OF WORDS

With love to Elizabeth
Adam and Rachel

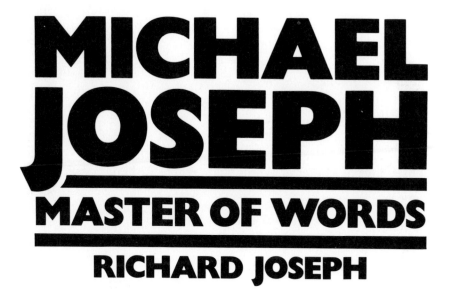

MICHAEL JOSEPH
MASTER OF WORDS
RICHARD JOSEPH

With a prologue by
Monica Dickens

Ashford Press Publishing
Southampton
1986

Published by   Ashford Press Publishing 1986
                      1 Church Road
                      Shedfield
                      Hampshire
                      SO3 2HW

Printed in Great Britain

British Library Cataloguing in Publication Data

Joseph Richard
    Michael Joseph: master of words.
      1.Joseph, Michael, 1897 – 1958 2. Publishers and publishing—Great
      Britain—Biography
      I Title
      070.5'092'4   Z 325.J7/

    ISBN 0-907069-66-5

Contents

Illustrations

Introduction

My father used to say that luck played a large part in his successes. On reflection he passed a little of this on to me, for I happened to be in the right place and at the right time to be handed a trunk of his memorabilia. This large chest was one of those used in the heyday of ocean voyages, bespattered with dirty Cunard and P & O labels, and filled to the brim with literary riches.

Amongst the many press cuttings of reviews, articles and stories, were draft typescripts and souvenirs of his literary achievements. Best of all, there were boxes of original home-made 16mm films, many of them now fifty-five years old, but despite their age, the images are intact and it has been possible to reproduce a few frames in this book. To those who can recall the nineteen-thirties they will, I am sure, invoke waves of nostalgia.

Having briefly examined the contents of the trunk, I thought at first, that it would be easy to verify the details, for the envelopes and folders were clearly labelled. However, the more I looked, the more difficult the task became.

I soon established one fact, that no other writer has yet attempted to write the life history of this well known publisher. Perhaps it was his residual fame, and the continuance of his publishing firm that made them hesitate, or possibly many of the authors who knew him well, were waiting for another to do the job.

As can be seen from the family tree, illustrated on the end-papers of this book, many of the relatives who knew him well have long since departed from this world. The information gleaned is at times therefore sketchy and to a very large extent, I've had to rely on information in letters, articles and books. Many of the anecdotes and stories recounted here are in print for the first time. And I'm sure you will agree that the extracts cited from his articles and books contribute to a better understanding of this quite remarkable and talented man.

Of Michael's sixty years I only knew him for eighteen, and of those, the first five can be quickly discounted, with his war activities taking priority. Thereafter his writing, running his business in London, and trips overseas, kept him occupied to such an extent that we had few opportunities to get to know one another well. Soon came boarding school for me, further cutting down our time together to my school holidays. Even from this short relationship, I acquired many vivid memories, some of which were sad, but others very happy.

With these restrictions in mind, I set out to prepare this biography, and it is through his hoard of press cuttings and other memorabilia, that I have been able to portray his early life. They demonstrate just how wide his talents were. He is best remembered, of course for his publishing achievements but less well known as the prolific writer he was. The extent and range of subjects he wrote about provided the idea for the title *Michael Joseph – Master of Words,* and before setting out to read this book, I recommend a quick look through the bibliography. It quickly illustrates that he was much more than just a publisher.

His varied interests led me to approach his biography on a thematic ·basis. Although the chapters are inextricably interwoven, this representation of Michael's life emphasises the strength of his abilities much more than a chronological one. Michael was an extremely gregarious man, with numerous friends all over the world. He became a very well known personality but like all of us he had a private life out of public view. This is where the book starts.

The main theme that stands out from all his achievements is that Michael should be remembered for his writing and penmanship, rather than for founding one of the country's most prestigious publishing companies. His first book was published in 1923 and by 1953 when he was 56, seventeen titles had appeared in his name. He began by writing about how one should set about writing short stories, and followed this up with other titles, developing the theme into other areas of authorship.

His first article appeared in the *Daily Express* in 1916, when he was just 19 and fighting in the trenches during World War I. From then to 1954 he penned over 300 journalistic pieces which newspapers and journals published both here and overseas. From the early twenties, when his articles about authorship first became a regular feature, he became an authority on a wide range of topics.

His influence in journalism and publishing was considerably enhanced when he became a literary agent, joining Curtis Brown in 1924. His command and mastery of the English language quickly enabled him to establish the respect of authors, at the same time gaining credence with successful publishers (among them Victor Gollancz) who soon realised that when he submitted a novel, it really was one that ought to be published. No doubt the success of his own books helped.

It is a fact that, as time passes, fewer people will connect him with anything other than the publishing company he founded. This year has seen Michael Joseph Ltd celebrate its Golden Anniversary with appropriate publicity, for it has indeed been very successful. The main reason for writing this book to coincide with these celebrations is to record though briefly and sometimes only superficially, the full range of Michael's personal achievements.

Throughout his life Michael adored cats. To him they were an antidote to the pressures of life and his affinity with them and his understanding of feline behaviour was second to none. Perhaps what endeared him most to cat lovers everywhere was the expression of his feelings for and empathy with Charles, his favourite Siamese, in his book *Charles – The Story of a Friendship*.

What follows is the first full biography of Michael Joseph, a master of words.

Richard Joseph

Cliddesden
June 1986

Notable dates in Michael Joseph's life

1897 Born 26 September
1909 Joined City of London School
1914 Left City of London School
1915 Temporary Commission 2nd Lt 8th Btn Wiltshire Regiment
1916 Transferred to Machine Gun Corps
1916 Promoted Lieutenant
1916 Served BEF France 56th Company Machine Gun Corps – July
      1917
1917 Promoted Acting Captain
1918 Married Hermione Gingold
1919 First son born, Leslie
1920 Left *Nash* weekly to join Hutchinson & Co
1921 Second son born, Stephen
1923 *Short Story Writing for Profit* published
1924 Left Hutchinson & Co to join Curtis Brown
      Journalism for Profit published
      Joined Savage Club
1925 *The Commercial Side of Literature* published
1925 *How to Write a Short Story* published
1926 Divorced Hermione Gingold
      Married Edna Frost
1927 First daughter born, Shirley
1928 *The Magazine Story* published
      How to Write Serial Fiction published
1929 *The Autobiography of a Journalist* published
1930 *Cats Company* published
      Complete Writing for Profit published
      Foujita – *Book of Cats* published
      Moved into 15 Regent's Park Terrace
1931 *This Writing Business* published
1932 *Puss in Books* published
1933 *Heads or Tails* published
1935 Left Curtis Brown
      Founded Michael Joseph Ltd
      Moved to Acacia Road, St John's Wood
1938 Severed financial agreement with Gollancz
1939 Visited America, sailing on the *Mauretania*
1940 Commissioned Lieutenant Army Officers' Emergency Reserve
      Third son born, Richard

1941	Invalided out of Army
	Moved to Copyhold Farm
1942	*The Sword in the Scabbard* published
1943	*Charles – The Story of a Friendship* published
1946	Moved to The Garden House, Stanford Dingley
1949	His second wife, Edna dies
	The Adventure of Publishing published
	Moved to 13 Gower Mews
1950	Married Anthea Hodson
1951	Bought first race horse, Midshipman Hornblower
	Visited South Africa
1952	Second daughter born, Charlotte
	Best Cat Stories published
1953	Visited America again
1954	Fourth son born, Hugh
	Sells publishing company to Illustrated Newspapers Group
1957	Visited America
1958	Died 15 March 1958

Prologue
by
Monica Dickens

Michael Joseph changed my life. He gave me my start as a writer, forty-seven years ago. Now, almost forty books later, the memories of that astonishing excitement are still very clear.

In 1937, having dropped out of the debutante scene, I was working as a cook and maid in many different basements, exhausted but fairly content, with no thought of ever writing, because Charles Dickens had done that for all time in our family.

At a dance at Paddington Baths, I met Charles Pick, then a salesman for the new firm of Michael Joseph.

"Why don't you write a book about what you're doing?" he said. "Come and see my boss on your next afternoon off."

Michael welcomed me at the top of the stairs, charming, amused, gratifyingly interested in this insignificant cook-general, who had almost been too scared to come. As he talked encouragingly, I began to see that perhaps this new world could really be mine. Captivated by this persuasive man, I was jealous of Daphne du Maurier's picture on the wall, signed, "To Michael, with love."

"Write the story of your adventures," he said, "and we'll publish it."

"All right." I knew enough to grab at an opportunity. After signing a contract (I thought that all new authors were wooed like this), I turned back at the front door to ask, "Suppose I can't write?"

"Then you tell us the story, and we'll write it."

If he meant to nettle me, it worked. "I'll do it myself," I thought, and went home and wrote *One Pair of Hands* in three weeks in pencil in old exercise books.

Michael's guidance was not editorial, but from one author to another. When I got bogged down in beautiful formal phrases, as new writers do, he gave me a superb piece of advice, which I've passed on to many new young writers.

"Don't try so hard," he said. "Just imagine you're bursting into a room full of people you know quite well, and you're saying, "Listen to what happened to me!""

We became loving friends. When I took him home, I introduced him to my mother as "My publisher". Afterwards, playing something seductive on the piano, he laughed at me.

"Aren't you allowed to have boy friends?"

He was happily married. He was playing a game, so I played it too, pretending, caught up in the fun and excitement of suddenly being an author.

He hung my picture alongside Daphne's, and when he went to war, as I did, he guided and encouraged me through many more books, and always did me the favour of laughing at me when I got too serious.

Chapter 1

The Private Life
of a Public Man
1897–1958

*'Authors are easy enough to get on with, if you are fond
of children'.*
Michael Joseph, Strand Magazine 1949

Moss and Rebecca Joseph were living at 130 Osbaldeston Road in North London when they decided to start a family. Moss, a man of many interests, had led a varied life up to 1897 and was to continue doing so. He was not settled in any profession, nor was he an academic and his life style was not one which was conducive to encouraging any literary minded offspring.

Earlier in his life Moss had been employed in the tyre business with the Davies Tyre Company. A restless man, he soon left this occupation for an entirely different one in the cinematic world. He and his two brothers, Godfrey and Lionel, were involved in running a cinema near Marble Arch but this turned out to be another short-lived venture. They received a number of criticisms from the audiences that the flickering images gave them headaches. Not surprising for the speed of the film through the projector was then only sixteen frames a second. Today, the standard speed is twenty-four frames. Hence the expression 'going to the flicks' became a common phrase. Moss thought about this and grew apprehensive that these flickering images on the screen might eventually make people go blind, and for that reason quit the business before the complaints became serious.

Another of Moss Joseph's ventures was connected with Wembley Stadium though this interest occurred many years later. The story illustrates Moss's colourful life. This magnificent arena, now much in the public's eye due to the riotous behaviour of football fans was built as part of the British Empire Exhibitions in 1924 and 1925. Moss, again with his brothers Godfrey and Lionel, won the concession to manage the cloakrooms, car parks and toilets for the two years involved. They sought an official company name which would reflect the nature of their business. A number of rather rude names for their company were suggested to the

Register of Companies but they were all rejected. Finally, they settled in 1924 upon *Cave (Wembley) Ltd,* and for the next year, *Park (Wembley) Ltd.* By reversing the spelling of the first names, you will understand their perverse sense of humour.

They were also on to a very lucrative enterprise. For Gibbs presented their companies with thousands of free bars of soap – and perhaps not surprisingly, the companies made a charge for the use of the toilets, and cloakrooms. The fee then was a halfpenny for the toilets, a penny for the cloakrooms and fourpence to one shilling for parking (5 pence today). They also had the management of the Lost Property Office. In 1925, over 272,000 cloakroom tickets were issued and at a penny a time generated quite some income for they only had to pay 10 per cent for the concession. Michael, very much aware of these stories and his connections, avoided mentioning them in the reviews of Wembley which he wrote for publication in the *North Staffordshire Labour News* and other local papers. It would appear that Moss and his brothers did very well out of these ventures.

Moss then decided to go to South Africa where he could study the precious stones business. He became very enthusiastic about the possibilities and returned home to set up his new company. He remained a diamond merchant in Hatton Garden until he died, when the business passed on to Michael's brother Lionel.

These are examples of the background against which Michael was brought up, and which did little to suggest that there would be any literary talent in the family.

*   *   *

The year Michael was born, 1897, Queen Victoria was celebrating her Diamond Jubilee. There were many celebrations that year and it may have seemed fitting for Moss Joseph to start a family then. He was twenty-four and though not well off, had a sufficient income. Rebecca gave birth to Michael at home and the arrival of Moss's first child was the cause for family celebrations, as he himself was from a large family, having three sisters and three brothers. However, Moss and Rebecca did not follow the family tradition and it was another three years or so before their second son was born. Michael and Lionel were to be their only offspring.

One of the memories that Michael had of his time in Osbaldeston Road, was the cat given to him as a pet which was much admired by all the family, particularly his brother. The long association with cats started

2

here, for he grew very fond of Zulu feeding and grooming him so much that at times they were inseparable. Lionel openly coveted Zulu and frequently quarrelled with Michael over him; he desperately wanted to own the cat and was prepared to do anything to achieve this. Michael was naturally not pleased about this but honour was satisfied one day when he agreed to transfer ownership for favours and jobs. Michael made the most of this situation. For each little job or favour Michael would transfer part of Zulu, first it was a whisker, then a paw, then a leg. It turned out to be a very long and drawn out process but finally Lionel had total ownership. Michael was learning how to trade, even if it wasn't for money!

Life for young boys was far more strict in those days. Formality existed, even in a close-knit family. No conversation was allowed at the dining table and discipline by today's standards was almost oppressive. Schooling was taken seriously and both Michael and Lionel were expected to study hard. At home misdemeanours, if discovered, merited punishment, and chastisement then was the norm. Michael was a frequent sufferer. When he felt really depressed, he would seek refuge and consolation with the mother of one his friends, Micky Goldhill, who lived close by.

Moss's sons both attended a local school, from where Michael at the very early age of eleven won a London County Council Scholarship to the City of London School. The fees then were eight guineas a term and the Scholarship meant that his father only had to pay part; no doubt Moss was delighted. Michael continued to excel, and was promoted to a more senior class twice in his first year. His major subjects were the classics and he consequently spent most of his time being taught by Mr F. W. Hill, a tall and hirsute schoolmaster who doubtless commanded respect wherever he went because of his stature. A diversion from these studies was the school's Officers Training Corps which became very popular in the years prior to the First World War. Michael, like many others, joined in for the fun and military activity. Apart from drill and parade-ground experience he had the opportunity to learn how to handle and use a rifle. Little did he realize at the time that this training was to save his life before he reached the age of twenty.

Micky Goldhill remembers him well, and recalls that he first met him as a teenager and their friendship developed. As he remembers, what exacerbated the strained relationship between Michael and his family, was that his education had made him a very determined young man, and the good schooling had given Michael a more wider and superior knowledge than his father's. It was not surprising then, that Michael could rout his father when it came to an argument. He, for instance wanted Michael to become a boxer, but this was far from being one of

Michael's ambitions and became a focal point for several major altercations. At the time Lord Kitchener was calling for volunteers and army life seemed to offer an opportunity for adventure and an alternative to the prickly atmosphere at home. These stresses encouraged Michael to volunteer for army service though he was only sixteen at the time. Micky Goldhill remembers Moss in those days as being very materialistic and completely unable to provide the emotional support and security that his family needed.

Osbaldeston Road is situated near Stamford Hill in North London. The street lay in an uninspiring part of the suburbs and was built like many others. Hermione Gingold, who was to become Michael's first wife, recalls that the house was decorated, in her words, 'in the worst possible taste'. She would, of course be biased. Michael's mother, Rebecca, was a teacher and she and her husband lived modestly but in relative comfort. Not that her husband's activities gave her much peace of mind.

One of the popular attractions for teenagers was then, as it is today, smoking cigarettes. Michael took to this social habit with gusto, eventually becoming a heavy smoker of up to forty cigarettes a day. He later experimented with a pipe for a short time, but found it much less satisfying. He tried many brands of cigarettes, collecting the 'cards' that were so popular at the time. Today he is remembered by his contemporaries for his favourite brand, du Maurier, which he liked not just for the enjoyment of smoking, but because they always reminded him of the du Maurier family and happy memories of the times he had spent with them.

Michael was therefore not an active sportsman but as a youngster he went fishing. This sport appealed to him as it required skill and patience to succeed rather than strength and energy. This became a regular activity for many years and in his early life he would take his brother Lionel with him. As a teenager, he enjoyed the odd game of tennis and later, when serving in the army during the First World War, he played football for a time until he was invalided out. In the late twenties, he took up golf but that too was a passing phase. However, fishing, and later game shooting, were the only hunting sports which he enjoyed, strangely contradicting his love for animals.

*   *   *

When World War I began, Michael, like so many thousands of others, was caught up in the excitement, patriotism and the sense of doing one's duty. He volunteered for the army, believing like so many others, that it was to be a short war. His wartime career is fully described in Chapter

A formal portrait of **Hermione Gingold**

A formal portrait of Edna

Michael and Edna 1927

Michael 1927.

4, but when at the end of the war he was on leave having recovered from typhoid, Cupid took a hand.

He was at an ice-rink in Bournemouth and whilst skating around he literally bumped into a beautiful young lady. Instantly attracted to each other, a whirlwind courtship and romance followed and – in the best theatrical manner – he married Hermione Gingold a few weeks later in Grantham. It was now 1918 and peace had been declared. The hasty marriage, which Moss thoroughly disapproved of, soon began to take its toll. And as the saying goes, it really was 'marry in haste and repent at leisure'.

At first Hermione shared Michael's love for cats but strongly disagreed with his method of training. She recounted with disgust that on one occasion he rubbed the nose of her little kitten in pepper, all in the course of house training. This infuriated her and did little to endear him to her or the cat.

Their marriage was destined to fail, for not only did Michael go against Moss Joseph's preferences by marrying an 'actress', the marriage simply did not go down well with the rest of the family either. Hermione was not someone to take life quietly, and according to her, she was as much to blame for the break-up as Michael. During their short marriage, he worked first as a sub-editor on weekly magazines, then as a keen young Advertising Manager for Hutchinsons. He devoted his energies to his career rather than his marriage, something that we all do at one time or another.

One of the curious features of Hermione's life is that even today, she does not like anyone knowing her age. For example, she still denies her age to *Who's Who* and yet from her book *My Own Unaided Work* it is easy to establish that she was the same age as Michael. In fact she was two months younger.

Michael and Hermione soon started a family, having two sons, Leslie, born in 1919, and Stephen in 1921. Hermione, a dominant and colourful extrovert, was determined to make the stage a full time career. Bringing up children and being a housewife with her husband away at the office was not one of her ambitions. So they separated, leaving Michael to cope with Leslie and Stephen.

When the divorce came in 1926, Michael's family couldn't resist saying 'I told you so' but that didn't help the situation. Michael had been fully aware of his parents' disapproval and they were now quite open about it, believing that Michael had married beneath his level in society. She, however, went on to carve out a wonderful career in films and stage, whilst he became a legend in the publishing world. It's a pity that the marriage didn't work for as so often happens there were two children, whose lives and futures were greatly affected by the break-up.

*   *   *

Michael, knowing his father's opinion of his first marriage, found Moss openly delighted at the prospect of his son's second marriage to Edna Frost. She was a complete contrast to Hermione, for Edna's parents lived in Cheshire and were established members of British 'society'. Edna had been presented at Court and afterwards as a débutante she spent a full season partying. In turn her parents provided Edna with a 'coming out' party, but Michael first met her at the famous Chelsea Arts Ball where this incredibly attractive and bright young girl was totally captivated by his charm. She was entirely sympathetic about his previous marital problems, unlike her family who did not appreciate her relationship with a divorcee, let alone someone with the responsibilty of two young children. They volunteered their views in no uncertain terms, but as Michael and Edna's affection for each other grew and wedding plans were discussed, I'm told that her parents would only allow the wedding to proceed if Michael undertook to have nothing more to do with his side of the family. If true, this must have been a painful decision, nevertheless they married the following year, on 11 March 1926. Thereafter Stephen and Leslie's upbringing became strained, for their presence as step-children was a constant reminder to her parents of their embarrassment. Michael's first marriage could not easily be forgotten.

The following year Edna presented Michael with the finest present ever for his thirtieth birthday, a daughter. Just what they both had wanted. Christened Diana Shirley, she quickly became very special to them both. As she grew up she was given numerous special treats, sometimes seemingly to spite the boys. In her formative years her photograph appeared in the press, she had books dedicated to her and was the star in most of the home movies that Michael made.

Although there were quite naturally, many scenes showing Stephen, Leslie, Edna and relatives, it was Shirley who featured in the majority. Michael had become a doting father. Naturally, several reels show the family's interest in cats, but the main theme that ran through those Michael had edited, was the family holiday. This was a major event each year, as in so many other families, it formed an important tradition. The Isle of Wight and Cornwall were regularly featured. Amongst the reels were many picturesque scenes of Seaview on the Isle of Wight, and Fowey in Cornwall. Other reels show domestic and various contrived scenes around the house and garden. Stephen and Leslie can be seen fighting which is clearly fixed whilst other sequences include animals playing. They behaved quite naturally but Michael's human subjects seemed ill at ease in front of the camera and in almost every scene, one or other would light up the ubiquitous cigarette. There is an interesting reel taken in 1929, completely devoted to a race meeting at Goodwood, which must be rare indeed. Amongst the collection are a few shots of authors, one of which shows Daphne du Maurier taken on the balcony at the Fowey Hotel. In the background are nostalgic scenes showing the harbour full with cargo ships, naval craft and sea-planes that frequented this seaport. And there is a sequence taken as he went upstream in a motor launch, showing the Ferryside Inn which is still owned by the du Maurier family.

Michael organised the annual holiday and sent the family down to their holiday home, where he would join them later. Seagrove Bay lies on the north-east side of the Isle of Wight and is thus more sheltered from the prevailing westerly winds than Fowey. The attractions there included a pier which extended into the sea on suspended sections not unlike a long road or rail bridge. The house overlooked the beach, which lay just across the road and made an ideal venue for his children. Stephen and Leslie were almost old enough to look after themselves, whilst Michael would take Shirley for short trips in the dinghy, which went with the house. Apart from mackerel fishing, cine-photography had become Michael's major hobby and he was very proud of his results. In 1931 he managed to take some film of the air race for the *Schneider Trophy* when Britain won for the third year, retaining the trophy. Taken in brilliant sunlight the planes were mere specks in the sky. There were no telephoto lens then, and they were difficult to film travelling at some 340 miles per hour. Leslie remembers the events well, for the pilots became national heroes, if only whilst the excitement lasted.

As I have said, there was far more film devoted to Shirley than to her two brothers. The films certainly reflect Michael's love for her, but in a perverse way they underlined the bias shown at home against her brothers and this went some way to alienating Shirley, who thought her parents were at times very unfair to them. Shirley sympathised more with Stephen who usually took the brunt of any criticism and as they grew up, they became the greatest of friends. For many years Michael outwardly disliked both his sons; it was not to be a permanent state.

Nowadays, psychologists could easily explain Michael's behaviour. His wife's attitude to her step-children, being influenced by her parents, and the pressures of Michael's venture into publishing with the gamble and the responsibility of employing staff, must have imposed untenable pressures on him. It is very doubtful whether he would ever have pronounced to the *Strand Magazine* 'Authors are easy to get on with, if you are fond of children', before his daughter was born.

In the autumn of 1930 the family moved to 15 Regent's Park Terrace, a smart London area, where they were to stay for the next five years. The architecture and location of their new home was definitely to Edna's liking, but for Leslie and Stephen it was not an enjoyable time in their lives. Michael, like his father Moss, was strict and the brothers did not see much of him either. He would devote time to them at week-ends and only then if he wasn't away socialising.

This was Leslie's and Stephen's first real home, a terraced house with five floors. The nursery was set as far away as possible on the top floor, where the two brothers and three-year-old Shirley had to spend most of their time. Below was Michael's bedroom and off to one side was the boys' bedroom.

The close proximity of their rooms led to one of Stephen's ill-fated escapades. In an inquisitive mood, and perhaps when boredom had set in, he decided to try out his father's safety razor. Unfortunately for Stephen, he left behind some residue of soap and hair inside and when next morning Michael discovered these, he was furious, for he was a methodical man and liked everything in its place, clean and tidy. The boys were accused and both denied being involved, but the finger of suspicion was pointed at Stephen who was most adamant in his denial. It led to a major family row and increased tensions. No one ever owned up and the affair gave Edna another reason for disliking her step-children.

As time passed, Michael grew to dislike Stephen, and not just for the affair about the razor. At first there was no particular reason. Edna was naturally always finding faults, but he put up with those. Shirley vividly remembers her emotions by the extraordinary line that was drawn between the two boys and herself. Sometimes there were terrible scenes, the root going right back to nursery days when the two boys had been fighting. Stephen had a very bloody nose and the nanny had to call for help. Michael came up to the nursery, and instead of attacking Leslie, for he had been the aggressor as usual, harangued Stephen. He was, as Shirley recalls, normally close to being a real pacifist. Michael reproached Stephen, for, of all things, not showing any spirit in fighting back. This attitude stemmed from an earlier occurrence when Michael had learned that Stephen had been using the sewing machine in the nursery to make marionettes. This to him was not a boy's occupation and totally alien to Michael's opinion of what they should be doing. He felt that Stephen was growing up to be, well, not quite a man's man.

It is possible that his feeling influenced Edna, who went on to bring them up with bad grace, for as time passed she seemed to have no heart for it. The boys naturally became curious about the whereabouts of their real mother and it was Stephen who one day ventured to discover where she lived in London. Shirley recounting the events now, can vividly describe her mother's reaction – this was the perfect solution, . . . 'How could he be so ungrateful, after I had brought him up? How unreasonable . . .' So Stephen and Leslie became *personae non gratae* – that is, until the war came.

Michael's feelings about Stephen were mitigated by his achievements at school. It was perhaps fortunate that both Leslie and Stephen had reached reasonably good academic standards, for poor results at the end of term would have been rewarded by a severe caning. Considering that Michael suffered many a caning as a boy, I was surprised to learn that he was so ready to wield the rod. No wonder they did well, but they never really enjoyed living at this their first home.

Down one floor from the nursery, was the drawing-room, lined of course with many shelves of books; and containing a grand piano on which Michael spent many hours relaxing and composing the odd ditty. He had great fun writing tunes for Shirley's birthday, something that he never did for the boys, perhaps because her birthday and Michael's were the same. Often they felt really left out by the family, whilst Shirley received lots of love and affection.

Meanwhile Michael had worked hard at becoming a very successful literary agent at Curtis Brown and his exploits are well covered in Chapter 3. He strove hard to ensure that both Leslie and Stephen enjoyed a good education, but it fell to Michael's second wife Edna, to provide for them. So both attended a good local preparatory school, Burstow in Horley. Leslie went on to Bradfield College which was close to Stanford Dingley in Berkshire, a village where Michael went to live in the forties.

However, whilst at Curtis Brown, Michael became extremely adept at crosswords, frequently entering competitions which offered prizes and one of those was in the *Spectator*. He would regularly have the correct answers but failed to win. It was not until many years later when he had offices in Bloomsbury Street that he inadvertently discovered a method by which he could win on a regular basis. The *Spectator* offices were adjacent to his and when delivering his entry one week, he established that the staff were never keen to burrow down into the bag for the winning entry. The first correct one taken from the top of the pile was the winner. So he used to pop round just before the offices closed on the final day and place his entry on the pile. Or he would so time the posting, that it arrived just before the closing date. Often as not, he would be in the winners list. So frequently did he win, that the Editor had 'words' with him. So *noms de plume* became the order of the day with all members of the family eventually winning some useful gift. On one occasion Michael asked Shirley if she would like a dictionary, which of course she would, and Michael sent her off to post 'her' entry. Shirley complained that it was all a great fiddle, but as Michael pointed out to her, she had posted it herself. Sure enough, she won a leather-bound edition of Chambers. The game could not go on indefinitely and the ruse of the *noms de plume* was eventually spotted.

Then Michael had the idea of using one of his cat's names – Mr A Binks. Yes, he too won, but the game was up when a cheque was sent made out to the cat for five guineas. Michael had to write back saying that he, Mr A Binks had not got a bank account and could he have postal orders instead? The editor spotted this ruse too. *The Times Crossword* was another regular feature in his life. Hardly a day went by without a completed puzzle laying beside him. He was quick to complete it too, once claiming to have finished in ten minutes. It was almost a ritual – for Michael was very much a man of habit.

One example of Michael's ability to win competitions for others is to be found in an old edition of *The Morning Post,* under the heading of Peter Piper's Potted Plots. The winning entry ran;

> Labour was a broth of a boy
> One Cook spoiled the Broth

This was the entry of a Mrs Michael Joseph, Mayfield, Oxted, Surrey.

*   *   *

Of the two brothers, Leslie was more athletic and also had a very good 'eye' for ball games. Cricket was one of his strengths, that is, until he was hit on the head by a ball. At the time just a very painful accident, but the damage caused, led later, to the need for a major operation to remove a tumour from his brain. This was a very anxious time for Michael and Edna who were aware that the operation was very risky and expensive. It was Hermione who came to the rescue with the vital funds. The surgery was carried out by Professor Cairns, the best known specialist at the time.

Edna, resenting the additional financial strains to her already well ordered life, was fearful that the operation would only partly succeed. The subsequent imposition of a step-son whom they might have to look after for the rest of their lives was a thought that played on her mind. She was increasingly growing to dislike the ties of her step-children. However, she need not have worried as the operation was a total success.

When Leslie left school he found himself a job with *British International Pictures* at Elstree. He does not recall why he was drawn to the film industry, but returning home one evening, Leslie was caught up in a delay on the London Underground (then as today, not an uncommon experience). When he finally reached home Michael was in a furious mood, no doubt incited by Edna who imagined he had been visiting his mother. Denying he had been to see her, he was forced into admitting that both Stephen and he had kept in touch with their mother. Michael finally acquiesced to his wife's persuasive nagging and asked him to leave home and find accommodation elsewhere. Whether he issued that classic phrase, 'leave this house immediately' is shrouded by time, but to Leslie his behaviour was extremely unreasonable and the hurt was to remain with him for over twelve years before the two were to be reconciled, Michael living to regret the day as much as the two brothers. This event and perhaps a sense of guilt was to create such a vacuum in Michael's life, that he later over-compensated for his behaviour by spoiling his third child, Shirley.

Though living in London suited Michael, Edna was very much a country lover, yearning for the tranquillity and beauty around her Cheshire home. There was nothing quite like the countryside there, where she would take her dog for long walks in the lanes and fields. So, to live in Regent's Park Terrace was rather claustrophobic, though her lifestyle and image were in keeping with her ideals.

She shared Michael's affinity for animals and because she lived so close to London Zoo, Edna was able to spend hours observing and befriending the creatures. Through her, the family learned of the many fascinating details of animal behaviour and because she was a Member of the Zoological Society – Edna was allowed special privileges. For example, she was permitted inside the pens to feed the animals. Her favourites were the penguins and they were so tame that they let her hold one of their wings to walk them along the edge of the pool like a mother and child. All the family went there, finding it an idyllic place to relax. But it was not a complete substitute for the Cheshire countryside she missed so much.

The evenings, though, were a very different matter. Edna enjoyed to the full the social life in London for this included attending numerous parties. In the process Michael of course made many new friends, some of whom became authors through his work at Curtis Brown, and in retrospect this period can be seen to be the beginning for his publishing company. He was at this time a member of the Whitefriars Club and he took Edna to their Christmas Banquet in 1931. The six course menu included 'Turbot Poche, Sauce Mousseline with Pommes Vapeur' which would have appealed to Michael. The toast for Christmas was given by Sir Philip Gibbs, the response from the guests, by Lady Cynthia Asquith, names which were to become familiar in later years when his publishing company got under way. The souvenir menu includes autographs from

Edith Sitwell and Cynthia Asquith. 'Friar' Michael, as he was called, enjoyed a grand evening.

He was by now a well known author and literary agent and through these and other contacts made at work, made the most of the new opportunities. One of his new-found friends offered him the opportunity to go flying. His first flight took place on 21 July 1933 when he flew from Stag Lane to Ryde, on the Isle of Wight. Stag Lane was then an aerodrome of some size, covering over 83 acres in Edgware, Middlesex. Now the area is residential and little remains to show that the aerodrome ever existed. It was here that Geoffrey de Havilland started building his famous aeroplanes, though by the time Michael went there, the factory was about to be moved to Hatfield. The aerodrome had been a very busy place with over a thousand people working there, and forming a relief aerodrome to Hendon. The flight in a Moth, piloted by Gabrielli Patterson, took only forty-five minutes but Michael made the most of his experience by describing the scene in a series of cryptic notes written during the flight. No doubt at the time, he harboured thoughts of including this experience in some future short story. As it turned out his experience also reminded him of the spotter planes he had seen flying over the trenches in the First World War.

Helmet (old and dirty – only kind borrowable), goggles pulled down over head. Earphones – plugged into connection with pilot's speaking tube. Rubber-mouthed speaking tube similarly plugged to pilots earphones. Difficult to make self heard in flight above noise of machine. Webbing strap – fairly tight, buckle fastened with split pin & string to pull out pin.

'Give me a swing' – Taxi across S . . . Lane aerodrome and up INTO the wind. Smooth rising climb to about 1000 feet. London on left in thick haze.

Average speed about 75-80 m.p.h. Seemed to be going SLOW. Country scrolls below in slow panorama. Cold in clouds . . .

In front of passenger two notices, 'Do not touch' – above two switches – and 'Do not smoke'. Rudder bar at feet. 'Don't touch it' had been Patterson's instructions. Also spirit level and speedometer. Luggage in compartment (raise lid) in body of machine . . .

Slight heaves upward in flight. 'Banking' in descent – over at an angle. Round and round in circles. Smooth landing and taxied across aerodrome on grass.

Sensations: Cold rush of wind (?"slip stream"), very noisy – but noise reduced by drop in speed to enable me to hear what Patterson was saying thro' tube. Curious 'upward heave' sensation as though to recover balance (or height). Sensation of solitude – slow progress though air though actually fast. Journey – Stag Lane to Ryde took ¾ hour exactly.

Could see on either side of aeroplane but pilot behind and invisible. Hot pipe on left. Had to avoid flying over Portsmouth Dockyard 'Prohibited Territory'.

Climb in and out of machine by stepping on track (? Name for this) on lower wing on right hand side of cockpit – slippery. Had extra cushion to enable me to see better. Wore blue sweater – not cold enough for overcoat/raincoat which is usually worn.

This was an age when flying was a real adventure. It was probably through Gabrielli that he met another pilot, a young and determined lady, Amy Johnson. She also learned to fly at Stag Lane and on one occasion, a few years later, flew Michael down to Ryde again, though this time he had the comfort of a closed-in cockpit. It made a fine start to that years's annual holiday with his family as it was more usual for him to travel by train from Waterloo, complete with servants and animals, which would take up a whole train carriage.

After one holiday in Ryde, with all the stresses of logistics and planning who does what, Michael took Edna up to Scotland for a further holiday – just for the two of them to get over it all. Those really were halcyon days, for they sailed up the west coast on a coastal steamer. He was like that at times, romantic but with a sense for the dramatic.

Back in London, Edna was not to be overburdened with housework – this was still the period of 'upstairs and downstairs' and at Regent's Park Terrace there were a cook, housemaid, butler and nanny. The children upstairs in the nursery were never allowed near the kitchens and that was a strict rule. However, look they did on one quiet afternoon, by using the food lift.

The staff were as much a problem then as they can be today. Michael for exceptional business reasons had to get up early one morning. Rising early was not his natural habit and while shaving, he thought he saw the figure of a man disappearing over the fence at the back of their garden – but he knew one's eyes can play tricks at that hour. He was sure that he'd seen someone though and the following morning set a trap and, surprise, surprise, he caught the cook's boy-friend. Well, boy-friend was not quite the right word, for they were both in their thirties. On questioning him, Michael discovered that he had been working elsewhere during the day, and slipping back to cook's bed each night. They both had instant notice and left, but this saga certainly made a good after-dinner story.

Another story that definitely wasn't talked about, was the affair that took place at the country home of one of Michael's friends in publishing. If Michael and Edna went off to socialise at the weekends, the children usually remained at Regent's Park Terrace. However, on one occasion, Shirley was asked to accompany her parents to their friends in the country. She was especially asked to go, as the host's young daughter would also be there and Shirley would be good company for her.

On their arrival, the weekend started badly for Shirley as she was instructed on being introduced to the nanny to call her 'nurse', a term which Shirley thought pompous (good for a six year old!), and their daughter, who was some two years younger, took her off to show her around the garden.

After a late tea, Shirley went to bid a 'goodnight' to her parents and to her hosts. Then she was taken upstairs to the children's quarters by the nurse where to her horror she found that she had to sleep in a cot! Now a six-year-old definitely would not be seen in a cot and she made sure that everyone knew her feelings. There was absolutely no way that she would sleep anywhere else but in a proper bed. Surely she thought, guests are supposed to be pampered and a cot was certainly not her idea of being made welcome. Shirley thought it was very degrading. Finally, the nurse conceded and arranged for her to sleep in the nurserymaid's bed next door. Honour satisfied, Shirley relaxed.

During the night, she awoke to hear her door being opened slowly. Thinking that it was probably one of her parents checking up to see all was well, she didn't move. Then she heard the door close and footsteps blindly shuffling across in the darkness towards her. Not a sound was heard, only the heavy breathing of the intruder. By now frightened and very alert, she froze and waited, then she felt a hand touch her feet, moving slowly upwards. At that point she screamed, her shouts bringing Michael and Edna running, followed by all the other guests, to her room.

There sitting at the end of the bed was their host, very much the worse for drink. Unfortunately for him he had not been informed of the switch with the nurserymaid.

Unlike Leslie and Stephen, Shirley did not enjoy the benefits of school education. Perhaps Michael could not bring himself to part with his beloved daughter, or perhaps he really eschewed the thought that a school might change Shirley into 'a pig-tailed girl' only interested in hockey. For her part Edna wanted only the best for her daughter, so Shirley was taught at home by a succession of governesses, which, although providing a good education, precluded her from having a wide circle of school friends. Once when no governess could be employed, Michael had an attempt at teaching her himself but he found the work much more

Edna at London Zoo walking a penguin

Stephen (far right) with 'Tish' and the crew of HMS *Newport*

difficult than he first thought. The curriculum he adopted revolved around the classics and languages at which he had excelled at school. These did not go down too well with Shirley for her lessons, of Latin for example, would last for two hours or so and regular tests took place. Naturally, Shirley failed to rise to his expectations and there were many rows. Failure to meet his standards, however, meant punishment – but in her case, unlike the boys, this meant that she could not go riding.

*   *   *

In the summer of 1935 the family moved to 38 Acacia Road in St John's Wood. I do not know why this road is so often quoted in plays but there it is, and every time it's mentioned I am reminded of this period. Soon after moving in, Michael started his now well known firm of Michael Joseph Ltd. The house was spacious and had a larger garden than 15 Regent's Park Terrace, a very important factor as far as Shirley was concerned. Now she could have more of the pets she wanted. During this period, the family's menagerie included rabbits, cats, and dogs. There was even an illuminated tank of small fish kept inside the house.

These were happy times, but tensions in Europe were beginning to affect Michael's future plans. War seemed inevitable and when hostilities broke out in September 1939 he sought to rejoin the army, though the family thought he was very foolish even to consider further service. It was different for the boys, though. Stephen quickly joined the RNVR and Leslie joined the infantry, whilst later on in the war Shirley joined the Land Army. She made notes of her experiences which, doubtless prompted by father, she drafted into a book. These made good reading and her book about those times, *If Their Mothers only Knew* was published by Faber and Faber soon after the war.

Their new home was not too far away from his father's home in Finchley Avenue. Despite his obligation to Edna's family they used to meet occasionally, and it was on one of these outings that Moss was involved in a serious car accident. He was, at 65, a slow and cautious driver but he misjudged a situation and knocked a motor-cyclist, Miss Sampson, off her machine. Unfortunately she had to have her leg amputated and Moss was very upset and showered her with gifts of fruit and flowers. She sued him of course, and despite there being no witnesses to the accident won £2,800 in damages. The press report includes the classic 'I've been driving for seventeen years, and it is the only accident I have had'. Still, the Judge in the King's Bench Division was reported as describing him as a 'gentlemanly motorist'!

The family only stayed at Acacia Road for a few years, moving out during the build-up to the War. During 1939 and 1941 the family became itinerant, moving from one house to another. With Michael away it left Edna, and Shirley, now twelve, to fend for themselves. Edna was also, after a long gap, expecting her second child, adding to Michael's worries. For everyone's peace of mind, it made sense for her to be well away from the intense bombing of London. However, she insisted on being attended by Doctor Jimmy Clark, who was a long standing friend of the family. This meant that she had to go up to London for the birth, and on 3 September 1940, exactly a year after war had broken out, she gave birth to a boy at 12 Briar Walk, Putney, in what can only be described as one of the worst air raids of the war. Michael proudly put announcements in the national press but more interestingly he added the news into the text of his book published two years later *The Sword in the Scabbard*. The addition marked in pen on the uncorrected proof copy, was his way of thanking Jimmy for all his care.

My birth was greeted with many congratulatory messages, amongst which were ones from Ursula Bloom, Curtis Brown, Richard Llewellyn and May Edginton. Michael bitterly regretted not being able to ensure that Edna had all the necessary nursery items. He felt very frustrated, having to do things from a distance, and even the pram's arrival was a week late; well, it was wartime and one very quickly became inured to that sort of thing!

During this period when the family were moving from one house to another, a chance in a million brought them in touch with Leslie. He was stationed at West Camp near Mayfield and his weekends there were very boring, as, unlike all his friends, he had no 'home' to go to when the company was granted leave. It was a case of killing time with anyone left at the camp.

He and his 'squaddie' friends got into the habit of walking over the hill and down into the neighbouring village of Mayfield for a pint or two. The company had gone on leave and on this occasion, his two Scottish friends remained behind too. So all three dressed in casuals, set off for a friendly evening pint at the Middle House. To get there they had to walk down a narrow byway known as Smugglers Lane which had a mass of trees overhanging making it difficult to see from the surrounding countryside. Nearing the bottom, on the right was a farm, and he suggested that they should call in to scrounge some eggs – and cream if possible.

Later, fortified with a pint or two inside them, they began the long walk back up the lane in the twilight. As they approached the farm, a lone girl came out from the cowshed, dressed in white overalls and cap. The light being poor, he completely failed to recognise her. Amazingly, it was Shirley. He had no idea that Edna and she were there and rather sadly, it reflects how easy it was during that time to lose touch with relatives.

*   *   *

Later, when Michael was invalided out of the army, he moved the family to a farm in Curridge, Berkshire. In the peace and tranquillity of this delightful Berkshire farm, he wrote *The Sword in the Scabbard,* followed by *Charles* and many other short stories.

Copyhold Farm held many delights for all the family. Michael could enjoy stalking and shooting rabbits, whilst Shirley had ample room to stable and school her horse, which she did quite expertly. Gymkhanas had become her speciality. But autumn that year was marred for Michael by his father's sudden and fatal illness. Lionel phoned news of Moss's illness through to the office, and it was fortunate (or maybe, was it telepathy) that Michael had travelled up to London that morning, enabling him to see his father for the last time that October evening. He died later that night.

There was a melancholy atmosphere at Copyhold Farm in the weeks that followed leading up to Christmas. Being wartime, the traditional celebrations were curtailed and Christmas in 1943 was no exception. Everyone tried hard to overcome the shortages of food and clothing, and fortunately, living in the countryside made it a little easier to obtain the necessary Christmas tree, holly and mistletoe than it was in the city. These at least created the atmosphere even if there were not many presents. Stephen had already taken his leave earlier in December, so he was away, which disappointed Shirley, for she liked having him around. Michael made up for her disappointment by presenting her with a new pony, by far the best present she had ever received, and her mother gave her a driving whip – so it wasn't hardship for everyone. Enthusiasm for equine activities was rampant and Shirley really did live for riding, hunting, and tending her horse, 'Cinnamon'. Boxing Day saw Shirley out with the local hunt with some forty or so other enthusiasts. She took part in many other events and her innate organisational abilities led her at the age of sixteen to become the secretary for a local Horse Show and Gymkhana. This was to be the first of many events.

A few weeks later many miles away, Stephen aboard HMS *Newport,* was about to enjoy an evening meal. Moored 'somewhere in Scottish waters', as the wartime expression goes, the ship was comparatively safe and the ship's crew was in a relaxed mood. He had been chilled by the bitingly cold wind whilst on watch and was now ready for a good hot meal. He had just downed some steaming hot soup, thereby restoring his circulation, when there came frantic shouts from on deck 'Tish's overboard'. This was serious, for 'Tish', the black and tan mongrel, was the ship's mascot. Sailor's superstition being what it is, if the mascot was lost, bad luck was bound to befall them. Bedlam ensued but no one seemed to have the courage to act. So Stephen, in his quiet laconic way, said, 'Oh well, if no one else is going to do anything about it, I will.' With that, he went on deck, took off his shoes and tying a line around him, dived overboard into the freezing water. Tish was only just saved from certain drowning in the the numbing cold water. They were pulled aboard to safety, frozen to the marrow, but much to everyone's relief, in one piece. However the story does not end there.

A member of the crew reported this story to a local paper and the next morning, the events appeared in several newspapers. The RSPCA and the PDSA both heard about the story but the RSPCA awarded him their silver medal. Michael was delighted to read the news.

But for Stephen, it took many months to live down the gibes 'Oh, meet our man with the gong – and yes, he got it whilst in harbour'. A good thing that he had a relaxed sense of humour.

Later though, he was to earn a medal of a very different kind. Stephen, now a Sub-Lieutenant aboard HMS *Avonvale,* was proving to be bright as well as practical. These attributes ensured that despite being a member of the RNVR, who were generally looked down upon by the sailors in the Royal Navy, he was sent on the training course for radar gunnery officers. Radar equipment was then a very new ship's aid and few understood or could trust the benefits of equipment not yet proved to be reliable.

It was late in 1944 and the ship was sailing on one of those 'hush-hush' missions in the Adriatic. Conditions were ideal for their operation, for they had been sailing through patches of heavy mist all day. Their mission was to rendezvous with a small boat and take aboard a number of 'guests'. Nearing their destination, the radar room reported that enemy ships had been spotted on the radar 'scope'. This was duly reported by Stephen as Gunnery Officer. The ships were closing and the enemy was coming into range. There wasn't a moment to lose, so Stephen shouted 'Fire', and fire they did which was contrary to Regulations. A few seconds elapsed before a muffled 'crump' was heard as a shell hit its target. The records show that Stephen was later awarded a DSC for this action.

When he returned home, Stephen delighted Michael and Edna with the full details of these events and as a result, his parents now saw him in a very different light. Michael and Edna made quite a fuss over him during his leave but more importantly, Edna now looked upon her step-son with pride and respect.

In 1944, when the tide of the war had turned, the countryside around Curridge was a quiet and relatively secure place to live. Michael, by then very well known, became a prime candidate for organisers of local events. Not that he minded, he had time to spare and in a way, quite enjoyed the new experiences. His involvement in cat shows, fêtes and gymkhanas was doubtless encouraged by Shirley's enthusiasm.

A major local event that year was the Annual Fête organised by the 26th Newbury Scout Group. This event, which is worth noting, was held on the town's football ground and saw over 2,000 people that sunny afternoon. There was an attractive programme of events consisting of a Scout demonstration of athletics and tumbling, a comic football match, a novelty dog show, a beauty competition and a display of firefighting by the National Fire Service and Fire Guards. For a few hours the war seemed a long way away.

And amongst this multitude was Michael who had agreed to judge the novelty dog show! Aided and abetted by Inspector F. W. Checksfield of the RSPCA, Michael struggled to adjudge the six classes, handing out prizes of 10/-, 5/- and 2/6d to the class winners. Not to miss a trick, he auctioned a copy of *Charles* immediately afterwards, which went to Sir Frederick Carden who had opened the Fête, but it cost him two guineas. And that was more than four times the retail price.

Frank Checksfield was also Michael's chauffeur. He used to take me, as a young boy, to school in the neighbouring village of Cold Ash. We would go there in a Ford Prefect and on rare occasions he would let me sit on his lap and steer the car down the country lanes. (He could not get away with that these days!)

The woods which lay adjacent to the farm, provided an area for exploration and adventure, and I made the most of it. My mother had given me the freedom to roam through them and one warm summer's afternoon, I managed to tread on an adder whilst stalking a rabbit. The shock gave me one huge fright and I ran home without stopping, where my noisy arrival put an end to my father's peaceful writing. It took a great deal of encouragement by my father for me to return to those woods and several days elapsed before I went with him again on one of his shooting forays. However, I felt a little safer with him but nevertheless I was very wary where I trod. Even today that moment of fright remains with me.

Michael, like his father, was always a generous man in the materialistic sense. As an example, he once gave me a pedal car which was to become one of the most treasured memories of my childhood, and of the time spent at Copyhold Farm.

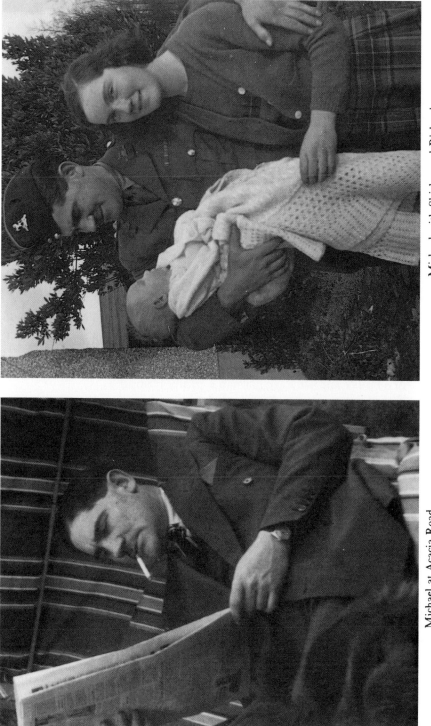

Michael with Shirley and Richard

Michael at Acacia Road

It was most probably a second-hand model, as there was a shortage of toys during the war, but never was a small boy so delighted. It had more care and attention lavished on it than any other present.

The gravel drive at Copyhold Farm sloped down to the farm's lane at the bottom, at the far side of which was a steep bank. With mother in the garden, I decided that I would show her what I could do and in a moment of extreme bravado I pedalled down the drive gathering speed. At the end, I was going too fast and couldn't turn the corner. I went straight across the lane and up the far bank, hitting my head on the steering wheel and knocking in one of my front teeth. This accident was also a pointer to my future, and it took frequent, and expensive, visits to the orthodontist in London to correct that ingrowing tooth. (Twenty-five years later, I was to be involved in a similar and spectacular motor racing accident at Silverstone, fortunately without sustaining any serious injury.)

Edna occasionally went up to London with Michael, and on one of those occasions she left Michael to stay overnight at Richard Llewellyn's flat. Edna recalls her impression of his flat in a letter to her mother.

Michael is in London for the night – sleeping at Llewellyn's flat again. I believe it's full of wonderful things. It's only three rooms but the contents are valued at £13,000. He went away leaving £7,000 worth of jewellery in the flat not insured! All out of *How Green Was My Valley* and we have not had a penny from it!

The summers spent at Copyhold Farm were few. The family moved on to Stanford Dingley shortly afterwards, though I still vividly recall the sight of Michael, 12-bore under his arm, standing patiently in the wheat fields being harvested behind the farm, while the tractor-drawn binder slowly reduced the standing crop. Every now and again the odd panic-stricken rabbit would race to the safety of the nearby woods, running helter-skelter through the stooks. Not many made it to safety.

*   *   *

Then came the move to The Garden House in Stanford Dingley. It was the epitome of Edna's style. Large, imposing and buried deep in the countryside, but best of all there was a river too. The only disadvantage was that the main garden lay across the road, but Edna was delighted. The house lay in a small and delightful village which is largely unspoilt today. It was once owned by George Henty, the writer of adventure stories which were the literary pabulum of every boy and girl back in the 1890s. Michael also thought that Jonathan Swift had once lived there. The house was much larger than Copyhold Farm, which made it

Michael and Richard

Michael with Shirley at Yattendon

Michael, Anthea and her father Mr Justice Hodson (later
Sir Charles Hodson) at Chelsea Registry Office. 5 November 1950

ideal for holding a wedding reception. For it was here that Shirley celebrated her marriage to Michael Savage in March 1948. Their wedding, like most, was a happy and emotional occasion, and among the guests were many notable literary figures including Cecil S. Forester, Monica Dickens, Eleanor Farjeon, Richard Llewellyn, Mark Hambourg and the cartoonist, David Low.

At the back of the house was the river Pang. It ran right across the rear, providing a natural boundary. There was a mill just upstream which formed a pool in the middle of our patch. Downstream, on both sides were reeds, providing a haven for the fish and trouble for the fisherman. Those reeds ensnared many of Michael's flies, for he had now taken to fly fishing in a big way. As soon as he came home at the weekends, and if it was not too windy, he would be out on the back lawn practising casting. Further and further he would cast for ten or twenty minutes at a time, until he was quite happy that he could cast across the pool exactly to where the fish were waiting in the warm, shallow water.

In the years we were there, many a good trout was had, but they were not always caught by the sophisticated fly. Worms and floats were to be seen, though Michael used to say that this was cheating. Cheating it may have been, but the rewards were there.

Downstream, and at the end of our stretch, was a small and low hump-backed bridge where the river narrowed to flow underneath. Michael had often hooked the 'big one' but it had won its freedom whenever the fight took the fish near the bridge. The dark waters beneath were a safe haven. The frustration eventually got the better of him and he hatched a plan with me as his co-conspirator. I was to start downstream of the bridge laden with a bucket of gravel and slowly wade upstream towards the bridge. Into action I went, slowly moving forward, throwing occasional handfuls of gravel into the water. Meanwhile Michael equally slowly and with infinite patience waded downstream towards the bridge, armed with a long landing net. It was a crude way to land the 'big one', and after some twenty minutes – success. A good seven-pounder was in the net. The family held several good dinner parties after that episode. The point of this is that Michael would not be beaten by a dumb fish and the attraction of a challenge got the better of him.

It wasn't long before I also became adept at knowing where to find the best worms in the garden and how to bait the hook. This was not as easy as one may think, as they do struggle a bit and tie themselves into tiny little knots. Michael, being a member of the *Piscatorial Society* was an expert and taught me well. On one particular weekend he presented me with a short stumpy sea fishing rod which was light enough to be used on the river. This became a prized possession but I soon discovered that I could not cast out far enough into the river to reach where the best trout were, and I began to plan how to build a longer make-shift rod. (It was whilst making this, that my mother had a seizure.)

I remember the day that my mother, literally, fell ill. It was one of those warm July days when all a young boy wanted to do was to go fishing or potter around in the garden. Those were the halcyon days of youth, when time seems unending and the days always hot and dry. For much of the time, I was left to my own devices and with the absence of my father who was busy in London, I was allowed to do very much as I pleased. The river running though the back garden was always tempting and my thoughts turned once again to fishing. I wandered around looking for a suitable supple branch and eventually found one. This, once fashioned into a rod, needed of course the line and hook. Line was easy, but the hook ... I could not find out where the collection of hooks were – my father kept things well locked away. So, finding my mother, I asked her to bend a pin ... This she did and whilst doing so, seemed suddenly to get the shakes and fell to the ground with a crashing thud. I drew away in fear for surely I would get the blame. At that moment I thought she had simply fainted, but I could not raise her so I started to shout for help. Very quickly someone – possibly the cook came to my aid and I was ushered away.

I did not know it at the time, but she was suffering from a cerebral tumour, and the outward signs were shaky hands, and partial loss of function in her right arm and leg. The type she suffered was not painful, but the tumour, which grew slowly, was one which the medical world could not easily remedy.

Michael moved out of the master bedroom, in order to make her nights as comfortable as possible. Though it should be said that the master bedroom was far from being on the small side. It was some forty feet long with every window overlooking the splendid gardens which lay across the road. This was some consolation for Edna, loving the sights and sounds of the countryside.

She was eventually taken to hospital for an operation and though she faced it with equanimity, her heart and morale sank when she saw the name on the surgeon's case of instruments – 'Professor Cairns'. She knew all about him, for it was he who had operated on Leslie, when he had suffered from being hit by a cricket ball. Her surgeon was Joseph Pennybacker, but obviously trained by Cairns. The very sight of his name stretched Edna's mental stability to the limit. Operations on the brain were extremely dangerous, and the chances of survival were not good. Survive she did for nearly two years, but her condition worsened. Edna was finding even the basic functions of living extremely difficult and the effort to simply eat and drink sapped all her energy. Eventually, Michael acquiesced to her doctor's advice, and she was admitted to

Newbury Hospital in April 1949. She faced it with calm but she despaired for her future, sensing that she would never survive. Despite the care and attention that was lavished on her, she died on 16 May aged only forty-eight.

It was, for her, a release from a very long and unpleasant illness. For Michael, it was a heart-rending end to a very happy marriage. It took Michael many months to recover from the shock; the finality of life is always difficult to come to terms with, and it was Anthea, his secretary, who understood and shared in his grief. Edna was cremated at Oxford with only a small group to mourn her passing.

Soon after all this, I was sent off to The Wells House, a boarding-school which was a very long way from home, in the Malvern Hills. No one had said anything about moving house, but I sensed, as I left and was driven away up the hill, that I would never go back to that house again. As I travelled to school I recalled the fun I had had racing from bedroom to bedroom in an effort to hide when I had been called. There were eleven bedrooms I think, but with two large drawing rooms, study, dining room, kitchen, scullery and copious cupboards, I tested their patience. Outside, there was a large barn running down to the river's edge. This was packed with rubbish and wood for the fire but there was space left for Checkfield's car, Michael's being garaged in another building and that was always locked.

*   *   *

Soon after I had been sent off to a boarding-school in Malvern, Michael married Anthea Hodson. Their wedding took place at Chelsea Registry Office in London on 11 November 1950. Their love affair had been a well kept-secret in the office, but not from her parents. They had been sharing a flat in Gower Mews for some months, a fact which Anthea had found impossible to keep hidden from her family. Neither her father Charles Hodson (later Sir Charles Hodson), nor Susan her mother, totally approved of this situation. To them it was definitely not 'the done thing' as they said, but by now Michael was quite used to critical in-laws. Their home was an intimate little two-bedroomed flat, convenient to the office in Bloomsbury Street, yet close enough to the theatres and cinemas in the West End. Number 13 was an excellent base for them and for that matter, for me during my school holidays. The flat was also close enough to the office for Michael to slip away when he was ill – or otherwise.

Anthea soon became very much part of the family, and took very easily to her new role of step-mother. By comparison to Edna's relationship with Leslie and Stephen, we had a much happier time. Right from the start she cared for my well-being both at home and at school and I recall that on one occasion, she sent £2 to me as additional pocket money. The Headmaster of The Wells House, sadly confiscated this handsome sum on the grounds that I did not need any additional money. Today this would be worth about £25.00, and though this, and other offers were very comforting, I did not enjoy the life away at school as the reports sent home confirmed. My achievements were a disappointment to both my father and step-mother for these reports indicated lack of effort and a lack of interest in learning. The letters I sent home from school reflected these reports and now, when I read them, I shudder with embarrassment. It was about this time that Michael had begun to plan the future of his firm and these letters, and reports, could never had given him any encouragement that I would ever have any ability to follow him into the publishing world.

In 1952 we moved to their new home – a farmhouse in Hampshire. Michael had already given Browns Farm, built in Cromwell's time, the nickname 'Cold Comfort Farm' – for it was really cold indoors even when the weather was warm outside. The solidly built house had a damp cellar with stone flooring, woodworm in places and there were damp patches in the kitchen. Michael immediately set about having these things put right and then extending the house. He wanted a study but it finally turned out to be a large library. Someone once calculated that there were between six and seven thousand books to choose from but the vast majority were of course, ones the company had published and there were many first editions.

Browns Farm wasn't really a farm, though there were some seven acres of land, most of which formed the bank of the disused Basingstoke Canal. When purchased, the fields had scattered clumps of brambles and thistles but amongst the trees on the banks, the rampant undergrowth provided ideal cover for Michael to have pot shots at the pigeons and rabbits. He spent many hours under the trees, patiently waiting for some poor unfortunate pigeon to fly past or alight on a nearby branch. And despite almost neurotic precautions against gnat bites he always managed to fall victim. His curses, and slaps of self-flagellation would often disturb the very birds he was stalking. You could always tell when they were getting through to him by the muffled 'damn' or 'blast' and the irritated sweep of his arm. Nevertheless, he seldom missed his prey and the cats rarely went without a tasty morsel.

Part of the land lay across the road from the house and Michael allowed a local and very venerable lady to graze her cow there. Mrs Williams and 'Daisy', a Guernsey cow, provided our family with a regular supply of cream, but the residue of farmyard litter in the back-yard was a constant source of irritation to Michael.

The main feature of the 'farm-yard' at Browns Farm was a very large, and ancient, thatched barn. The thatch was always in need of repair and a haven for the birds. Rats infested the murky dark interior and were a constant concern to Anthea who always worried about such matters. Not that she was afraid of them, just that she could well do without them. Naturally, they became the target for my youthful quest to kill, which was no doubt one of the reasons behind the acquiescence to my badgering for an airgun.

The barn was pretty well complete, but in poor condition. One of the main front doors was hanging on one hinge and seldom opened, the other permanently open, the hinges seized with rust. Over the years, the part tiled and part thatched roof had sufferd the ravages of the elements and had become in many areas a network of birds' nests. The occasional strands of straw blowing round the yard added further to the place looking unkempt, something that Anthea, like Michael, found very irritating. No longer a farm, the building was used for storing wood, old furniture, coal, bicycles and any other clutter. It was the dump for anything that did not have its place and really deserved to be pulled down. Unfortunately, it became the subject of a preservation order and Michael was stuck with the maintenance costs. Adjacent was another thatched building, but in much better condition, which formed a double garage and garden shed.

It was scenes like this that Clemence Dane, the author and painter, found fascinating. Michael had known her for many years, indeed he had published one of her books *(A Hundred Enchanted Tales)* as early as 1937. She occasionally visited Browns Farm to spend a few moments of relaxation with Anthea and Michael. Clemence, who had been a long standing friend as well as an authoress, had made a lasting impression – for he had written of her before he embarked as a publisher: 'I take my hat off to Clemence Dane, surely the most energetic and brilliantly versatile author of our time. Whenever I meet her, she is planning and writing new books, plays, lectures, scenarios and broadcasts. Her mind is always scintillating with new ideas. And she works like a Trojan. At five o'clock every morning she is up and out of doors, protecting herself from the early morning dew by piles of cushions, revelling in the clear air . . .'

*   *   *

Michael never really liked driving but the Humber Snipe was soon sold to make way for a more stylish Bentley. Michael, when he was home, used to drive up to Malvern in this and I recall that the car ranked among the better ones visiting my school. Few parents realise that to boys at boarding school, it really does matter which car their parents own – and is a very important status symbol.

However on one occasion, Michael went up to Malvern by train from Paddington, leaving his car parked at the station where he thought it safe. On his return he was very 'miffed' to find that he had contravened a by-law. He was duly fined and, not a man to miss the opportunity to express himself in writing, this is part of his letter that appeared in both *The Times* and the *Daily Telegraph*.

Too late I learned from the railway police that many others have fallen into this trap. I was duly fined.

But do British Railways play fair? The by-law, which they say, perhaps cynically, 'operates for the convenience of the travelling public', sets a time-limit for the parking of cars, but no notice is displayed for the enlightenment of fare-paying passengers.

Yours &c.   Michael Joseph

At least he had the last word.

Michael devoted more leisure time in the latter part of his life to game shooting. He had, through Macdonald Hastings, been introduced to Churchills, the famous firm of gunsmiths. Mac, whom he had known for many years, persuaded him that he would achieve better results if he had a gun made to fit him, rather than use one with a standard stock. He grew very fond of his acquisition and his standard of shooting certainly improved as a result.

This was the age of the *Eagle* – a weekly comic that stirred the imagination of every young and not-so-young reader. I was an avid follower of Dan Dare, the hero in the main feature, but once I had been introduced to Mac, his articles, as the *Eagle's Special Investigator* became much more absorbing. Each week he wrote about his adventures and experiences that every youth yearned for, yet had very little chance of ever attaining.

When Macdonald Hastings came to stay for the weekend as Michael's guest at Browns Farm, I would volunteer to stay in, which was unusual. Fortified with a large gin and tonic he would regale me with stories that hadn't yet been published and there were many that involved shot-guns. I wanted one too, so Michael took me to Churchills where he bought me a second-hand 12-bore. For the next few years, I literally trod in my fathers's footsteps and learned that patience was essential in stalking prey; fortunately and to my father's envy the flies and gnats that bothered him never came near me. He completed the job by teaching me after a successful shoot, how to to deal with the gutting and skinning of rabbits.

The family at Home in Hampshire

ILN Pic Lib

When Macdonald Hastings' book *Eagle Special Investigator* was published he presented me with a signed copy. There is nothing unusual about this except that he inscribed:

I send you this book in the sure belief that when you are a man you will have a far more exciting life than I have had.

A generous thought but very unlikely to come true.

Another visitor to Browns Farm was Arthur Street who was one of those people blessed with such a rich country voice that you could never forget it. Known to all his friends as 'A. G.', the use of initials being a practice that was much in use amongst his contemporaries. But it was A. G.'s voice and country knowledge that was his signature. Others too, thought much of his 'voice' and he was often heard on television advertisements extolling the virtues of Batchelor's peas. He became another firm friend of Michael's and on at least one occasion, when on holiday from Harrow School, I remember being invited to join them on their frequent weekend fishing trips to the River Test.

In this private pool there were fish a'plenty. Huge salmon were there to be caught, and what catches they were too. The excitement of hooking a large salmon and then 'playing' it seemed to take up so much energy – let alone skill. Michael enjoyed these outings despite tiring easily. The rewards were often memorable as the evocative photograph on page 35 shows, this one taken on a day when I was not invited. Three good fourteen pounders.

Browns Farm was the focal point for numerous visitors. It was often just like a hotel, for not an hour would pass without some friend, acquaintance or relative dropping by and weekends were especially busy. Occasionally, Anthea would persuade Michael to leave Browns Farm for a weekend, and because he shared the same birthday as Shirley, he was, on one occasion, easily persuaded to visit her in Suffolk to celebrate the event.

She lived on a small farm near Framlingham, the farmhouse being in much need of repair and though it was 1951, still had its own generator for electricity. Early autumn evenings meant that the diesel engine was started as dusk fell and the friendly thumping was strangely reassuring as the evening wore on. Retiring to bed for the night was marked by the ritual of 'Lights out' but this was only called when everyone was safely in bed. The unusually early dying thud of the diesel ... and the succeeding peace that settled around the buildings became extremely pronounced.

During one of those evenings, Shirley was putting her son's baby clothes away in the cupboard, for he was now fourteen months old. She

Michael and Macdonald Hastings with a good catch

Michael lands a salmon at Testwood with Jack Terry, the keeper

and her husband Michael were planning ahead and naturally, having had a son, now wished for a daughter. Closing the cupboard door, she remarked to Anthea 'Those will do nicely for Charlotte.'

'That's very generous of you', was Anthea's instant reply. Shirley was taken aback and chided Anthea for being greedy as she did not yet have a child and was not even pregnant. Anthea's retort was 'Nevertheless, I'm going to – and I have chosen Charlotte for her name.' The chiding continued and Shirley became quite prickly. 'Well, as you haven't a daughter, and I have also chosen the same name, we'll have to see who is first and whoever wins can adopt the name.'

Two weeks later, Anthea telephoned full of excitement, saying that her doctor had just confirmed that she was pregnant – wasn't it marvellous – and 'it seems that I can claim the name'. But still Shirley wouldn't concede, retorting testily 'Well, you don't know that you will have a daughter yet, it could be a boy. You'll have to wait awhile yet', not suspecting that she would shortly join in the race.

A few more days elapsed and it was a very elated Shirley who telephoned Anthea to announce that she too was now pregnant – her doctor confirming the anticipated date of birth, which was about a fortnight after Anthea's. And if I repeat the first experience, I'll be ten days early, so you could still lose the race.'

And of course, all this rivalry and family teasing went on for months, prompting Michael to relate the story and events to one and all with a gleeful smile. Bets were laid and the odds shortened when the doctors both anticipated the result. Dick Francis recalls that he and his wife, Mary were amused by these family antics – especially, when Anthea gave birth to a daughter late in the evening of the 4 June 1952 and Shirley's daughter, arrived only a matter of hours later, but alas, after midnight! Not satisfied, Shirley called the result a draw and named her daughter Charlotte, too.

Two years later Michael's son Hugh, was born joining his sister at Browns Farm. As soon as they could be left with a nanny Anthea rejoined Michael at the office and as events were to turn out, her presence there was important; but leaving her children in the care of nannies minimised the close family ties that normally exist. And when the weekends came, off Michael would go shooting or fishing. In his latter years his literary output declined, as he preferred to devote his energies to these sports and horse racing.

My school days at Harrow were fast coming to an end, but I didn't know it at the time. In my father's last letter to me he wrote:

Michael with Anthea, Richard, Charlotte and Hugh

Caricature of Michael in North Africa

...there's a Meeting at Newbury on Friday and Saturday which I hope to go to: and next week a day's fishing (Thursday 13th – hope it will be lucky!) before we fly, early on the 14th to Stockholm ...

As events turned out, he didn't fly out on the 14th nor the 15th. He was due to meet Charles Pick in Stockholm and Charles remembers those eventful few days well. Michael never made it to Sweden.

He died on the 15 March 1958 at the London Clinic. After all the medical help he had sought for most of his life, Michael believed that, if he was patient, he could recover – but it was not to be and this time his ulcer finally won, pumping the poison into his blood. The doctors strove to heal him with every remedy known but despite the good efforts of Dr Dickson Wright, he succumbed.

His death caused many to mourn, for his passing was the end of an era in publishing. Times change and we shall not see the like of him again. He died, leaving a complex Will which effectively minimised any death duties. He and his good friend Graham Smith, his solicitor, and Martin Dubois, his accountant, had seen to it that his Trusts and Legacies for his heirs avoided, as far as possible, the obvious death duties.

He also left a legacy of literary effects most of which have lain undisturbed for years. One of the objectives of this biography has been to highlight the lesser known achievements of this man and who in his life-time achieved more than most.

Chapter 2

Master of Words:
An Author First and
Foremost
1916–58

*'It is with books as with men; the very small number play
a great part, the rest are mingled with the crowd.'*
Voltaire

Throughout Michael's life, he wrote prolifically, and yet most of his writings have now largely disappeared into oblivion, with the exception of his books on cats, which if you are lucky, can still be found in second-hand bookshops. He wrote many more articles than books, as well as short stories, reviews, and forewords, and last but not least the odd poem, music, and film script.

As an author, he is without any doubt best remembered for his books about cats, but in fact he wrote more books about the art of writing and journalism than any other subject. In all, he wrote seventeen titles, but in numerical terms the total of articles and short stories alone, dwarfs all the books put together. One of Michael's habits was to hoard every little scrap of print that he was in one way or another, involved in. His scrap books include cuttings of over seventy essays on the art of writing, 220 short stories and articles, together with numerous reviews of other books for the literary press both here and overseas. In the period from 1916 to 1958 the total appears to be over 300 though it has been an almost impossible task to accurately establish the total amount of titles. Those that have been discovered are listed for the student of literary history at the back of this book.

*   *   *

But where did he start? Almost certainly with an account of the effectiveness of the then new 'Machine Gun Corps' in the *Daily Express,* dated early 1916. Naturally, this was carefully pasted into his scrapbook and annotated with the inscription, 'My First Article'. And several more followed, under the guise of 'No 1', but authorship and journalism had to take second place until after the war.

The records of *Who was Who* show that he went to the University of London. Technically, this is correct but he actually spent only a short time there before volunteering to serve in 1914. After the war, he went back to take a part-time course at University College. This was one which was started after the First World War to help those leaving the forces find gainful employment. The Diploma of Journalism was a two year course of evening lectures. The group Michael joined included forty men and three women. All those who took part in this course were later to take up journalism and work for the national and local papers; except Michael, whose destiny lay with writing and publishing books. Records show that only three took the final examination, and what's more, only one student passed. Michael was not mentioned, for quite early on in the course he became disillusioned with the academic approach to journalism. In an article about journalism written years later, he maintained that journalists write and teachers teach, but journalists could not teach their subject. He was very cynical about that course. Whether he always felt that strongly about the Colleges's efforts is not clear, but he very definitely did not take the examination.

Michael was just twenty when he returned to civilian life from the First World War. His first post, as a junior sub-editor, on a weekly magazine in Fleet Street, was to be a rude awakening. The sub-editor, under whom he was to be initiated, not only could not speak the King's English; he could neither write nor spell it. His first introduction to the methods of the sub-editor, was to watch him correct proofs with the aid of a well-thumbed dictionary. When Michael disclosed that he could save him the time, he became very welcome. They worked on an 'Answers to Correspondents' column and as he became absorbed into the work, he realised that it was far more important to be able to cut and edit proofs, and to verify references, than it was to be able to write academically good English. He was to work in succession for three weekly magazine publishers as a junior sub-editor and *The Nash Weekly* was one. There, he helped edit a half dozen short stories each week, many uninspiring and far from well produced as no illustrations adorned the pages. They made heavy reading but were, nevertheless, popular. Numerous other new magazines were started in the 1920s to satisfy the public's demand for fiction, many failing to survive. He wasn't very happy doing this work as it failed to stretch his mind, and consequently as boredom set in the inevitable happened, Michael sought employment elsewhere. Civilian life was very flat after the intense action in the trenches.

Joyce Lambert of *Woman* magazine interviewed Michael in January 1950. She reported that Michael, 'shudders slightly when he mentions these three weekly papers, then, with a happier note in his voice, that they are no longer in existence'.

However, in the early twenties he began to write on a wide range of subjects, including reviewing books. One of his first book reviews appeared in *The Globe*. The public, it was thought, had become apathetic to war stories and in the article, Michael highlighted the fact that publishers still had these titles on their lists, indicating that they thought that there was still an appeal for such works. One possible explanation for the apparent apathy was the singular omission of all such 'war' based articles and short stories from the popular magazines. Almost every author at the time found that editors of fiction magazines refused to take such articles. They said that the public wanted to forget about the war. Books were different, especially serious works. Two extracts demonstrate that Michael had already grasped the marketing importance of publishing books.

War books cannot be ignored. As I have pointed out, there is, fortunately, sufficient demand to enable publishers to put such works on their lists . . . Publishers, like theatrical managers, must give the public what they want, and the number of new war books promised suggests a revival of interest which should be welcomed by every thoughtful Englishman. *(The Globe 22.11.1920)*

He also wrote about the cinema – in an article appearing in *Family Circle* he appraised the progress of the film industry, then in its youth, and enthused about the entertainment values. Many thought that there were defects in too many films. These criticisms focused on the excessive display of expensive motor cars and sometimes, the quite unnecessary use of the telephone. The article appeared in 1921 and the subject must have had more than a casual interest for Michael. His father, Moss, together with his brothers Lionel and Godfrey had once been involved in the cinematic world.

In 1921 Michael saw many more reviews appearing under his own name. For example, he wrote a lengthy appraisal of Rider Haggard for *John O'London's Weekly,* entitled *The Romance of Rider Haggard.* Haggard recounted to Michael that the strain of writing and rewriting his manuscript in just three months was excessive, so much so that he had to finish the manuscript in a darkened room. I wonder if Michael took any note of this, for his first book was to be published two years later. Nevertheless all the effort became worthwhile for Haggard's book was none other than *King Solomon's Mines.* Gilbert Frankau was another author whose books he reviewed.

In appraising Frankau's book, *The Seeds of Enchantment,* published by Hutchinson, he wrote:

There is something of the quality of Swift and Anatole France, but although satire is the predominant flavouring, this does not detract from the enthralling interest of the story. For above all, Gilbert Frankau can tell a rattling good story. *(John O'London's Weekly 5.2.1921)*

Other authors included Colonel Arthur Lynch and Miss Winifred Graham. The fact that most of the books he reviewed were published by Hutchinsons may have missed the attention of the less discerning reader.

For he had joined Hutchinsons as Publicity Manager in September 1920, but his flair for writing led him to produce these reviews. One subject that appeared in a number of press cuttings was the value of book jackets.

In an interview he gave to the *Evening Standard* in May 1922, he enthused about the American invention of the book jacket, believing that it was an ideal method of protecting the book on dusty railway stations, whilst providing the prospective reader with a pictorial and alluring picture which would stimulate the purchase. He commented that 'the work of designing and painting of jackets is pleasant and lucrative . . . specially well adapted to women's talents . . . very often a new author will owe his first acquaintance with the reading public to the fascination of a jacket that excites curiosity or awakens some chord of sympathy that is irresistible.'

Sound marketing advice.

*　　　　*　　　　*

His first major work as an author appeared in 1923, *Short Story Writing for Profit*. Hutchinsons, of course, published it, which was only to be expected as he had been working for them as their Publicity Manager for some three years. In that time he had established himself as a capable promoter of books – indeed it may well be that he was responsible for the innovation of the four crosses which were the hall mark of Hutchinson's advertisements for some years. Perusing through old cuttings during my research, I find they are as eye-catching now as they obviously were then. The style is certainly memorable. (see illustration on page 51) His experience of advertising titles and promoting a large list of books to the reading public must have made his commercial experience as a fledgling publisher with Victor Gollancz, all that much harder to bear.

He had by now, clearly got his feet well and truly under the table, and apart from arranging the advertising, Michael devoted his remaining time to reading stories and manuscripts for publishing. 1922 saw the upsurge of the 'short story' and during that year thirteen new magazines were started to meet this new demand. Amongst the better-known writers was Stacey Aumonier who was at the time considered to be a master of the short story and had a huge following of avid readers.

Very few of the stories submitted ever reached the printers, for the vast majority simply were so badly written, that no matter what the sub-editor could do, he could not turn it into a worthwhile tale. Doubtless it will not surprise you to know that Michael grew so tired of the poor standards and the repetitive errors, that he sat down to write a book on how to write good stories. He believed that, if the quality of manuscripts could be improved, then he would have a wider choice to select from for publication. So who better to write the foreword of his book than Stacey Aumonier. He was to become, like so many other authors, a very good friend.

His first book was the forerunner of a theme which continued for some years. This was that authors, and journalists for that matter, should always write for 'profit'. He returns to that theme time and time again throughout his books on writing and publishing. In *Short Story Writing for Profit* he set out to show authors just how to write fiction which would be bought by editors. In this book, Michael dissects and then analyses the component parts of a story. Finally he advises the aspiring author on where to sell his work. In his Introductory Note Michael cites that rather unkind phrase: 'Those who can, do; those who can't, teach.'

Stacey Aumonier highlights this aspect in his foreword.

They [the editors] are deluged. But unfortunately barely one-tenth of that deluge is in any way worth serious consideration. I suspect that Michael Joseph's motive in writing this admirable and helpful book is to raise the percentage from ten to say twenty per cent. It can be done . . .

Michael was in effect passing on his expertise so in a sense he was both teaching, and doing. And for profit as well.

The reviewers made much of Aumonier's foreword, but in an interview with W. R. Calvert for the *Daily Graphic,* Michael said,

He [Michael] is convinced that the heavy percentage of worthless short stories which swamp the modern magazine editor's desk can be reduced, perhaps one-third, by a careful study of the techniques of the craft.

The book was widely and enthusiastically reviewed. Only one paper published a cynical opinion, that was the *Daily News,* which suggested variations on the title such as *Politics for Profit, Song Writing for Profit* and *Play Writing for Profit!* Michael, being the squirrel that he was, kept all the cuttings and there are over a hundred and six. Not bad for his first 'book', and one which blazed the trail for aspirant authors.

I quote one such review from *The Sunday Times:*

We commend it as not only being a brilliant work on the art of the short story, but as a work of art itself. Mr Joseph has rendered the greatest service to a very large public.

The contents and advice were eminently sensible and practical for the time and he encompassed in the book all the features that hopeful writers were constantly getting wrong. Guidance on the composition, dialogue, style, and the plot was explained in detail. Stacey, as I said, enthused about the book and its contents, but the main attraction surely was to be found at the back of the book. For Michael had included as the last chapter, a most comprehensive list of magazine publishers and what sort of stories they were buying. What's more, he listed the prices paid to authors. For example, *Bow Bells* – offered £1.1.0. (£1.05) for fifteen thousand words; *Lady's Companion,* £1.5.0. (£1.25) per thousand words; *Boys' Own Paper,* £1.1.0 per published page of two to four thousand words. All of which were nearly double that novelists were earning. This reference section was one of the best and most useful parts of the book. It was a stroke of genius to include this topic and with the overt support of one of the leading short story writers of the day, the book's recognition was guaranteed.

Michael completed this, at twenty-five years of age and after only five years in journalism and publishing!

The book was published on 5 October 1923 and Hutchinsons must have been very happy as they produced a *second* edition that month, a *third* in December and a *fourth* in the following May. There were at least six reprints and in publishing terms, Hutchinsons' timing and their judgement of the subject's appeal was impeccable. Not many authors strike success so soon. The whole experience must have greatly added to Michael's confidence and encouraged him to write another, which he did.

Journalism for Profit was published the following October (1924) but by this time Michael had grown stale at producing advertisements. The yearning for dealing with authors and publishers had grown and he was more than delighted to receive an offer from Messrs Curtis Brown the literary agents, which he accepted with alacrity. For undoubtedly it was to give him a wider knowledge of book publishers and the type of work that authors could produce and, above all, he would be in a position to help new authors achieve their literary ambitions. In the summer of that year he succeeded Mr Savage as head of the English Book Department.

Michael repeated the format that had been so successful for *Short Story Writing For Profit* by obtaining Sir Philip Gibbs to write the foreword, and he also included a chapter with contributions from his colleagues. The subjects he covered included News, Interviews, Humour and Verse and Pictorial Journalism. Michael reiterated the useful, and no doubt publicity-appealing chapter in which he had twenty-two leading journalists write 'How I make Journalism Pay'. Two of these were Gilbert Frankau and Hannen Swaffer, both well known writers of that period. A sure way to obtain good reviews!

Michael wasn't the only one to tap this particular readers' market. Others were in on the act too. Competing with him for sales were a small group of authors all of whom had the same idea. The others I must mention were, Low Warren's *Journalism,* A. Baker's *Practical Journalism, Popular Guide to Journalism* and A. Bull's *How to Write for the Papers,* proving the point that it was a market worth pursuing in view of the public's demand for guidance in becoming writers.

Good reviews duly followed. Again Michael managed to file away some hundred press-cuttings from a wide variety of newspapers and magazines. By now he was receiving reviews from overseas which included Australia, Egypt, India, Ireland, Italy and South Africa. The book was widely acclaimed by his fellow journalists, which was praise indeed and very satisfying. Amongst the reviews were the odd humorous comments. For instance the one in the *London Opinion,*

> Michael Joseph . . . offers the budding journalist a lot of sound, horse-sense advice; tells him to go where the money is and how to get there, and does not hesitate to give away such trade secrets as that 'book reviews and theatrical notes are – more or less – the work of literary and dramatic critics'. Oh, Michael, Michael, isn't that more or less unkind! *(28.6.1924)*

And the *Humorist* wrote:

> In our opinion the book is of considerably more practical value than all the schools of journalism combined *(6.24)*

Michael had previously declared his hand about his feelings for courses on Journalism, whether at The University College of London or elsewhere. He was definitely not enamoured with the current teaching methods and the reason that he did not take the examination is to be found in the text of his book *(Journalism For Profit).*

It is unfortunately true that there is still no recognized or approved training for the would-be writer. In spite of the establishment of a few commercial institutions which no doubt do excellent work despite the handicap of dealing with the majority of their pupils by correspondence, and of the newly created University of London Journalism Course (which at present is sadly academic and hopelessly unpractical), the ambitious writer has absolutely no guidance at all.

One of the arguments that he started, was whether the role of the journalist was a 'trade' or a 'profession'. He believed at the time, that journalism was more a trade and several reviewers took him to task on this point. Another quote which attracted attention was that allegedly attributable to Lord Rothermere:

If there is a fire in the city and £5,000 worth of merchandise is burnt, that's a news item worth three lines. But if at the same fire a fireman risks his life to rescue a black kitten from the top storey – that's a human touch worth half a column. *(Newspaper World 2.8.24)*

Such were the comments.

Whilst Michael was basking in his well-earned limelight, Curtis Brown had left to visit America and the *Sunday Times* noted that in his absence, Michael was now acting as General Manager. Talent has its rewards and promotion obviously came quickly.

More books were published in 1924 than ever before, indicating that there were good prospects for any new author. It is hardly surprising that books on this subject were selling well.

With two successful books under his belt he followed with *The Commercial Side of Literature,* which was published in 1925, again by Hutchinsons. Much of the advice given then is still valid today and although numerous books have been written on these subjects since, these titles are still well worth reading.

One extract worthy of being repeated demonstrated that news items, to be effective, should be brief, and he quotes an American reporter recording a fatal accident,

John Dixon struck a match to see if there was any petrol in his tank. There was. Aged 56.

Succinct, and illustrating the point precisely. All his books were described by reviewers as practical, sound, covering every aspect and providing the help and guidance that writers and journalists require.

Thus, his third book sold even better than the first two. For it ranked with the best sellers of the day. *Publishers Weekly* (New York) included it with such august titles as *John Macnab* by John Buchan, *May Fair* by Michael Arlen and *Tales of the Long Bow* by G. K. Chesterton; and in England it ranked with the top eight best sellers in the summer of 1925.

Curtis Brown must have been duly proud to have such an authority on writing with him. No doubt, when Michael gave advice to any author, it would probably have been followed without question or dissent. Agents in those days spent much of their time editing and advising authors on how to rewrite parts of their work, if they wanted to have the manuscript published, a practice that today is not repeated by all. The art, for that is what it is, gave many new authors a chance to have at least one book published, and in later years, when he was a publisher himself, he never lost that art, as authors today will attest.

1925 also saw Michael become a regular contributor to *The Writer,* a magazine solely devoted to authors. It was natural for him to contribute, bearing in mind the acclaim he received for his books on the subject. Articles carrying the headings of 'The Dialogue', 'Composition', 'Climax', 'Selling the MS' were just a few. He managed to maintain a regular feature every month, in addition to which, he was also writing for *T. P.'s & Cassell's Weekly.* A year of prodigious output!

Two of Michael's quotes were highlighted in *Eve,* one of which is worth noting:

> Somebody once said that at some time or other in his life, every man has the ambition to write a play. 'And nearly all of them write it', said a cynic. *(22.7.35)*

Years later, Michael was also to fall for this trap and wrote a play called *Discovery*. It was in fact published by Gollancz but never sold very well. What an understatement, for one royalty statement shows an income of 4d. (four old pennies, about 2 new pence today). Even he had his limits!

Michael was not forsaking other areas either. His reports on what novelists were earning (about 10/-per thousand words – on an average novel of 80,000 words) were not only published in this country but they were repeated overseas as well. For example, the comments on novelists' earnings were reprinted in the *Adelaide Register* in February 1926.

Consequently he was becoming more than adept at writing. He was the guiding light to many new authors and a useful reference source for practising editors as well. The appeal to authors was, I think, mainly that they could see that he fully understood their problems. His empathy was a tool which he used with the precision of the surgeon's scalpel.

The new author would not necessarily earn the average of 10/-per thousand words on his first novel. It was more likely to be less. Michael was quoted in the *Daily Express* as saying:

> The author's gross return is, roughly, 6s (a shilling – worth about five pence today) per thousand words, a rate which would be scorned by any self-respecting provincial journalist. I emphasize the word gross; for, from this meagre return, the wretched author has usually to pay typing bills – £5 or so – agent's commission (ten per cent), cost of paper, ink, postage of manuscript, and other sundries. *(9.12.1927)*

At the time he was still acting as a literary agent and would have quite easily understood the author's point of view. And obviously a wide knowledge of authors' earnings would be essential, if ever he was to become a publisher himself.

Michael always counselled that the writer, and for that matter, the publisher too, should study and understand the markets to which his books were aimed. There seems no doubt that part of Michael's success lay with the steady purchase of his titles by the lending libraries. *Boots Library* for example, was a frequent purchaser, as were the main lending libraries throughout the country. The subjects Michael covered in his books were popular with them, because writing was a widespread activity, and the books likely to be in demand for some time to come. The libraries insisted for obvious reasons, that the books had a secure binding, which resulted in a higher price of 7/6d a copy.

The popularity of libraries came in for criticism though, for in 1930, one James Fieldhouse believed that they produced thoughtless readers who 'skim and never delve into books. A book worth reading is worth buying . . . Michael Joseph suggests that until we become a book buying nation it is better to continue the borrowing system, but I think that if the borrowing system was curtailed, more books would be purchased, and certainly, greater discrimination would be shown by the reader'. The argument continues today.

Whatever the discussion, the libraries certainly helped Michael to become well known.

Michael frequently offered advice to others but occasionally he ignored his own words. On one classic occasion Michael recommended that authors should never reply to reviewers when they wrote criticising their work. Sound advice. However, Michael broke with his own rule, but then in his eyes, he had to.

The *Author, Playright and Composer* took him to task in their review and levelled the accusation that his book was propaganda for the literary

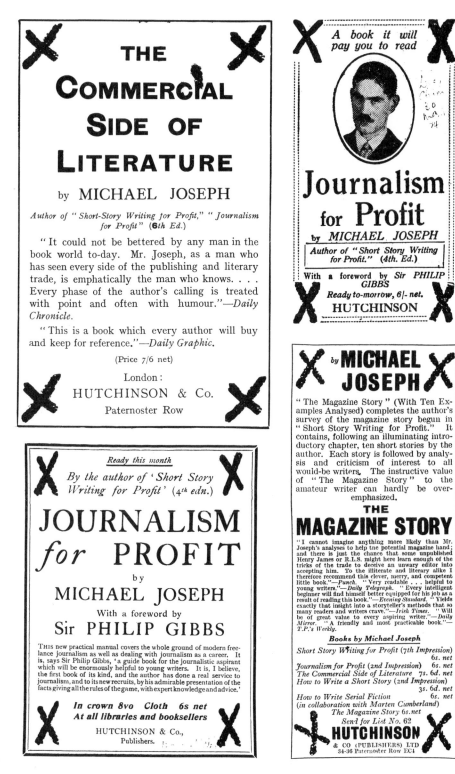
Hutchinson & Co's advertisements with the famous crosses

agent. This was a sensitive area as Michael, still in the employ of Curtis Brown, had become a very successful literary agent and it could be said that he was acquiring publicity for the company.

His reply to the journal was lengthy, but his response to the criticism left nothing in doubt.

> The penultimate paragraph of the review suggests that my book is propaganda for the literary agent. Your reviewer implies that on almost every page I recommend the use of an agent. That is simply untrue. Apart from the chapter on the subject, there are not half a dozen references to the literary agent in the whole book. He agrees with the statement made by a publisher that an agent is unnecessary to the majority of authors. It is true that many authors (among them most of the writers of educational books, to whom your reviewer quite truthfully refers earlier as being 'sweated labour') do not employ an agent. It looks as if they would be better off if they did. But the significant fact remains that nearly all the successful novelists and experienced members of the Society of Authors chose to be represented by agents. That speaks for itself.

The reviewer 'D. K. R.' replied to the letter and though he wrote a spirited defence, did finally concede that Michael was right. So sometimes perhaps it does pay to respond!

Some years later he was to become a regular book reviewer himself for *Pictorial Weekly*. So he crossed over to the other side, and some of the comments he was to make are really worth noting. These are recounted more fully in the next chapter.

However, life was not all about literary agents, authors and publishers. In 1925 Michael took himself off to tour parts of North Africa with his old friend, Stacey Aumonier, to celebrate the success of *Short Story Writing for Profit*. During their holiday they visited Morocco, and Southern Algeria, and Michael used some of the time in researching local events, no doubt, with an eye to a future story. On occasions they stayed in hotels, moving from one *Hotel Transatlantique* to another as they travelled from city to city. However, they journeyed overland by camel to visit lesser known parts of Algeria. They reached Laghouat, on the edge of the Sahara where Michael took a photograph of the very impressive Christian Cathedral. This later appeared in *The Sphere* as did another in *The Morning Post* which won him a guinea in a photographic competition. In search of back-ground material they visited the holy city, *Ben-is-guen*. From the notes made on *Hotel Transatlantique's* writing paper, he recorded detailed observations on the city, including comments on the local food, wine and women.

Kous-Kous – the staple Arab dish consisting of wheat rolled by hand and steamed for hours. *Lagmi* – the sap of the palm tree, taken from the top only, fermented for 24 hours becoming very potent. Cool and tasted like coconut juice but more syrupy. *Ouled Naïl Girls* – who prostitute in order to earn their marriage dowries.

His next book, *How to Write a Short Story,* came out in December 1925. So that holiday was not wasted after all! He had written about the techniques of writing short stories before and he needed to update the work. Also he had penned notes for the aspirant author of novels and for the journalist too. So now he felt it was necessary to help the short story writer again, especially as the public still craved for good short stories.

In the book, he covers all the subjects that are germane to this style of writing. Nothing was left out, for Michael knew every aspect and he was methodical about covering each detail. There are chapters on the plot, character, dialogue, composition, climax, and style. And he included the types of magazine story which were popular, and preparation of the manuscript. Critics at the time considered that the young authors had nothing more to ask – simply go away and write. If they followed all the advice given, then they would succeed.

Amongst the reviews was this one from the *Western Mail,*

Mr Joseph bids fair to become the standard "guide philosopher, and friend" of all literary aspirants. This latest addition to his series of practical manuals deals with the technical requirements of the modern magazine story. Construction is explained in a manner which should make the essentials plain to the merest tyro; all the difficulties which beset the amateur's path are fully considered. "Indispensable" is a strong word to call into service; let us say, then, for anyone less than a genius Mr Joseph's book will be of the utmost service.

If this laudatory review appears to the reader to be too fawning, then so be it. The reviewers were overwhelmingly in favour of his publications and generally welcomed all of them. You should not be left in doubt as to the strength of the literary world's feelings. This, and all the other titles, were essential books for all librarians. Understanding the needs of the lending libraries was fundamental to Michael's considerations.

Having exhausted that particular market he turned his attention to stories for magazines. In 1928 he had two books published, *The Magazine Story* and *How to Write Serial Fiction,* both again becoming essential reference sources for libraries. The latter was written in conjunction with Marten Cumberland, but as you can imagine, producing two books in one year could only be achieved at the expense of home life and his second marriage was beginning to make demands on his time, leaving him less time to write. Writing about serial fiction and magazines was the logical conclusion to the series and in a way, rounded it off nicely.

The theme that runs throughout his books, writing for profit, and not prestige, is nicely proved in *Magazine Story*. He takes ten of his own previously published short stories, and reprints them in book form. At the end of each story, he sets about analysing and criticising the structure, content and composition. All of which was done with the intention of helping the beginner! Using previously printed stories as examples really was making profits out of short stories.

By April 1928 Michael realised that he really had made a permanent mark in the literary world for *How to Write Serial Fiction* had begun to sell well. The success of this and the previous titles on the craft of writing and his work at Curtis Brown led people to say that he was the 'most authoritative source on the subject'.

How to Write Serial Fiction was to be the last in the series, but there is another aspect to this title. Again, he had used the formula of including other experienced and famous authors to illustrate his points. In one chapter, there are contributions from twelve established serial writers. Significantly, amongst them was the international writer, May Edginton. She was one who, later, invested in Michael's company when he wanted to buy himself out from Gollancz. Moreover, this title made up the fifth in the omnibus edition *Complete Writing for Profit*. This enhanced his reputation even further as the literary expert.

One of the points he stressed about writing serial fiction was that the earning potential was much greater. The authors believed that it was possible to earn £240 from two 60,000-word serials, which was much more than could be earned from books or short stories. Since he had written so much on the 'how to' of writing, it is tempting to include extracts. There are simply too many but I have included a selection of his own efforts which reflect society in Chapter 3. During his relatively short writing career he managed to compose articles on a very wide range of subjects. He was really pleased to have so many published, but greater satisfaction was realised when his work was cited as good reference sources by Mrs May Byron's family advice column in *British Weekly*. For several years, a frequent event.

Michael had not stopped writing, though. The successful formula on *How to* being almost exhausted, he turned to the human side of journalism, an aspect of authorship which he had missed and one which seemed to him to be so important that he went to great lengths to emphasise it. His contacts with Fleet Street led from one thing to another,

A Book of Cats by Foujita, Michael wrote the text (see over)

PASIPHAE

❦

Sleep, coquette, your blandishments avail no more. Now I am delivered of your tyranny awhile.

You do not love me. When, furred siren, you tempt me from my work it is to gratify your vanity. Cajole me as you will, I am familiar with your flattery.

Yet you succeed. How should I write when you disturb my papers? How well you love to thrust a gossamer paw beneath the sheet on which I write and gently disengage it from my hand. Think you that baby mice lurk underneath the surface scratched by my industrious pen?

The sheet is spoiled and so I make a paper ball and throw it for your capture. You seize it fiercely and begin the ancient sport of toying with your prey. But if I work anew you spring upon my knee, proclaiming mischievous intent.

You know I would ignore you; capriciously you coax from me expressions of my love. Your soul delights in praise and adoration. Now upon my knee you play a part, you feign affection to excite my love.

Then you will perambulate my desk, with mincing step avoiding my possessions. Will you not betake yourself elsewhere? You smile at my exasperation; compose yourself for rest and stretch your limbs complacently at length.

Your saffron eyes compel my love but mock my pleading. You will not suffer me to touch your bronze-flecked fur which I admire. Why then torment me?

But now I am released from bondage. Sleep on, coquette Pasiphae. In peace I work, but 't is of you I write.

and he was persuaded to edit a book, written incognito, by a Fleet Street editor (*The Autobiography of a Journalist,* published in 1929). As the editor said at the time, 'If I had put my name to this document, I could not tell half the story, and I want to tell it all'. One review by the *Spectator,* was praise indeed.

> This book is one of the most remarkable human documents we have come across lately, and is valuable, moreover, as a truthful description of the various aspects of journalism.

The sales, though, never ranked amongst the best sellers, which was a great personal disappointment for Michael.

And I wonder how Michael felt, when Henry Holt and Co., the American publishers, announced on 1 April 1930 the publication of *The Commercial Side of Literature* and *How to Write a Short Story.* They were publicised with the slogan *Insure yourself against rejection slips!*

*   *   *

Another book that Michael played a large part in is one of the lesser-known titles. *A Book of Cats* was published, as a limited edition of 500 copies, in 1930 by Covici Friede, an American publishing house, with superb drawings by M Fsugoharu Foujita. The book is very much a collectors' item and is now highly sought after. An extract appears on pages 55–6. Strangely, this book escaped the notice of the compilers, when the *British Library Catalogue* was put together, as there is no mention of this work with Michael's entry. Each book also contained an additional run of illustrations printed on Japanese vellum, one of which was signed by the artist. An expert pointed out to me that Foujita always signed his books in pencil, which was his special medium.

Through the years his love for cats inspired him to share it with others in a medium he was best at at – writing. Not only short stories, such as *The Yellow Cat,* but full-length books too. Among them were the well known *Charles – The Story of a Friendship, Cat's Company* and *Puss in Books.*

For *Puss in Books* he teamed up with Elizabeth Drew. This book, published by Geoffrey Bles was an anthology of twenty-one stories – not the first time this has been done, but this was Michael's first. The stories collected in this volume exhibited cats in all their various phases, with attendant circumstances of humour, sentiment and pathos. The success, it has to be said, was probably due to judging the right moment to have the book published. Some of the authors were quite well known even then, and with such names as Compton Mackenzie, Mark Twain and Émile Zola, a well illustrated book was bound to succeed. One of Michael's favourite cats, Minna Minna Mowbray, was also featured. At the time, Michael thought that the book would not have been complete without her!

This followed *Cat's Company,* also published by Geoffrey Bles, in which Michael recounts the life of Minna Minna Mowbray and others. These books are still read avidly today by friends of the feline species.

In *The Adventure of Publishing,* which was produced by Allan Wingate in 1949, Michael returned to the theme of *How to* and in this case, *How to survive* as a publisher. In this book, he set out to help those who had been harbouring thoughts of becoming publishers, and for those who had done so, how to stay in business.

One of the more interesting points he raised, was the amount of capital he considered essential for starting up. Michael quotes the then late, Ivor Nicholson of Nicholson and Watson who stated that he would not dream of starting a new publishing company with less than £100,000. Now of course, inflation had taken its toll on the pound but in relative terms, this was still very much more than Victor had set aside for Michael. Sound advice for the newcomers.

Then, as now, accountants had to contend with difficult circumstances. One was inflation. (Yes, it was occurring in those days too.) There is an interesting comparison of the production costs of a crown quarto 320 page title in 1938 and 1948 – £249 in 1938 and £665 in 1948, an increase of 166 per cent. This prompted Michael to campaign for an increase in the price of books, which, as he said at the time, had only increased between 13 and 23 per cent over the same period. Doesn't this sound familiar?

Michael also put nine pieces of advice in the book on *How to Survive* as a publisher. His main point was the tendency to produce too many titles. He returned to this theme in articles, speeches, and broadcasts over many years and it was a message that he repeated again and again in what amounts almost to a crusade. He believed that investing in too many speculative titles often contributed to a publisher's downfall.

I wonder if he reflected on his early days when he announced to the trade that he intended to put out some hundred titles in his first year. Who had the courage to pull his leg? Certainly, a number of people wrote to him, and, not surprisingly, there were several librarians amongst them.

After he was invalided out of the Army during the Second World War, he convalesced at a quiet farm in Berkshire. There, in the peace and tranquillity of the countryside, the war seemed very distant and it was here that he put pen to paper and wrote *The Sword in the Scabbard*. Apart from recording the events which now must be a useful reference to historians, he gave vent to his critical views which had developed over the previous two years. The lack of arms and the poor direction of the country's armed forces were two subjects that came in for his acidic comments. And in parts he even criticised the generals. Surprisingly, it was passed by the Censor. Looking through the the book today, the impression it gives me is that it could have been the forerunner and a major reference source for that splendid television series, *Dad's Army*, for the descriptions embrace all those fascinating and humorous aspects which the programme lampooned.

As far as the publishing profession was concerned, the war prevented excessive advertising so, much to Michael's delight, the book won fame through *word of mouth* recommendation. One of Michael's oft-repeated thoughts on advertising was that *word of mouth* was the most effective and influential kind. News of Michael's book spread, and for the first time, some of Michael's authors wrote to him to air their views. Amongst them were Clemence Dane, Joyce Cary and C. S. Forester.

Forester, writing to Michael from the USA, said that he had enjoyed reading the *The Sword in the Scabbard* enormously, though doing so engendered much homesickness. The book had puzzled him, as he could not understand why a publisher should ever bother to write books, but assumed that it was a sense of duty and public spirit that had got the better of him. He went on to say that in his experience over there, where he had met many generals, he believed that the British Army had come a long way since 1918. For one thing they all read *The General* and told him that they liked it! That had cheered him up whenever it was mentioned in conversation, though he remained cynical about it all.

He went on to say that he had not got one single criticism of Michael's book, much as he would jump at the chance of paying off old scores!

Joyce Cary also wrote to say that he enjoyed reading the book for its straightforward account of the situation after Dunkirk, especially the eye witness approach, whose details one could trust. The book certainly presented a very clear picture of the desperate position in those months.

Historians are far better qualified to expound on this aspect. Michael had highlighted several major weaknesses and attitudes which were out of step with the then modern needs of warfare. He repeatedly expressed his frustration at the lack of arms – and ammunition. And even the building of pill-boxes, where in one case, the firing window slit faced directly into a bank precluding its effective use.

With such accurate descriptions it would seem that Michael was fortunate to get it through the censors, having flagrantly flouted authority and risking the wrath of officialdom. The only stipulation being that towns, places and officers' names were to be printed with the first letter only. All of which was rather a waste of time, for if one knew the area it needed only simple deductions to trace the locale.

This was the first title that Michael had published through his own firm. The book was reviewed in a wide variety of papers and magazines, for the topicality of the subject was 'good' copy, and so was the fact that he used the book as a platform from which to criticise the Army ... especially for the stupidity of the routines of discipline. The *spit and polish* attitude received special attention of course! And his colleagues who had suffered with him must have been delighted by his achievement. No doubt a subject well aired in the mess bars!

The reviewers had a field day. H. M. Tomlinson, in *The Observer* wrote;

> This sober account by a company officer of service with an infantry battalion, guarding a stretch of coast when invasion seemed at hand, ought either to be censored for telling our troops what they know, as well as for worrying civilians with doubts, or else made [sic] compulsory reading at the War Office. Could the Home Secretary manage the latter? *(26.4.1942)*

Although many reviews were complimentary and laudatory, some were critical. John Brophy suggested in *John O'London's Weekly* that;

> If Mr Joseph has a fault, apart from his sentimental preoccupation with cats, it is an excessive desire to be fair to everyone with whom he has personal relations. He quarrelled with his commanding officer on details of training and routine, yet he admires him for showing once or twice an interest in books and music – *(10.4.42)*

And this wasn't the only criticism – *The Listener* was quite acidic;

> The book will entertain all whose military education has been similar. But the author should have been advised to omit the last section, which is devoted exclusively to military criticism of military organisation. For the trouble is that almost all his criticisms are invalid. Like a true-born Briton Mr Joseph cannot see beyond his own company commander's nose. That his battalion was part of a brigade and that brigade part of a division of a corps is hardly perceptible in the whole length of the book. Here is a small microcosm only, not the proverbial cog. How very British! And so we see the army only as one small

I

On a sunny Saturday afternoon in August 1930 I set out for Thames Ditton to choose a Siamese kitten.

I had for some time cherished the ambition to add a Siamese to my collection. The word "collection" is here used deliberately, for the reigning favourite in my household, Minna Minna Mowbray, was an enthusiastic mother. Her kittens were as charming as they were numerous and the house was usually over-populated with (if a self-respecting cat-lover dare use such a disparaging word) with young cats and kittens. I found it hard to part with them at any age.

Minna Minna Mowbray, a demure

company. And that frankly, gives Mr Joseph little basis on which to criticize the army as a whole.

Though this is strong comment, it was only one review of many, and largely out of step with the rest of public opinion. Suffice to say, that the book sold well and he received many accolades from his peers and colleagues.

Then came *Charles, The Story of a Friendship*. If there is one thing that guarantees the public's attention, it is a well-written and emotive account of an animal, particularly a cat. It is an intimate story of a man's close understanding of his cat, in a way, almost a human appreciation, each of the other. He looked upon Charles as a friend not only to whom he could talk and address his problems, but as an attentive ear for the articles he was writing at the time; above all, a playmate and marvellous companion that he could comfort and be comforted by. The book certainly attracted a great deal of attention then, and it remains popular still gracing many library shelves.

Michael wrote the story of Charles with a fountain pen, and much to the amusement of Charles, who thought that the moving pen top was a toy solely to exercise his predatory skills. There are quite a few deletions and insertions which are no doubt due to his antics. It is very easy to imagine the scene, Michael sitting at his desk scratching away on the paper, Charles leaping on to the desk swiping the wobbling pen top with his chocolate brown paw. An idyllic period for Michael when his health was returning to normal, and his writing and business activities going well for him.

When Michael wasn't writing books or articles, he was far from being idle. In 1951 Faber and Faber asked him to edit an anthology of cat stories, to be entitled *Best Cat Stories*. This he did and also wrote the introduction to the book. Being a well known ailurophile, naturally many reviews followed. So did the letters!

Eleanor Farjeon was quick to acknowledge the appeal of the stories. And Hettie Gray Baker, the champion of cats everywhere, writing from New York in October 1952, expressed her admiration for the book. There were nineteen stories on cats – some from well known authors – T. S. Eliot, P. G. Wodehouse, Selwyn Jepson, Walter de la Mere and Paul Gallico being amongst them. The book was liberally illustrated by Miss Eileen Mayo.

Though many of the letters and press cuttings make good reading, there was a letter from one upset reader;

I have just read the first story in your book *Best Cat Stories*.

I immediately closed the book and posted it back to my library (Smith's of Lambeth). I dare not read any more in case there were other heart-rending yarns of the same kind, which there quite likely may be, seeing this is your idea of a *Best Cat Story.*

It is a beastly stinking story and should never have been written at all or published, let alone included in any book. Do you realize some misguided person may innocently buy your beastly book and give it to some unsuspecting child for a present only to have to have his little heart wrung in the very first story . . .

You cannot please everybody, even cat lovers.

Friends Michael made through his affection for cats were persuaded to write as well. Two such were James Mason the film star, and his wife Pamela, who wrote *The Cats in Our Lives.*

It is one huge achievement to actually write a single book, let alone seventeen, and this in a period of thirty-seven years. To do this whilst creating and nurturing an internationally known publishing company, living a family life and going to war, is an achievement which outranks many in the literary world. Nothing comes easily though, and there were sacrifices to be paid.

Leaving a legacy in the form of press cuttings, letters, books and articles, he made the whole job of recounting his life that much easier. It is to his credit that he took so much time – and patience – in preserving these cuttings. I can visualise him – meticulously cutting them out with his folding scissors, which he kept in a small and worn leather pouch. Whenever he saw an item of interest, he would almost ritualistically take out the brown leather pouch, unbutton the flap, returning the pouch to his pocket, and then neatly cut out the press item, without damaging the surrounding articles. There were times when he took great pleasure in cutting out headlines which amused him, or which had double meanings especially to his family or friends.

But what drove him to write in the first place? Having researched the period, I believe that he was genuinely sure that he would encourage others to improve their writing. Perhaps he had an enduring sympathy with those editors he left behind on those weekly magazines. Above all, he thought that he could do better than those around him. The formula he used in his books was repeated often, but it always worked. The inclusion of other well known authors in part of his books ensured that they were always read.

The reviewers could hardly ignore them.

Chapter 3

Master of Words:
The Creative Challenge
1923–58

*'The bad journalist seldom, if ever, gets into print, but
the bad novelist – oh, my lord!'*
Michael Joseph 1926

As the years pass, it will be far too easy to assume that Michael was just a successful publisher, but his books on authorship and writing will testify that he was more than that. A man of much creative ability and erudition, his journalistic achievements were so numerous that I believe they merit a chapter of their own for they all contribute towards the picture of the whole man.

On publishing, authorship and related subjects, he was considered in his time to be the authority, but he also wrote about horse racing, reviewed books, wrote plays, poems and even had his own column in an American newspaper. During my research, I compiled a list of these published stories, reviews and other material which are to be found in the Bibliography. Some of his memorabilia include drafts of stories and articles which do not seem to have ever been published. None of these came up in discussion when I was a young boy and it has been absorbing for me to retrace his career through them.

As I have said, his efforts encompassed many aspects. His earliest, and serious achievements were extracted chapters from his book *Short Story Writing for Profit* adapted for *The Writer* (published in 1923). Two years had to elapse from the book's publication before these selected articles appeared, but once started his contributions continued on a regular basis for the next five years. Even after 1930, he had the odd article published. These went a long way to enhance Michael's reputation as an authority on the subject.

In addition to the books on writing and publishing produced whilst at Hutchinsons, he also turned his attention to writing stories and articles for the press. He was after all, practising what he was preaching – writing for profit. One such article concerned an entirely different subject, the cinema. In 1921 he wrote a short piece entitled 'The Rise of the Cinema for' *Family Reader*. There is no mention of his father's interests here either, but he took a nice swipe at Moss's concern about the flickering screen which he thought would ruin people's eyesight and equally, affecting the audience's minds.

Every popular movement is, in its early stages, inevitably subjected to severe and antagonistic criticism, and especially is this so in the case of forms of public entertainment. The cinema was no exception; at first the critics vigorously denounced it as a 'blood and thunder' creation of the worst type, prophesied its evil effects on childish minds *(a prejudice which still survives in certain quarters)*, cheerfully anticipated its early collapse and condemned the movement generally.

Not all the articles carried his name. Unknown to the public there were family links to several major feature articles that appeared under his name. One example concerned Wembley Stadium and the family links with this are described in the opening chapter.

At the start of the twenties, the government and press made much of a new and very large exhibition planned for Wembley. It was to be known as *The British Empire Exhibition* and for the time it was a massive undertaking requiring 12,000 skilled men to build the exhibition halls which stretched over 216 acres. The national press played its part but Michael managed to write a preview of this great event for *Pictorial Weekly*. This was also published in the *North Staffordshire Labour News* and the 1,600-word article with illustrations covered a full broadsheet page.

Michael pointed out that Mr Rudyard Kipling was to have the responsibility of naming the fifteen miles of streets. One item of information which must have been savoured by his father, 'The visitor to Wembley – and you and I and everybody will be flocking there from April onwards not in our thousands but in our millions . . .' Curiously there is only a passing reference to the catering and 'accommodation' for the visitors. I wonder what Moss said when he read the review; it seems likely that Michael's attention to this aspect was highlighted by his father's business interest in the exhibition.

Michael had several different jobs in the immediate post-war years (1919 to 1924). Whether it was due to the lack of excitement or unsatisfactory employment is not clear, but he once really let off steam about the younger generation in a way that is remarkably similiar to many current observations. The article, 'The Younger De-Generation', was published in *The Smart Set* in 1925;

Poster – Our Farmer Prince

Poster – Kissing Cup's Race

The 'flapper' and the 'nut' of pre-war vintage have been replaced by the 'sweetie' and the 'tin of fruit' (I understand that these are the really correct labels) of today. The embryo flapper and the nut had, however, the advantages of sound disciplinary handling from their elder brothers, and experience has convinced most victims that elder brothers all the world over rarely hesitate to apply corrections when necessary (i.e. often) to the exuberant new idea.

Our modern 'tin of fruit' however, is the product of a highly emotional, artificial time. During his childhood there were no elder brothers, or younger uncles or fathers. They were doing an unpleasant, but exceedingly necessary, job of work. And most women, too, were busy with war-work of varying usefulness but time absorbing in its demands. Consequently, the very younger generation grew up anyhow. No one was there to spank them, or impress on them the relative unimportance of their existence or keep them in order generally. They grew older in an atmosphere charged with unnatural excitement, panic sometimes, amid houses and streets darkened at night, while searchlights flitted across the sky . . .

The gap which separates the war-scarred generation from its immediate successors is not one of years. There is a huge gulf between those of us who went to the war and those who were too young to go. The men and women who were jerked out of gear for nearly five shattering years and came face to face with the war feel a little bitter today, and sometimes a little afraid, to think that they fought and suffered so that today's spineless, irresponsible youth might flourish in safety.

To survey the modern young people of our acquaintance is pro-foundly depressing. To hear them talk one would think that sex was the only important topic in the universe. They mistake licentiousness for frankness, and stimulated cravings for natural impulses. They want to be free, and they are simply loose. To look at them would be amusing if it were not rather pathetic . . .

Good Housekeeping, one of the popular magazines at the time, as it still is, persuaded him to review the current and popular women writers in 1929. I have mentioned elsewhere his susceptiblility to young ladies, so understandably he accepted this task with alacrity. He knew many of the better-known writers and he liked to be associated with their literary successes. Of women writers he observed;

And the conclusion that I have come to is this; women writers are more honest, less 'catty', certainly less vain and altogether more likeable than their masculine rivals.

> Women . . . are candid, sensible, practical, not above taking advice, and fundamentally more sincere. In their business dealings they are direct, clear-thinking, sometimes shrewd, rarely dull. Outside an office they are content not to talk 'shop'.

Michael managed tactfully to mention most of the popular writers of the time, including Rose Macaulay. Of her he wrote, 'a most stimulating person to meet. Her conversation is as witty as her novels. I am a little afraid of her, for I suspect her of deriving impish satisfaction by luring one into dangerously profound discussions'. Others included Beatrice Seymour, Naomi Royde-Smith, who became the wife of Ernest Milton the actor, Clemence Dane, Rebecca West and Storm Jameson;

> Margaret Storm Jameson is one of my favourites. One of the most attractive things about her is her voice. Like Rose Macaulay she has a sense of humour and a gift for shrewd, penetrating comment. She is probably unaware, but I have found it to be so, that she is popular among women. Women who write are much more loyal to each other than men; there is less jealousy and infinitely more appreciation. It is not surprising that Storm Jameson is popular for I don't see how anyone, knowing her, could help liking her.

Doubtless Michael received appreciative letters from all those he mentioned. Certainly when Mrs Guy Chapman read the article, she wrote to Michael, using her pen-name Storm Jameson.

She was moved to comment, as one of 'Michael's favourites', that the publishers of the article really ought to have included a photograph of him. She knew him as a young and charming publisher for whom she had the highest regard, and went on to encourage him to ensure that the following issue of *Good Housekeeping* rectified this sad omission. The caption, she suggested, should reflect his good luck and good fortune to marry Edna, whom she rated as one of the most charming women she had ever met.

Michael and Edna did enjoy a very happy marriage and they shared many interests together. They were both also heavy smokers and like so many at the time, wanted to give up the habit. It was the journalistic streak in him which prompted an article in August 1930 which *The Daily Mail* published;

> I suppose most heavy smokers have discovered that the only satisfactory way to reduce one's consumption of cigarettes is to buy them in smallish packets. Fifties and hundreds make a tempting display and

disappear in no time. So now we usually buy our cigarettes in packets of twenty. This led to The Great Discovery . . .

It was my invention. I decided to secrete, squirrel-like, a few cigarettes in queer, out-of-the-way places against the frequent occasions when my case is disconcertingly empty and there isn't a packet in the house.

It was a triumphant moment for me when my wife looked woefully at my empty case, as if to say, 'Now we haven't any cigarettes and the shop is shut . . .'

This time, however, with the bland air of a conjurer about to produce rabbits from a hat, I led the way to a corner cupboard which we seldom use. A neat little pile of cigarettes was hidden away in the drawer. We seized them gleefully.

But when I next went to the cupboard I found that my wife had been there before me. So I had to find another cache for the reserve cigarette ration.

From that time onwards, the concealment became a battle of domestic wits.

A real game of hide-and-seek, but inveterate smokers will recognise the game which I'm sure is regularly played throughout the civilised world. Whilst many played the game, Michael wrote about the rules, and got paid for his efforts. The final hiding-place was, naturally, the obvious, the silver cigarette box on the drawing room table.

It was not until his first two sons were old enough to be involved with a school's OTC (Officers' Training Corps) that he gave vent to his personal feelings again in print. It was the *News Chronicle* which carried in 1934, a half-page article, 'Schooling for Soldiers'. Michael had been informed that his son would shortly be joining the OTC. Michael checked the prospectus and indeed it did state that 'all boys *may* join at the age of 15' (my italics). There was no mention of any compulsory rule that boys had to join – if that had been the case, Michael would, as he wrote at the time, have looked for another school. He felt most strongly that his son should not join and said so. It was not surprising that he later received a letter from his son's housemaster asking Michael to 'state his reasons', and adding 'it does seem such valuable practice in leadership, taking charge of things, unselfishness and responsibility'. The *News Chronicle* article ran;

My objection to the OTC is that it is fundamentally a training for war. So far as it lies within my power as an individual I will do nothing which prepares for war, which I now regard as futile and wrong. I was brought up to believe in 'Si vis pacem, para bellum', [if you wish peace, be ready for war] but I am now convinced that this is a false doctrine. Nor do I believe any longer that war is waged in self-defence. All the nations in the last war were convinced that they were 'defending' themselves.

Please let me make it clear that I have no personal grievance. I did not suffer (except perhaps in health) as a result of the last war. In many ways I benefited. I had comradeship, responsibility (I was in command of a machine gun company when only three years older than my son is now), valuable discipline and opportunity.

Nevertheless, I am today strongly opposed to war and, in principle, to anything which is even remotely preparation for it.

Several letters followed in the succeeding issues of the paper, some in support and some against. Those who had survived the First World War were in sympathy, whilst others thought that the country needed the continuity of good soldiering to provide a national defence. In this article he was referring to his son Leslie, who went to Bradfield College, near Reading in Berkshire. Leslie recalls the occasion well, for he received a letter from Michael ordering him to resign from the OTC 'with immediate effect'. He did.

Only six years later Michael felt it necessary to leave the business that he had founded to go away and fight once more, but he never mentioned this article again.

*   *   *

In his role as a journalist Michael's prolific writing led him to correspond with and write about many notable people. One was Noël Coward whom Michael knew very well; when he was studying the earning potential of authors he cited Coward as an example of one who was then earning a high income. Not that he thought Coward did not work hard for it. Michael described him as 'a serious, tremendously hard-working man who has had years of opposition and failure to overcome. His high spirits and enthusiasm are deceptive; under the surface he is a man very much in earnest.'

Magazine editors asked Michael to write appreciations of many authors – a privilege and a challenge that he made the most of throughout his lifetime. There were many such essays, not only on novelists but also on the wider spectrum of writers. Sydney Horler the writer of many thrillers published by Hodder and Stoughton was one. In the late twenties he had ten thrillers all selling well and the point that Michael stresses at the beginning of his commentary is that fashionable novelists come and go, but the writer of 'thrillers' goes on for ever. He reminded readers of *The Bookman* that the constant popularity of the mystery – adventure story made its own point and he posed the question of whether this satisfied the majority of readers. Critics were not likely to provide the answers but buyers for libraries and booksellers would. The critics were not Horler's friends either, for his success came from word of mouth recommendation. This only goes to show that Michael had that point clearly in his mind many years before he started publishing.

Another story teller whom Michael interviewed and subsequently wrote about, was Gilbert Frankau. In the twenties, he was one of the most popular writers, especially of short stories. Michael had not the same empathy with him as with other writers of the day, but they did share one experience. He was, as he said, 'one of us during the war' and Michael was struck by his appearance, which was totally unlike the public's image of a writer. In the article, Michael described him as well groomed, with a dark moustache and an unmistakable soldierly stance. It was, for Michael, a short piece unlike the one he wrote about P. G. Wodehouse.

Pelham Grenville Wodehouse was some sixteen years older than Michael, though Michael's appreciation of his writings, published again in *The Bookman,* indicates that he knew him very well. Michael was a gregarious man but whether he went out of his way to meet his subjects or whether his editors sent him out is unknown. Probably a little of both, but he managed to meet many authors, and for a period of two years commencing in November 1933, he was a regular book reviewer for *Pictorial Weekly*. This meant contributing about 500 words a week – together with a photograph as they were always illustrated.

One of the titles he reviewed is historically very interesting. On *My Struggle* by Adolf Hitler, Michael commented that 'the story of Hitler's triumph is, however, in itself a dramatic narrative, and not even the author's frequent lapses into rhetorical street-corner abuse detract from its interest. The book contains some interesting sidelights on British war propaganda, to which Hitler pays a bitter tribute.' And this, remember, was in 1933. Glancing on through the cuttings other familiar, and less oppressive names, appear, Yeats-Brown, Arthur Wragg, T. C. Bridges, Hessell Tiltman and Philip Gibbs.

During the Second World War Michael took issue with Bernard Shaw over his criticism of doctors. Though he would correspond with authors and publishers in the professional sense, he seldom wrote to criticise or compliment. However, his letters to Shaw were the exception. These are illustrated on pages 79–80.

It was well known that Bernard Shaw hardly ever replied to letters and it was therefore gratifying to receive a reply, even a postcard. They make provocative reading for Michael's corrections were accepted.

*   *   *

The urge to be creative began to show in Michael's life when he was at Curtis Brown, and not just in the pure literary or journalistic sense either. Apart from composing music, writing the odd poem and play and pencilling a sketch or two, he often lectured on the subject of publishing. And surprisingly, he turned his hand to adapting novels and poems for film scripts.

One tangible sign that he was interested in the cinema at an early age was the recent discovery of his collection of 16mm films. Taken in the late twenties and early thirties, they are now quite brittle, but some of the scenes are very emotive, despite the poor quality. Most of the films cover a relatively short period, roughly from 1929 to 1934 (many reels are undated), though when colour film became available after the war he made and edited at least two more. All, of course, in the best of silent movie traditions, and complete with captions. Rediscovering the films was a lucky break for they had not been seen for at least thirty years, but they are important, apart from the family interests, for they reflect his serious approach to the subject.

Once the *talkies* arrived to entertain the public on a commercial scale, Michael began to consider writing scripts for them. His interest in home movies and writing helped and it was not long before he attempted writing the dialogue for a commercial film. His first venture was to adapt Campbell Rae-Brown's novel and poem for a film entitled *Kissing Cup's Race*, which made a full-length film of some 6,700 feet. Produced by Butchers Films it lasted for about two hours, but unfortunately no copies of the film remain, the nitrate covered cellulose on which the images were stored having deteriorated with time.

It will come as no surprise that the story centred around the horse-racing world. A reviewer describing the film's strong points wrote in 1930,

> An exceedingly well-staged and capably characterised racing drama .... The story is a trifle obvious, but it leads up to popular dramatic situations and provides good entertainment.

The stars were Stewart Rome, Madeleine Carroll, John Stuart and Richard Cooper. Stewart Rome so the review ran, playing the part of

Jimmy, son of the Marquis of Hillhoxton, finds that he is destitute when his father dies. His fiancée, Lady Molly Adair, played by Madeleine Carroll, persuades him to run his horse Kissing Cup, in a big race and so retrieve the family fortunes. However, Lord Rattlington, (Stuart Rome) an unscrupulous gambler, also in love with Molly, had entered his horse in the same race. The film comes to a happy conclusion with Jimmy and Molly 'living happily ever after' and the family fortunes restored.

Fired with this successful attainment, Michael went on to write the commentary for *Our Farmer Prince*. This ran for forty minutes and was also produced by Butchers Films. Two years were then to elapse before this film made it to the big screen. However, it attracted a wide audience because the star was the then *Prince of Wales,* later Edward VIII. It was a film, patriotic in sentiment, which illustrated his activities and interests, and of course, his support for the Cornish Estates and Scilly Isles. The commentary for this 'U' rated film was given by R. E. Jeffrey. It is conjecture now, but perhaps it was this early contact with the Prince which enabled Michael to become the accepted publisher of The Duchess of Windsor's book *The Heart has its Reasons*.

Another year was to pass by before Michael's screenplay for the film *Account Rendered* was published. This drama involved the neat story of a magnate ensnared in his partner's financial jugglery, and how he saved the life of the lawyer briefed for his prosecution. This 'A' rated film had a stronger content but only received average reviews and *The Cinema* casually declared that it was only a 'useful second feature for the popular halls'. These were exciting times and Michael certainly made the most of this period of his life.

But this was certainly not his last film. He wrote the story for another, the working title of which was *The Reckoning,* but this film was made by a new company, Triumph Films. They announced with a flourish that they intended to make eighteen films, now with sound and work would start in February 1934.

Michael also contributed to the dialogue for the remake of a musical, *Brewster's Millions* which appeared in 1935. Produced by Herbert Wilcox, the 'U' rated film ran for eighty minutes and starred Jack Buchanan and Lili Damita.

It is regrettable, but the British Film Institute confirmed during my research that they do not, except for *Brewster's Millions* hold copies of these films in the National Film Archives and the existence of copies is unlikely; unless of course anyone reading this book knows otherwise. I harbour the thought that somewhere someone may have a copy.

One of Michael's other hobbies was playing the piano, but he did not, like so many people, just 'tinkle the ivories' occasionally. It was another antidote to life's pressures and the time spent playing was to him enormously relaxing. He started to play in the twenties at his home in Regent's Park Terrace and there became a proficient pianist. He enjoyed entertaining both friends and authors, though many of the former were authors as well. His approach to music was similar to his approach to films, and for a time he threw himself into this area of the arts, too.

One of his friends who was interested in music was Penelope, the wife of John Mortimer, who had written a novel which Michael had published, entitled *A Villa in Summer*. This had given her the encouragement to write another and she was one of many ladies who had captivated Michael's attention and he really enjoyed the fun of entertaining them. Michael once played most, if not all the songs in Noël Coward's *Song Book* to her. This was typical – he loved to charm the fair sex, but he took risks. On one occasion at Regent's Park Terrace, he was playing a duet with Angela du Maurier when Edna walked into the room and, seeing them, asked tetchily whether it was necessary 'to sit quite so close together'.

He really did like all women, but if he had a preference, it was for those in their late twenties whom he found irresistibly attractive. Not as he would admit, because they were at their physical prime, but that a girl of that age was still in love with life, oozing vitality and confidence, and enjoying the freedoms society had hitherto denied them. In his experience they were at that age intelligent and frank, and could talk knowledgeably about politics, religion, art and society with inspiring confidence.

This is the background which led, as I can establish, to his first piece of music being published. The tune appeared in a popular magazine *Womans Weekly* as early as January 1927, but what Curtis Brown thought is not known. Presumably he did not object to his colleague's extramural activities. The refrain for *Valley of Love* was put together by Draycot Dell and must have put Michael in a very romantic mood for now the words do seem very apt.

> Just you and I in the gloaming
> Thro the sweet valley of love.
> Over the heather come roaming, roaming, homing
> To that sweet spot in the valley;
> And when the stars shine above
> O perfect night, time of delight,
> In the sweet valley of love.

The following September his first daughter was born.

Playing the piano enabled him to relax in the same sort of way as he did when he had his cats around him. (Though the cats would often leave the room, because the noise upset them.) In later years, when married to Anthea and living at Browns Farm, he would play whilst she sang. These moments created an idyllic harmony for being very much in love they felt in that brief moment, an even closer bond. Besides *The Valley of Love* he composed other tunes, once putting together a melody which he managed somehow, probably in one of those do-it-yourself booths, to record and cut a 78 rpm disc. I don't believe that there were many copies made, probably no more than two, but the pleasure it gave him to bring it home and play it to the family was immense.

Not satisfied with writing, lecturing or broadcasting, he turned his hand to drawing. However, this was something that he did not take up seriously though several sketches survived him. One, a caricature of Mohandas Gandhi (known to his followers as Mahatma, meaning Great Soul), was drawn in the early thirties and I think shows that he was never destined to really succeed as an artist. However, he put more effort into sketching his cats.

It is not my intention in compiling this biography to idolise Michael, but he did have more than his fair share of talent. My research of his life unearthed records of many varied activities, interests amd achievements. For example, he turned to writing plays, though only one was published. *Discovery*, a three-act play, was published by Victor Gollancz in 1934. Sales were modest with two editions priced at 3/6d and 5/-, and his income from this was small. However, the subject is really quite significant. In *Discovery*, the plot centres on a woman who is capable of dreaming the future. She is married to a doctor who misuses her powers for greed and financial gain.

The idea for the plot came from Professor J. W. Dunne who had studied this possibility and wrote a book entitled *Experiment with Time*. Michael shared this man's belief, for he had personally gained from dreaming about future events. In an article published in *Pictorial Weekly*, he disclosed that he had successfully picked the winner of the Cesarewitch, a rank outsider, by memorising the event from one of his dreams.

There is another play in draft entitled *Account Rendered* but the plot and characters are entirely different from the film script with the same title. One can only conjecture as to whether this was ever published, but I would think not, as there are no reviews to be found and Michael was such a squirrel for mementoes. However, the script does make good reading

Poetry was another art to which Michael turned his hand. His poem dedicated to Charles is shown in Chapter 8, but this was not the only poem he wrote about cats. Another, naturally entitled *The Cat* ran to two verses. He composed one entitled, *The River* which was even longer and is worth including, for it is very apposite.

> Man is like a river
> Born a stream
> Of liquid crystal
> Sparkling into life,
> Tossing, tumbling gaily
> Through his infancy.
>
> Adolescence steers
> A troubled course
> Diverging, growing painfully
> Into a swift and rushing brook
> Which presently becomes
> A flowing river
> Placid and serene
> Breasting its burdens
> With an easy grace.
>
> The burdens grow
> As man flows on
> More sluggishly with time.
> The waters deepen
> Leaving stagnant pools
> In idle places.
> Weeds and flotsam cling
> And crease
> The once smooth surface.
>
> Slowly now the river flows
> Past buildings,
> Wharves and sheds
> Symbols of servitude
> Whose grime
> Discolours as it falls.
>
> The tired river
> Broadens slowly
> Age and toil have done their part.
> The sea awaits
> The deep obliterating sea
> In which all rivers flow
> And lose identity.

There is no record of this ever being published but judging from the way it was typed and the paper it is on, I think it must have been written during his days at Curtis Brown.

*   *   *

In addition to these challenges, he went on to become first a lecturer and later an ambassador for the world of authors and publishers. As his career in publishing grew he was asked to speak more often, sometimes formally but more often informally at luncheons or dinners.

His career as a lecturer began, as far as I can trace, in 1928 when he addressed a large audience at Foyle's Bookshop in May that year. He began his talk entitled 'Some experiences of a literary agent' with the statement that, 'A publisher can recognise a good book when he reads the manuscript, but it is impossible for him to predict whether the book will be a success.' He highlighted how difficult it was for authors to succeed, citing, for example, the difficulties of American authors in finding publishers in England, and equally those of English authors wishing to be published in America. Elizabeth Bowen's *The Hotel* was rejected by thirteen publishers in America. The fourteenth accepted the work and proudly announced that, because it had won the award of the Book of the Month Club, 50,000 copies had been sold prior to publication. Today, there are many similar stories, but it is the year this occured that makes it so fascinating. Another interesting fact emerging from this talk is that out of fifty books placed by Michael whilst he was at Curtis Brown, only fifteen were really successful.

Later on in 1936, he was invited to speak to members of the Leicester Writers' Club on another subject on which he was well qualified. It was entitled 'Authors and Publishers'. At this time he had been a publisher for less than a year, but the Club made much of his visit with posters circulated advertising the talk. I note with interest that members of the public were invited too, but they had to pay a fee of 6d – 2½ pence today. The audience included members of the local press for the *Leicester Daily Mercury* commented the following day, 'he stressed the point that only through hard work and regular hours for working could success be attained.'

The Leicester Writers' Club was not the only provincial club he addressed. He was Vice-President of the Birmingham Booklovers' Society – at least for two years, in 1938 and 1939. The programme announced that he would talk to the club in February 1939 on 'The Books I want' and that he would take part in a two-day course in March on 'Books, Authors and Authorship.' In his talk on the books that he was looking for, he mentioned biographies, citing Herbert Hodge as an

7th-October 1944

Dear Mr Bernard Shaw,

Except for professional reasons I do not write to authors about their books. One of the disadvantages of being a publisher (which I am in a small way) is that any letter he writes to a well known author is suspect. I am however writing to you merely as an interested reader of "Everybody's Political What's What?", which I bought for my son as a corrective to the influence of a naval ward-room.

The book is a remarkable performance even for you. But you know that. It is twenty worth-while books rolled into one, with autobiography for good measure - and what good measure! The best part of the book for any reader who, like myself, agrees wholeheartedly with much that you say and disagrees violently with you in certain matters.

Your attack on doctors, for instance is ungenerous to a profession that by and large is doing its hard-working best. Although I am not yet fifty I have had more experience than most men of doctors of all kinds: some eminent but inefficient; others, overworked but intelligent, supremely kind and humbly aware of their limited knowledge and skill. If you want to see the typical doctor, turn your back on Harley Street (as I have done) and have a good look at the country doctor with a large practice. I have found more "sense of honour" among medical men than in any other occupation. And the statement (page 316) that " a doctor who cures his patients loses them" is less than a half truth. A doctor who cures his patients gains many others.

But your chapters on Banking and the Money Market are first rate. Did you ever come across Frank Tilsley's "First Things First"? Not since that book (which I published, unsuccessfully) have I read anything on the subject so forthright and salutary. Tilsley is almost as good in his assessment of democracy and capitalism, although his vision is that of the common man and not of the Sage.

There is much more in your book that I read with admiration and delight (mingled at times with exasperation) but I will restrain myself from writing a long letter.

I noted a few mistakes. On page 112 you say, "After the race all the money staked on the winner is divided among its backers. The machine keeps the rest." It is surely the money staked on the losing horses (less the 10% deducted by the Totalisator) which is divided among the backers of the winner. Page 302, Jim Phelan, not Whelan; and page 351, Magna Carta - please!

Your reluctance to reply to such letters as this is understandable. But please let me thank you for writing "Everybody's Political What's What".

Faithfully yours,

(Michael Joseph)

G. Bernard Shaw Esq.,
4, Whitehall Court (130)
London, S. W. 1.

Letter to Bernard Shaw

Mr. Bernard Shaw, though he is always glad to receive interesting letters, seldom has time to answer them; for his correspondence has increased to such an extent that he must either give up writing private letters or give up writing anything else. Under the circumstances he hopes that writers of unanswered letters will forgive him.

I have never attacked doctors. I have criticized their efforts to be "scientific"; but I have not depicted them as unamiable, ungenerous, or dishonorable. I have made the best, not the worst, of them personally.

I have never before heard of Tilsley. Is he still in print?

Many thanks for corrections. They have all been made.

G. Bernard Shaw

(4, Whitehall Court, London, S.W.1.)
Ayot Saint Lawrence, Welwyn.
11/10/1944

16th October 1944

Dear Mr Bernard Shaw,

Many thanks for your postcard. I did not expect a reply to my letter.

Tilsley's book is out of print but I have traced a wrapperless copy of the cheap edition, which is being sent to you from my office today, with my compliments. It is no disrespect to Tilsley to say that I have the better of the bargain, with a Shaw postcard in my possession.

I still think that your condemnation of the medical profession is too sweeping. The mischief done by the General Medical Council and by such people as Pavlov deserves all the hard knocks you give them; but you seem to me to give the ordinary practitioner less than fair treatment. However, you would no doubt argue that the ordinary citizen should be blamed for the sins of Government and criminals!

Faithfully yours,

(Michael Joseph)

G. Bernard Shaw Esq.,
Ayot Saint Lawrence,
Welwyn.

Bernard Shaw's reply and Michael's riposte

example, travel books (if they were good) and fiction, but not short stories.

He told them that publishers buy books for profit, to enhance their reputation, to seek attention of reviewers, and because certain books fitted their lists. Lastly, and by no means least, publishers played their 'hunches' for luck always played a large part in success.

In 1946, he gave a talk to the Associated Booksellers of Great Britain and Ireland's Second Year course at the Polytechnic Institute. His theme again covered authors and stressed that there were two kinds of authors. The first were those who wrote to please themselves or because of some inner compulsion. They cared little or nothing for the prospects of publication and if they were unsuccessful, they would pretend that it did not matter. If the publisher and the public were willing to buy and read their work, well and good; if not, it could not be helped. The second kind wrote quite definitely with publication as a primary objective; they wrote what they hoped and believed people would read, and studied the public taste and publishers' requirements.

Michael went on to emphasise that it would be wrong for anyone to assume that the first kind was the artist and the second, the commercial hack. There were good and bad from both types.

In the fifties, he gave a number of prestigious talks, for example, The British Council arranged for a course on Publishing and Book Production which ran for two weeks. He was one of several eminent speakers and his subject was 'The Selection of Manuscripts'. Other speakers and chairmen for the course included Sir Stanley Unwin, Richard de la Mere (of Fabers), H. J. Jarrold (of Jarrolds) and interestingly, his friend Walter Allen, who was one of Michael's readers and authors. Then there were the series of lectures put on by The Royal Society of Arts in May 1953, entitled *The Novel*. Michael's talk was to encompass all aspects of publishing, whilst Christina Foyle spoke on 'The Bookseller and the Reading Public'. However, it fell to Dennis Wheatley to open, describing 'The Novelists's Task'. The fact that The Royal Society had asked Michael to represent the publisher in such distinguished company is an accolade in itself.

Michael's lecture for The Royal Society was a classic, embracing every aspect of publishing and given by one who had matured to become, if there were such a qualification, a master publisher. In describing authors, he was, however, momentarily frivolous.

Authors, as I said at the beginning, are individuals. Some are modest, some are not. A few are intelligent. Many are temperamental. I sometimes think that a publisher and a trainer of racehorses have a great deal in common. Some authors are selling platers, but does that matter so long as they win races? Others are potential classic winners and have to be carefully nursed for success. Which reminds me that the late Lord Rosebery, speaking at a literary dinner, declared that authors were like racehorses: they should be fed, he said, but not fattened.

Perhaps a better analogy would be for the publisher to regard his authors as a large family of adopted children. They are like children in many ways; all smiles one minute, tears the next; unreasonable, greedy, charming, pig-headed, suspicious, trusting and unpredictable. They are an unruly family, all clamouring for attention at the same time; but a source of immense satisfaction if you can steer them through their teething and their growing pains. But in one respect they are not like children. They are like Peter Pan, for they never grow up.

It is perhaps, a good thing that not all his friends went to these lectures as for instance, Christina Foyle giving the third, recounted a comment made by Michael which so easily might have been misconstrued. 'Mr Joseph', she stated, 'once confided in me that everyone he ever met turned out to be an author. People he looked upon as personal friends and with whom he could relax and forget all about business sooner or later revealed confidentially that they had a manuscript: "It won't take more than an evening or two to read it." ' Most if not all Michael's authors grew close to him, even if they were not friends at the start. He passionately believed that a close relationship would enhance their work. It is not true that all his friends were authors though they might have liked to have been.

*　　　　*　　　　*

Throughout Michael's life, he dallied with various competitions. He liked the challenge of crosswords, but the literary standards were not always an important consideration. If the challenge appealed to him, he would 'have a go' and I have described elsewhere his yen for crosswords for these were a daily routine.

A good example of his ability to enter humorous competitions appeared in the *Morning Post* which ran a competition for back-handed testimonials. His entry came third, winning him half-a-guinea. 'Scotsman (writing from Aberdeen): "I always smoke your tobacco, and can safely invite my friends to try it." '

His dabbling in competitions was only fleeting for his greatest challenge remained the art of writing, and of course publishing books that 'ought to be published'. It was his nature, when he saw his own authors being ground down by forces outside his direct influence, to rally to their defence. In this case it was the Inland Revenue that he criticised.

*   *   *

In the immediate post-war years, publishers were still constrained by the shortage of paper, and it was not until early in 1949 that the restrictions were lifted. Thereafter publishers began to produce more titles, but authors still had their problems. Michael, who was always one to look after authors, took up their cause.

For them, the market took an abrupt turn towards the end of the war. It was Section 24 in the 1944 Finance Act that hit them. The Chancellor made a change to the taxation rules relating to their earnings. Before this time, the author, who might have taken several years to research and write his work, was allowed to average his subsequent earnings. Section 24 changed this and it was only his advance on anticipated royalties that was allowed to be spread. His actual earnings as royalties were taxed in the normal way as annual income. In some cases, this took the author into the surtax bracket and one example cited was a dramatist whose play netted after deduction of 28 per cent entertainment tax, £9,000. Tax and surtax then accounted for £6,000, and it should be remembered that this was a handsome income for the period. The author, it was reported, had not written a successful play before or since. The position so disadvantaged the author that a champion had to come forward. It was into this argument that Michael stepped, an argument that was to take over six years to win.

Championing the author was not something new for Michael; he felt that somebody had to start the hue and cry. He was, you might remember, living at Stanford Dingley and writing that objective memorandum to his co-directors on the precarious state of the publishing world. And it was in March 1948, whilst he was home nursing his sick wife, that he was motivated to write an article which set the stage. Paper at that time was still rationed, and publishers were constrained by the need to keep the saleable books in print by excluding work from new authors. Unless of course, the book was very exceptional. Even when an author was lucky enough to have a book published, it might have taken him two or three years to write it. And if the book was a runaway success in its year of publication then the royalties poured in, but so did the tax liabilities. Michael and others argued that this income should be treated as capital or part capital and not wholly as income.

For his case, Michael put together a strongly worded but well thought out article for publication. He sent it to the editor of the *New Statesman and Nation*, Robbie Willison, who read it sympathetically and published it; further, he agreed that a committee should be formed to do something about the tax. Robbie suggested that he, Michael and V. S. Pritchett should form the nucleus of such a committee. He agreed that they should not set themselves a task to help the J. B. Priestleys or the Shaws of the literary world, but rather those who were modestly successful, and who previously would have made a living by writing.

Less than a week later the group met. With Michael were Robbie Willison, V. S. Pritchett, A. D. Peters, W. Belleny and M. Hodson and at that meeting they agreed on the state of affairs, but not the action that was needed. Then, it seems not much was done, until in January the following year, a letter from one of the literary barons appeared in the press.

Bernard Shaw was the one who also made a impassioned plea in his letter to *The Times* on 18 February and once he started, others followed. Michael added his weight to the cause by sending in a letter in which he stated that in his opinion, Shaw had underestimated the case and went on to illustrate his point. Others were similarly moved to write, including Charles Morgan, Compton Mackenzie, A. A. Milne and Bob Lusty. But it was Michael's article appearing in the *New Statesman* that drew a comment from the tax inspectors at Somerset House. What they said is not known but they hinted that should a deputation attend their offices, then that deputation would receive a sympathetic hearing. To add weight to the presentation, which Michael and friends had started, a figurehead was needed and it was Bob Lusty who wrote to John Masefield asking him if he would help. He agreed. This was a coup because in addition to his role as an author, he was President of *The National Book League* and Poet Laureate. H. E. Bates, A. D. Peters, W. Belleny, V. S. Pritchett, K. Roberts and Michael made up the rest of the deputation, which duly gathered at 26 Bloomsbury Street, the offices of Michael Joseph Ltd. There they rehearsed their parts and set off for the meeting in a black Daimler specially hired by Michael for the occasion.

It would have be pleasing to record that they succeeded, but another five years were to elapse before the position was finally reformed. And throughout that time, Michael maintained his contribution to this cause.

Chapter 4

Military Matters
1914–41

'At the top was the most terrifying thing I have ever seen.
A sallow-faced desperate German, his rifle pointed
straight at me, his eye screwed up over the sights. In the
fraction of a second death greeted me.
Michael Joseph

As a fifteen-year-old, one of the diversions that Michael allowed himself to be distracted by was the City of London School's Officers' Training Corps. Most of his friends had joined and judging from the group photograph of the corps, he was one of the few who was able, at that early age, to grow a moustache. He enjoyed the training, for it seemed at the time to be fun. Patriotism was popular, and though there was talk of war, it seemed likely to be a short one. He, as I have said, had joined in for the fun and military exercises. Apart from drill and parade-ground experience he had the opportunity to learn how to handle various weapons including the rifle. He little realised at the time that it would be vital if he was to survive the forthcoming war.

Michael had planned to go on to the University of London after leaving school in 1914, but because war was declared in that month and mobilisation ordered, his future instantly became very uncertain. He went on to join the University of London OTC and it was from here that he volunteered for service in the army, leaving his younger brother Lionel behind to complete his own education at the same school.

Michael applied for a commission and the initial interview was before a Recruitment Board. The story, as the family recalls, was that on entering the interview room he was surprised to see a familiar face amongst those sitting on the panel. It belonged to Pelham ('Plum') Warner who was the chairman, a writer, and known internationally as a recent captain of England's cricket team. Realising that he was known to the chairman, Michael appreciated that he had no option but to answer all the questions truthfully, including the one about his age. Being only sixteen he was not surprisingly promptly turned down. Disappointed at the outcome of the interview, he thought he would remain in the hall, in order to speak to Pelham when a break occurred. His moment came and Pelham's subsequent advice to Michael was that he should rejoin the queue and say that he had 'remembered his right age'. With mounting tension he rejoined the queue and once more faced the panel. At this point I think he should tell the story from his book *The Sword in the Scabbard,* 'I gave my age as twenty-six instead of sixteen – thus anticipating Hitler's theory that a big whopper is more likely to succeed than a little one. I suspect that I was helped by the precocity of my juvenile moustache.'

He awaited his commission with eagerness and when it finally arrived, he was surprised and amused to find that he had to pay a 'postage due' on the envelope. Commissioned as a 2nd Lieutenant in the Wiltshire Regiment, Michael found his training in the school's OTC had stood him in good stead, enabling him to pass over the basic training quickly; and he found himself assigned to a new fighting force, the Machine Gun Corps. This was to take him to Arras, the Somme, Flers and Ypres.

The first few months were spent training and learning how to handle the new Vickers machine gun. In its day, the gun was a formidable weapon, firing five hundred rounds a minute and bringing a new dimension to warfare. The training soon ended and he found himself on his way to France and the front line. He saw all the worst horrors of trench warfare about which much has been written. Men blown apart, or buried alive in the mud by exploding shells. It was a brutal war, for the artillery had their say and it was the infantry that suffered.

It was whilst fighting in these foul conditions, that he wrote, when lulls in the fighting permitted, copious notes about his experiences. He was encouraged to submit them for publication and to his surprise and delight the censors passed one of his first efforts extolling the fighting capabilities of the Machine Gun Corps. His first report appeared in the *Daily Express* in 1916, (duly annotated in his personal scrap-book) and several more were published that year. Greatly encouraged by the appearance of these, he continued making notes, including descriptions of colleagues who had fallen in battle.

In the First World War, everyone who served on the Western front, certainly those who saw action in the trenches, had experiences to tell. Michael was no exception, and amongst his memorabilia, I found a draft of a story which epitomises the horrors. I have not been able to establish whether this was ever published, but his brief account is graphic. I'll let him describe the event;

July 1916. Mametz Wood, in the expressive phrase of the time, was 'unhealthy'. The night before the attack I lay with my men in a so-called trench, deafened by the noise of our howitzers (they were firing from just behind us) and plastered at irregular intervals by the earth

Fit for war 1915

thrown up by German shells. I was fortunate. Several of our men were hit, and Bramer, my section officer, was badly wounded in the leg and carried away somehow into the blackness of the night by the overworked stretcher-bearers. I was left in command of the section.

The machine company I had joined as a junior subaltern then had eleven officers on its strength. Nine of us were in action in that first Somme battle. A few days later I was one of two surviving officers.

On the morning of the 14 July I headed a single file procession towards the wood of Bazentin le Petit. We walked through a barrage. It was no use hurrying. I was past the sensations of all ordinary fear, and the men stumbled blindly after me across shell-holes, wax-like corpses and twisted wire. The indescribable stench of rotting human bodies, high explosive and the curiously bitter-sweet tear gas clung to the shell-pitted ground. We had about half a mile in the open; with stoppages due to casualties it took us nearly an hour to cover the distance.

I was drenched with sweat and realised only afterwards that I had carried a Vickers gun tripod and four ammunition boxes in addition to my own kit.

We worked our way into Bazentin Wood (does it suggest green-leaved trees? Actually it was a wilderness of broken ground) and passed through the shattered but still cheerful remnants of our infantry. Our objective was the village of Bazentin le Petit which lay to the east of Mametz.

Except on the map the place no longer existed. A few bricks and the shreds of a mattress were the only indications of its comparatively recent habitation. We were now reduced to crawling from shell-hole to shell-hole. Our numbers were less than half but luckily the four guns were intact. My map showed approximately where we were to take up our positions. The enemy, occupying the higher ground as usual, made this difficult and we had a taste of our own medicine from their well-placed machine gunners.

We managed to get two of the guns into position without further casualties but the third gave us a job which can only be described by the unprintable epithet of my section sergeant. This provided me with with my narrowest shave of the war.

It was necessary to explore a long concreted dugout in our rear which had been used by the Germans as a dressing station. Accompanied by my sergeant I climbed down the entrance into the darkness. We had no bombs and dared not use a torch. It was rather like feeling one's way through an unfamiliar room in the dark, and I think my hair literally rose under my steel helmet during the few minutes it took us to pass through that dugout. There were several wounded Germans crying pitifully for water but that was apparently all.

A gleam of daylight revealed the entrance at the other end and I at any rate made for it with a sensation of profound relief. But as we slithered up the steps towards the daylight I stopped short. At the top was the most terrifying thing I have ever seen. A sallow-faced desperate German, his rifle pointed straight at me, his eye screwed up over the sights. In the fraction of a second death greeted me. A deafening explosion – then realisation that I had fired my revolver. Gathering my wits, I found I was unhurt. I scrambled to the top. Then I found that I had missed, but that in the instant when that poor devil of a German must have been about to press the trigger a large fragment of shell had caught him in the back. The German shell that killed him had saved my life.

The night before the attack, Michael was promoted to Lieutenant – and he was then only 18 years old. (He didn't lose touch with 'Bill' Bramer, for they regularly corresponded to each other over the next two decades.)

The bloody war, an apt description with so many being killed, continued, with many of Michael's own colleagues falling in enemy action. There were all manner of ghastly weapons being used, not only the effective machine guns, but also gas and 'Minenwerfers' – flying mines which were nick-named 'toffee-apples' or 'minnies', and tanks. The latter appeared for the first time in 1916 and Michael was present when they first went into action. The surprise and shock of seeing these new and noisy chariots of war left a vivid and lasting impression on his mind.

It was 15 September at Flers when he witnessed this action. Just after 'stand-to' his sergeant alerted him by a shout of astonishment. 'And there – looming up out of the early mist – I saw the astonishing sight of the first tanks going into action. I had no idea that we had anything like them in France – their secret had been well kept.' History books record that of forty-nine tanks detailed for the attack, only thirty-two reached their starting points. It must have been an awe-inspiring sight – and a great boost to our troops' morale.

Michael's own morale received a boost too. His batman Lewis, a waiter in peace-time, took a keen interest in the correct method of serving wine and the other 'restaurant' ceremonies, which the younger subalterns cultivated under difficult conditions. Later in September, Michael was lying with his Vickers gun in a shell hole beyond the front line near Gueudecourt. The Company's transport officer, remembering it was

Michael's nineteenth birthday, sent him a large cake and a bottle of port by a runner.

He fought his way through with his messages and gifts, whilst the 'Boche' maintained their strafing of the area making the last stages of the runner's journey a series of running jumps from one shell-hole to the next.

When Lewis spotted the bottle of port under the runner's arm, he shouted, 'Hi, you! Stop shaking the officer's port. Don't you know better than to shake up port, you idiot!' (This anecdote apparently ranked as a joke and won Michael a guinea in *The Star's* selection of 'The Best Jokes of the War!'

The moment passed and the war continued unabated. They advanced. They retreated, and advanced again. Fighting in the trenches near Arras, he adopted a kitten, or rather the kitten befriended him. Scissors would be seen strolling across the lines blissfully ignorant of the human strife – only sure that as long as he returned to Michael, he would get a tasty morsel of bully beef. His coat of glossy black fur was marked with a white waistcoat and his presence soon made him a popular pet with everyone, and an antidote to the horrors they were witnessing. He would often follow Michael and his orderly along the poppy lined communication trenches, leaping up playfully onto the parapet and picking his way along the top, keeping pace with them. It was a dangerous practice as it was obvious to the enemy that the kitten was accompanying the officers on their rounds. But Scissors's incredible luck ran out and he was eventually wounded by a piece of flying shrapnel. Michael who could not stand to see or hear cats in pain, positively welcomed the opportunity to bandage his leg and cosset him until he recovered. Sadly, Scissors was missing when the division moved on – leaving Michael forever wondering whether he survived.

He wrote, like so many others, about the gas attacks but fortunately managed to avoid the worst effects himself. However, towards the end of the war he contracted a serious case of typhoid from drinking contaminated water, and was hospitalised in 1917. After a long period of convalescence, his duties were confined to training others to use the Vickers machine gun, a task which lacked the excitement and danger of the front line. He found it all very boring and in an effort to find a new challenge, tried to transfer to more active sections but without success. Nevertheless, he was promoted to the rank of Captain in June 1917. The aftermath from typhoid and 'gas' contributed largely to his 'tummy' problems from which he was to suffer throughout the rest of his life.

Peace returned in November 1918 and Michael was 'demobbed' on 11 January. A new chapter in his life was to unfold in journalism which was interrupted again in 1939.

*   *   *

In the years that led up to the Second World War, the numbers of volunteers' applying for re-enlistment had been growing. Historians have aptly described the tensions which mounted across Europe, and as the media carried the stories, so the numbers increased. To meet the persistent requests from veterans of the previous conflict, the Government formed the Army Officers Emergency Reserve. It was this organisation that Michael attempted to join, for, this being the age of patriotism, he believed that his experiences of combat would be of infinite value in training new recruits.

But why re-enlist? – Hadn't he had enough of fighting in the previous war? The answers, which are many and complex, are to be found in Michael's book *The Sword in the Scabbard*. This book was based on his experiences, having succeeded in re-enlisting, and serving again for just over a year. He had been invalided out of the army once again and took the opportunity of writing a book about it all whilst convalescing. He made some caustic observations and despite the strict censorship that was then in force, it is possible to pin-point where he and his colleagues were, and where the criticism was directed. Anyone reading the book now, will be surprised that he 'got away' with some of his statements.

His publishing company had continued to flourish in the years between the wars and at forty-one years of age, with the trappings of a succesful business, came a relatively comfortable lifestyle. It was quite normal in those days for Michael to arrive at the office at 10 in the morning to do a day's work. (How would he fare now?) He would quietly set about his tasks, giving anyone who met him the impression that he eschewed hard work. Nothing was further from the truth, but his enjoyment of good food, trips overseas to America and Australia, as well as writing and devoting much of his spare time to his hobbies, had misled many.

I was puzzled about his reasons for re-enlisting. For a start he was not a fit man, and at his age, not one likely to run around the forests or go for ten mile route marches! His friends were volunteering at a rapid rate and possibly one reason could well have been the 'Didn't want to feel left out of it all' syndrome. Stirring posters frequently caught the eye proclaiming *Your Country Needs You*. Patriotism and war fever were in the air again and the nostalgia of comradeship, of sharing and surviving hardships together, were forces which were difficult for ex-servicemen to ignore. It was a war which seemed inevitable and as Michael saw it, quite simply a matter for self-preservation. If Hitler succeeded with his expansionist plans and England should be overrun, there would be little hope for his company, let alone his life, with such an overtly Jewish name. Of course he faced a great deal of family pressure not to rejoin, but nevertheless he pressed ahead. His family pleaded with him, telling him that at the age of forty-one, he would not be of much use anyway. It could not have been an easy decision for him, but once his mind was made up, he became stubbornly determined;

> My own case typically discouraging. For several months before war was declared I had been trying to get into the Army. I was forty-one which was relatively young, and as I had served practically throughout the last war I thought it would be an easy matter to rejoin. I was wrong. The War Office was invariably polite, even if it took a long time to acknowledge offers of service, but evidently veterans were not in demand. I was able to compare notes from time to time with several of my contemporaries who were also trying to get back. Their experience was much the same as mine. Writing letters to the War Office was clearly a waste of time and it seemed that the only possible way of rejoining was to pull strings . . .

That says it all – at least for the start. The treatment he received for his efforts made him think that it was going to be more difficult to enlist than for the First World War.

There cannot be many middle-aged men today, who would willingly throw up civilian life and leave the safety and comfort of their homes. In Michael's case, this also meant leaving a menagerie of pets and in particular, his beloved cats behind. Months later, his favourite Siamese, Charles, was to be allowed to accompany him on his tours of duty, which was a great consolation. Michael's account of the war, *The Sword in the Scabbard,* is dedicated to *Charles O'Malley, Comrade in Arms,* who provided a welcome reminder of more pleasant times amongst the rigours and harshness of battalion life.

In fact he *wanted* to get back, for he missed the discipline of the army. Civilian life had become far too comfortable lacking the adrenalin-pumping dangers of the front line. He had also become incurably lazy – with not even enough time for a round of golf! Certainly no time was allowed for those all important early morning exercises. (Still unheard of in the family, I may say!) His desire to re-enlist goes to show that there was a mild masochistic streak in him but it may well have been partly a result of a tough home upbringing (of which I go into more detail elsewhere). Being a heavy smoker, one of the rules he was to benefit from in army life, was that of no smoking when on duty. He was to discover that working a fifteen-hour day without a smoke really tested his patience, as many an ex-smoker will readily testify.

Another explanation for his determination to re-enlist can be gleaned from his brief but sardonic view of commerce.

After twenty-six years of competitive life it is not surprising if one becomes a trifle cynical about the value of human friendships. There is so much self-seeking, so much jockeying for position, so many base motives behind people's actions that one may be forgiven for doubting. Perhaps it is true that one of the compensations of poverty is friendship: anyone with a shilling in his pocket is enviable and must beware of flattery and false friends.

Curiously appropriate, even today!

In the summer of 1939 there was still the business to run and manuscripts to be selected. Authors still had to be sought and if the company was to succeed, then agents and publishers overseas had to be visited. On 17 June that year Michael sailed on the maiden voyage of the *Mauretania* to New York, where the hot weather of New York made the impending war seem a long way away. The newspapers there portrayed a different story – 'Englishmen in Japan were being harassed and some challengingly slapped in the face, whilst others were physically searched.' The guarantee given to Poland by France and England had nearly been forgotten and it was said that Hitler would never risk his army and air force. . .

He returned to his home in St John's Wood during July, and when war was finally declared in September, he moved out into the countryside. Michael found a pleasant furnished farmhouse, snuggled tightly in a little valley in Mayfield, Sussex; the countryside, affording relative safety.

In moving house, the menagerie of animals had also to be considered. The poor budgerigars had to be destroyed but Shirley his daughter, pleaded for Peter, her much loved but aged rabbit to be spared. Peter was certainly not a friend of the rest of the family, for he could only be approached if you had a stick or golf club to ward off his attacks. He had become an exceedingly vicious animal, biting any passing ankle, and walking around the garden could be a very dangerous experience. In her absence, Shirley's pleadings were discussed by Michael and Edna, with Shirley winning the day, but alas, Peter died shortly after the move.

The 'town' cats of Acacia Road were certainly not amused at the move, for the house lacked adequate heating and their new territory had many new and frightening animals around. It wasn't until the end of November that Michael received a letter from the War Office requesting that he should attend for an interview! Five months later he received another letter. . .

As far as can be foreseen at present it is hoped, as and when your services are required, to offer you a post in connection with Infantry (Machine Guns) and you have accordingly been noted in that category.

Frustrating for Michael, for it was already April 1940, but at least this was progress. He had to wait until June before he was asked to attend another interview and a medical inspection. At the medical, the usual specimen was given, his eyes and ears tested, but the doctor who was treating everyone with briskness, noticed he had two scars on his stomach. Questioned about these, he answered 'more or less truthfully'. I wonder what he said for had that doctor known about his previous medical records from the First World War and his typhoid, he would have doubtless probed more deeply and the course of his life may well have been very different. As it was he was passed *Grade 1*.

This was followed by a further brief interview by a Colonel bedecked with ribbons ... and three weeks later Michael received a letter 'requiring him to report to the Queen's Own Royal West Kent Regiment in ten days' time'.

*   *   *

The first few weeks were taken up with the task of re-establishing the routines ... completing the numerous forms... getting a new uniform ... and learning many new terms. For, in his absence from the forces, the pace of change had quickened. The jargon had changed too. 'Taking a poor view', 'laying things on in a big way', 'browned off', 'are you fit?' – were amongst the *in* phrases then, making him feel out of the swim of it all.

Another aspect that sapped Michael's confidence once he was established back in the army, was the realisation that he knew little about modern weaponry. Of course, he was familiar with Lewis guns, but Bren guns and mortars were new and more powerful.

Then on 24 July the men who were to form 'B' Company arrived. Once again, there was the copious paperwork to complete and the recruits, a motley bunch from all walks of life began their training. Digging trenches, drill and basic training were easy, but as many readers may know, there simply were not enough rifles to go round. As Michael commented, 'a pathetic reminder of Dunkirk'.

The recent popular television series shown in the United Kingdom, *Dad's Army* accurately portrayed the dramatic lack of weaponry in the Home Guard. But this was not confined solely to them. Training with the Royal West Kent Company also included broomsticks for rifles which would have been comical but for the seriousness of the situation. The supply of automatic weapons, grenades, mortars, Bren guns, and ammunition was almost non-existent. Had there been an invasion in those early days, there would have been hardly enough ammunition to last an hour . . . and 'B' Company could only muster twenty rifles and dummy ammunition.

In 'B' Company, as with others, there was much to do but it was compulsory to take part in PT – a feature of army life that had worried Michael in volunteering again. It was, therefore, to his considerable relief that the Colonel had expressly excused all officers over the age of thirty from taking part in PT, but they were all expected to supervise. Lady Luck was smiling down on him once again.

One of Michael's more pleasant duties, or so he thought at first, was to write the Battalion's contribution to the *The Queen's Own Gazette.* The contribution, a mere 500 words a month, seemed to be an easy task. However what he had failed to take into consideration was the censorship that prevailed at that time. This example says it all.

The battalion welcomed 2nd Lieutenant A. B. S —, 2nd Lieutenant B. C. D. S — and that General P. Blank, C. B., D.S.O. had honoured us with a visit.

This practice of naming people by initials only was to become a major aspect of official life at the time – for everyone was exhorted to watch what they said or wrote. Portents of things to come, for his book, also published during the war suffered the same censorship.

In addition to being the Officer in charge of Battalion Correspondence he was made Entertainments Officer; after all, Michael could play the piano and his first wife Hermione Gingold would surely have passed on a few tips. This would have amused his son Stephen who had excelled at the Central School of Speech Training and Dramatic Art, where his talents were developed to the extent that he became, in later years, a leading producer and director. Hermione would also have chuckled about these activities had she known, but in the army, you must expect to play, literally, any number of different roles.

The Colonel had ordered, 'Two entertainments a week – and lay them on in a big way'. That said, the problems were naturally far greater in the army than in civilian life. Just obtaining the equipment was one major hurdle. First one located what was needed, then borrowing or more often than not, purloining, became the accepted challenge for the honour of the Company. Such items as benches for the audience to sit on, a piano, scenery, stage curtains, props and furniture became regular challenges. Then of course there was the vexed question of who was to entertain the troops. Live shows were difficult, whereas film shows were relatively easy. When live shows were put on, they were usually groups which were on tour, and being wartime there was little notice of their arrival. All this led to the belief that 'it'll be all right on the night'. Often it was. But on one occasion, a professional concert party was to appear, and at short notice. The usual frenetic activity followed, everything had to be organised and with just half an hour to go, all was set. However, within ten minutes of the 'curtain up' the benches were sparsely covered. Only a few men had turned up, of the expected four to five hundred. Having 'laid things on in a big way', the Colonel certainly wasn't going to appreciate the lack of support so Michael organised the NCOs to rush round to rustle up an audience. With minutes to go, a steady trickle of men entered closely followed by the NCOs. Michael could breathe again but it was a close run-thing. After the strain of that evening, Michael retired 'hurt'; his tummy had started to play up again.

These tensions were generated by the lighter side of army life. Other kinds arose out of the age gap between himself and other officers. When Michael had rejoined and was posted to 'B' Company, he was acutely aware that the officers' ages were considerably younger. It was a sobering thought that he could have been father to two out of every three of them. Naturally, he was sensitive to this age gap, but in turn, he was cynical of his elder officers, especially those who were incompetent. Those, for example, who were appointed Corps Machine Gun Officers, whose job it was to co-ordinate activities. One such venerable officer had the habit of issuing instructions which verged on the farcical. One of his circulated instructions read;

> It is a well-known fact the first round fired by the Vickers Gun will go wide of the target even if the sights, etc., have been correctly adjusted, as the barrel of the gun does not begin to vibrate until after the first shot has been fired. In future, therefore, the first round will be removed from every belt before firing.

Michael thought that there was bound to be someone who might just take him seriously.

Shortages of arms and equipment being a major concern, the task of training became very tedious. For example, there were still no prismatic compasses in the battalion – a fact which seems ludicrous today. And this was in August 1940, less than a year after war had been declared.

Meanwhile the German Luftwaffe had been bombing London and many witnessed the daily battles taking place in the air. This was the period which became known as the Battle of Britain. At times it was an everyday – or nightly event. Large areas of London were devastated, and Michael received constant reports of the damage to the Bloomsbury area from his business colleague, Bob Lusty. Fortunately, the offices at 26 Bloomsbury Street survived. From these reports and the accounts in the newspapers Michael was able to form a pretty accurate picture of the current state of affairs in the City.

His wife Edna, although living in Mayfield, had to travel to London frequently, experiencing the daily events. The fact that she was expecting a child must have added to Michael's concern for her and his family. To him it seemed very unreasonable that, there he was, in the army and well away from the real area of conflict, worrying about the lack of equipment, the organisation of entertainments and the petty events of the day, and his family were more at risk than himself. There was little he could do about it but worry, and naturally, like a ratchet being turned, his health had to suffer.

It was on a clear night when Hitler's Luftwaffe had thrown a particularly heavy bombing raid over London that I was born – to the 'sound of many guns' as he annotated the proof copy of his book. I don't suppose mothers-to-be had to have their babies induced in those days! Michael was the type of man to include this statement in his book and to announce the birth in *The Times*. How unlike his own father, but he did not have long to celebrate.

For on 5 September Michael was sent on a course at Aldershot. The journey from Maidstone was made in an old and tired Austin which he had recently bought, and thanks to his good friend Hugh Molt-Bignell, a motoring expert, the car had been made fully roadworthy and respectable again. Life in Aldershot was one round after another of intense training exercises. Thre were some called TEWTS (Tactical Exercises Without Troops), lectures by the score – and on every possible subject. They ranged from anti-gas drill to attack, defence, artillery co-operation, and intelligence and communications. At the end of the day everyone was fit for an early night. (Except those with families in London who listened intently to the wireless for any news of the raids, and especially the areas on which the bombs were dropped.)

Across the Channel, it was reported that motorised barges were gathering and rumours of an invasion circulated. And with the constant aerial attacks and bombing, the rumours gathered in credibility. Despite all leave being cancelled Michael managed to get a 36-hour pass, and was naturally delighted to get up to London to see his latest son. It was a memorable night for another reason too; the London Docks suffered a major bombing raid and the ensuing fire lit up the sky for miles around London.

In October, Michael returned to Maidstone. The word was that the battalion was on the move. The gossip was correct this time and he learned that they were all to take part in guarding the country's coastal defences – and the area assigned to them was part of the Dorset coast. A marvellous location in peace time, but in wartime, with barbed wire, pill boxes, patrolling sentries and mines, the area was anything but welcoming.

Even the defences that had been built were not up to scratch. On a tour of the seven mile stretch that they had been assigned, Michael recalls observing some pill boxes,

> One was several inches deep in water in wet weather and posed a nice problem for the storage of ammunition. Another was so exposed to view from both air and sea that it was impossible to camouflage and I for one would not have liked to be inside it in the event of trouble. But the prize specimen, which was being completed when we arrived, was a hexagonal pill box with three loopholes. The front loophole had a field of fire of about twenty yards. The left hand loophole enabled us to fire into a steeply rising bank of turf five and a half yards away (I measured it); and the third loophole offered as a target a few yards of trench which it was intended to be occupied by our own men.
>
> These and other pill boxes which I saw at various points on the coast were a scandal. Each costing several hundred pounds ... sited by the local infantry commander ... the work had been carried out by civilian labourers ...

It was a good thing that Hitler had decided not to invade, for it would have been relatively easy to knock these out.

The seven weeks or so that Michael spent at Lulworth were some of the most rewarding of his army service. He derived tremendous satisfaction from organising the defences and patrols and from motivating his Company. Although at times the weather was really atrocious, the work was always somehow completed. There was a real sense of purpose to the routines that had to be carried out. Taking an active part in the defence of one's country stimulated Michael's sense of patriotism and when a shortage of materials prevented work being finished, certain members of the company were dispatched to 'acquire' them.

When duties permitted, there were opportunities for beach-combing, though it was not always prudent for there were many new and dangerous items washed ashore in those wartime days. But on one occasion, a large quantity of timber drifted ashore and the men grabbed every piece for shoring up some of the defence structures that had been built.

It was to Lulworth that Charles O'Malley, Michael's better-known Siamese cat, arrived from his temporary residence inland, laying Michael open to much leg pulling from all his friends. Here they were, guarding the nation's coastal defences and their commander was to be seen cuddling a cat ... Charles was competition for the company's own kitten brought with them from Maidstone. Many names had been suggested, and doubtless some were rude, but it was Michael who in the end insisted that the kitten should be called *Ticki-Wee*. Left to their own devices,

The Dorset Coast, Durdle Door

Fit for war again 1940

cats, of course, sort out a pecking order and naturally, the eleven-year-old Siamese won the day. Cat lovers in the company lavished their attention on them, and they strutted around full of their own importance.

With Charles came the family and Michael was especially pleased to see his infant son again. Getting extra leave was difficult, consequently it was decided that I should be christened Richard, in the local church at Lulworth. The date was duly arranged and the first of December 1940 saw Michael and Edna at Morden Church where the Vicar of Lulworth performed the ceremony. The occasion had a heavy literary overtone as the Godparents included Richard Llewellyn and May Edginton. Llewellyn presented a generous gift – a half pint silver mug, suitably engraved on the bottom, only he got the date wrong, 1939 instead of 1940! Another gift, from my aunt and uncle, was a silver cigarette case! Obviously relatives with a sense of humour. It was a brief but welcome interlude.

A further note on the strength of the company's armoury was that at Lulworth they still had only two Tommy guns, with limited amounts of ammunition, and not a man among them had even fired a mortar or an anti-tank gun. This underlined what Michael felt at the time, that had Hitler decided to invade, his troops would have easily succeeded in penetrating inland.

After what had seemed a very short stay, the battalion received orders to move again. The December weather had been growing colder and moving and transporting the men in those winter conditions meant careful planning, for every contingency had to be considered, not least of which were icy roads. Getting lorries away up the steep lanes from Lulworth involved organising teams to spread sand on the roads, for there was no salt to melt the ice, as we have today.

And just before they were officially to depart, Michael went up to London to do a broadcast for Roy Rich on the subject of Cats. His voice coming over on the wireless sets caused much merriment but there were, it should be said, a few complimentary remarks as well.

That night after the broadcast, Michael fell ill – for as he ruefully reports,

I arrived back from London wondering whether it was the oysters or burgundy that had dealt me a knock-out blow. For some time past I had not been feeling too well, and now I had to spend a couple of days in bed. Doc Walters came to see me, gently reproachful, and offered his usual good advice about the folly of trying to anaesthetise my tummy. He, evidently, thought it was the burgundy.

Oysters and burgundy – was life that bad or had the BBC been over-generous! Isn't it strange that life always kicks you when you've been having a happy time. In war or peacetime this rule seems to apply.

Back on duty, Michael was soon finalising the move to Lambourn in Berkshire. The journey was made more arduous, for bad weather had now set in and the roads were extremely difficult to negotiate. His battalion was the first to arrive in this sleepy little town which was then, and still is, famous for the breeding and training of racehorses.

Michael was fortunate to have been billeted with Mr and Mrs Cook (Mr Cook was head man to the trainer Captain 'Ossie' Bell at Delamere who had a string of well known horses), but his men were encamped in the actual stables which had been converted to barracks with bunk type beds. These stables are still in use (as stables!) today and Delamere is a well known name among the *cognoscenti* of the turf.

Meanwhile, Michael was being royally looked after by the Cooks at Lambourne House. They kept two Jersey cows in the small paddock at the rear and it was to Michael's great delight that he discovered the Cooks were in the habit of providing cream at every meal as a matter of routine. Many a frosty morning was made more tolerable by this little luxury on hot porridge! And Charles never missed out either. I'll wager that the men never knew even though Michael's Maltese batman helped around the house.

Private Galea, continued to perform his everyday duties, but he went out of his way to teach Mrs Cook how to iron men's trousers, something that she couldn't master until he had taught her.

Apart from his army life Michael also found time to read manuscripts and he was kept topped up with a constant supply. They were often piled high in his bedroom, one of the few places where he could sit quietly and read. Michael, of course also had Charles to keep him company, and was frequently joined by Stooky, the Cook's cat. Stooky was a very good-natured feline and did not object to this stranger moving in. Their friendship was made easier by the attention of Mrs Hilda Cook's baby daughter Jennifer, who spent many happy hours playing with Charles. At least for the cats it was a good life, even if confined to the house by the cold. But Michael's brief billeting there left a lasting impression that he never forgot.

After the war, and hearing that Stooky had died, Michael sent Frank Checksfield over to see Mrs Cook with four kittens and he asked her to choose one for herself. She selected one which looked remarkably like the famous 'Mr Binks'. This was only one token of their friendship, for Michael was also to send a beautifully ornate doll's house to Jennifer, complete with all the furniture. His generosity did not stop there, for every year he would send Mrs Cook a book list asking her to choose those she wanted, which he promptly despatched to her.

However, here at Lambourn, the Battalion Mess was the centre of activities and the friendly atmosphere of the Company Mess was long gone. The Colonel believed in 'everything in the right place and in the right order'. The Mess was a very formal affair. In addition the Colonel was one of those who emanated intense dislike for anything that was not quite perfect (surely his birth sign must have been Virgo!). At the time, he was described as being a dictator. So it was with much trepidation that Michael found himself in charge of the Mess. The tasks included the requisitioning of those much sought after extras, wine, flowers and table-cloths – all of which went towards making life more comfortable for the officers, (though in 1941 these were not easy to come by in Lambourn). Newbury was 13 miles away and Michael had to rely on getting provisions from the shops there. For when there were important dinners in the Mess, all these niceties were 'de rigueur'. The pressures to maintain the standards were a constant nag in an already busy day.

Their stay in Lambourn was also short-lived, and in March they moved again, but this time to Bedfordshire, where once again training, giving and organising lectures were the norm. It was to be the last tour of duty for Michael as he in his own words states; 'For some time, I had been feeling rather odd inside' and was soon taken to a Bedford Nursing home where X-rays were taken. Doctors then confirmed that he could no longer continue in his capacity in the army and would have to be invalided out. In those days this went under the rather curious phrase 'reverting to unemployment'.

So July 1941 saw Michael's return to civilian life once again. Although disappointed and frustrated himself, his family were very relieved and glad to see him home again. His army career was now over and he had time to meditate on everything that had happened. The war was still on, his daughter was in the Land Army and his two oldest sons were away serving their country. So he wrote notes on his own experiences which seemed, when he read them through later, to have the possibilities of a good book. In any case, he was tempted to record his displeasure with the counter-productive nature of officialdom. *The Sword in the Scabbard* (published in 1942) was the result; it encompasses all his experiences and concludes with criticism of the army and its various practices. Discipline he thought was much overdone and unnecessary petty require-ments reduced the men's fighting capabilities. This is a book certainly well worth reading for it gives an insider's view of life in those troubled times, which as I have said, despite the censor, actually achieved publica-tion and portrays a battalion which suffered the same handicaps as the *Dad's Army* series portrayed on television.

Chapter 5

A Literary Agent
of Note 1924–35

*'There are too many literary agents in this country, in
my opinion. Some, I regret to say, have little or no
qualification for their job.'*
Michael Joseph

When peace returned in 1918 Michael sought employment like so many
other survivors. One of the main contacts he had with commerce during
the war, if not the only contact, was with Fleet Street. It was, then,
natural for him to seek employment there, which I have described earlier.
Apart from the excellent educational achievements which he could show,
all he could muster by way of qualifications for a career in journalism,
were the press reports of his writings from the trenches that had been
published. These undoubtably helped him secure his first job.

Although he eschewed the experience on those weekly magazines, he
gained an ability to discern the good and readable, from the rubbish.
Having to edit many articles and short stories he realised after a while
that he could write them just as well, if not better. However, there were
now many other new magazines created to meet the expanding demand
for short stories. Michael joined the ranks of authors as he had a number
published under his own name.

Then in 1920, he joined Hutchinsons as Advertising Manager. Not
an auspicious job, but one which for an aspiring publisher, was essential
if he was to learn the business fully. He worked with a modest man,
James Blyth, who recalls that Michael's time in that department was
brief and he soon joined the editorial department, where he felt more at
home. There he spent most of his time working on their, then well
known, fortnightly part-works *Bird Life, Animal Life,* and *History and
Astrology.*

*   *   *

In 1924, when Michael was twenty-six years old, he made a major
decision and left Hutchinsons to join Curtis Brown, the literary agents.

By now though, he was an author in his own right, and being a literary agent he thought, would further his career in journalism. As an author, he was now eligible to join the Savage Club where he knew, there would be many more contacts, prospects and friends to be made. He was formally proposed for membership in June of that year by Herbert (Hessell) Tiltman and seconded by Stacey Aumonier (not surprisingly as he had written a foreword to one of Michael's books), and T. C. Bridges.

Hessell Tiltman was a close friend, known to Michael as 'Bill' and he reciprocated by referring to Michael as 'Mitch'. He was a natural person to propose him, for they had known each other for years. Stacey Aumonier earned his success from writing short stories and T. C. Bridges a professional freelance writer, had worked almost exclusively for the popular weeklies. Mark Hambourg, Reginald (Reggie) Pound and Michael Arlen were also amongst his contemporary 'Savages'. As a club member, he was a frequent diner, and though not a great wit himself, he enjoyed the repartee of others. He is remembered for being full of gusto but he nearly always managed to avoid being the centre of gossip unlike some stage members. A popular figure, his membership reached a zenith when, in later years, he chaired one of those grand dinners for which the club is renowned. On each of these occasions, the menu would be original and for Michael's evening Ronald Searle created a splendid caricature of him dressed as a 'mermaid' and served on a plate. Three hungry cats were looking on which was a suitable send up, for Ronald Searle had neatly captured Michael's love for cats combined with the company's mermaid logo. But this wasn't the first time Michael had been shown on the menu. When George Whitelaw was in the chair, Michael had already become a popular member and he was depicted as one of the escorting natives!

He was frequently found sitting and listening to the current stories before the regular games of poker and bridge started. The huddles in the drawing-room would include Benno Moiseiwitsch, Arthur Street, whom Benno always called 'Farmer', Louis Sterling and 'Wee' Georgie Wood. Michael, not a keen player, would often make a polite excuse and quietly depart as they set up the tables.

On one social occasion, he was dining there with Cecil Forester and his agent A. D. 'Gus' Peters. Forester was known at times to be very frugal with his hospitality and Michael picked up the tab, but then of course, as a keen literary agent, he would anyway. It was all very different, fifteen years later, when Michael was Forester's publisher and the *Hornblower* books were best sellers. Then, Forester when visiting London, would insist upon staying at the Savoy.

Menu from Savage Club Dinner 1931

Menu from Savage Club Dinner 1954

One aspect of Michael's role as a literary agent intrigues me, for once he was established, he pronounced against the subject of sex being included in novels. He thought that the inclusion of this topic was counter to public taste and unlikely to enhance sales. He wrote to the *Daily Express,*

> The truth is that the general public is indifferent to sex novels. This fuss about them is childish. The public for unwholesome fiction – ask any reputable publisher – is negligible. What people chiefly want, now as always, is a good story. (7.11.1927)

However strongly he opposed the mention of sex in novels, he believed that censorship as such would not help the cause. Book censorship defeated its own object.

> It can never abolish the lascivious minded, who, immediately a book is labelled 'banned' will rush to read it. Equally because immorality does and must exist in any social community, no legal machinery could abolish pornographic literature ... As to the opinion that these so-called 'indecent' books corrupt the morals of the younger generation, that is nonsense. The younger generation lives in a reactionary state against the prudery of its parents, and is altogether more sane and sensible then they ever are. *(Sunday Dispatch 21.10.1928)*

Would he not be saying this today – some fifty-eight years later?

When he gave his statement 'what people chiefly want, now as always, is a good story.' to the *Daily Express,* he had been married to his second wife Edna for only twenty months. She was of the 'old school', with a very Victorian upbringing, and would have encouraged him in this belief; whereas had he still been married to his former wife, Hermione Gingold, she might have helped Michael acquire a more balanced outlook.

He did however write about the sex novelists. His very descriptive article, describing the sex novelist, and how you can recognize them, appeared in the *Smart Set,* in June 1925 and it is worth quoting part of his article as it exemplifies his attitude.

> It is quite easy to recognize a sex novelist when you see one. There are two kinds: the old school and the new. They are both amusing. Contrary to the general belief, it is very hard to make a fortune out of sex novels, and one ought to be sorry for those purveyors of passion who, when they are not actually poverty-stricken, seldom succeed in making more than a respectable living.
>
> First, the old school. These are gradually dying out, but several specimens still obstinately flourish, they are worthy of consideration.

The sex novelist of the old school is almost invariably an elderly maiden lady, very elderly and very maidenly. She usually wears worsted woollen stockings, a shapeless skirt and a black blouse which looks like satin and is probably worse. This blouse conceals her arms and continues so far up her neck that you wonder whether the poor dear is quite comfortable . . .

The new school is an entirely different proposition . . . The worst of the tribe are the University-reared specimens. They are really excrescences on sound and decent institutions. They don't play games. They take to livid shirts and horn rimmed spectacles as a duck takes to water. They talk in squeaky voices, sit on the floor, discuss Freud (poor Freud! if only he earned a royalty every time his name was mentioned!), with an earnestness which conceals ignorance, and settle down to write their sex novels out of the depths of their own experience (usually one barmaid, a couple of parlour-maids, perhaps a chorus girl, and maybe an amorous lady or two, old enough to know better).

After prodigious mental flagellation [what!] they produce their masterpieces . . .' (6.1925)

I have laboured the point about his attitude, certainly as far as the public was concerned, to sex in novels for one good reason: D. H. Lawrence. Curtis Brown were his agents. Shortly after this article appeared in the *Smart Set,* he published abroad his new novel *Lady Chatterley's Lover.* As Michael handled some of his work, and being so outspoken, he found himself greatly embarrassed.

There had been rumours that Lawrence was writing such a book. His guardian and agent at Curtis Brown was Laurence Pollinger, who suggested to him that the book, as Lawrence had conceived it, could never be printed in this country without some editing. Lawrence did not feel inclined to make any cuts, and decided to print it himself in Florence. It was full of typographical mistakes but then the Italian printers did not read a word of English, which must have been convenient.

It was a limited edition of only 2000 copies, each of which was numbered and most were sent direct to purchasers, some of them in Britain. The book caused a sensation and certainly offended the puritanical, and brought the subject out into the open.

The press were quick to condemn the book and because Michael had been so outspoken in print, he was again called on for comment. To the *Evening Standard* in October 1928 he said: 'I read the book [Lady Chatterley's Lover] a short time ago, but I do not possess a copy. So far as I know the book was printed in Florence, and about a thousand copies were printed. They were all subscribed for. I do not think that they will ever be put on sale.'

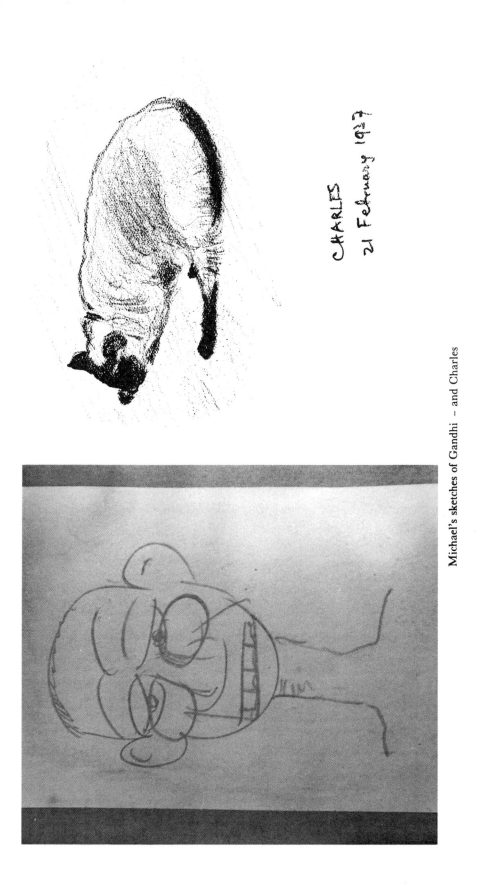

CHARLES
21 February 1977

Michael's sketches of Gandhi – and Charles

Ever be put on sale – how life changes! And this was *less than a year* after he had pronounced that sex in novels would not make for good reading, and certainly not 'what people chiefly want'. The condemnation naturally helped to create its own market and, as events turned out, copies of an American edition were on sale in this country some three months later, though it was hotly denied by anyone connected with the book. In today's liberal climate I wonder what he would have said. (Incidentally, a copy of this edition was at one time part of his library at Browns Farm.)

This book received so much public attention, that it caused the authorities to focus their minds on the subject. They took exception to Lawrence's work because of the lewd nature of the text and he was furious when a few days later The British Postal authorities, who objected to his views and free vocabulary, confiscated the manuscript of his poems. When news of this event broke, it only served to heighten the public's hunger for his books. All, of course, helping the publishers of his existing books and creating a larger market for the future.

*   *   *

The offices of Curtis Brown were in Henrietta Street. The building, number 6, was leased from Barclays Bank, and the place was always a hive of activity. The pace in 1924 was such that with holidays approaching, the directors had to take on a temporary secretary. Juliet O'Hea was the lucky girl, for due to the depression jobs were still hard to come by, and the company's staff levels were kept to an absolute minimum. She joined the firm in July that year as a temporary secretary, remaining longer than she could ever have anticipated. It was at the behest of Nancy Pearn that she worked on for the next two months. It was indeed, work she was grateful for, but Juliet announced to her colleagues that despite her temporary position, she really did want to take her fortnight's holiday as planned and was about to leave when Nancy Pearn remonstrated with her. 'You can't leave now,' she said, 'Michael Joseph wants a permanent secretary and has asked for you'. She stuck to her guns though and insisted that she would take her holiday. Reluctantly Michael agreed, providing that she took the holiday as unpaid leave. On conveying the news, Nancy Pearn ruefully exclaimed that she was 'a very lucky young girl'. Her wage at that time – two pounds a week! It was the beginning of a long and very harmonious relationship which endured many difficult phases. She was to share Michael's love of cats and other interests whilst they worked together. As I have said, the offices were a busy place and above the general hubbub a cat's miaowing was often taken for granted. Michael regularly brought his cats into the office, and if asked why, his reply would invariably be because 'they are an extremely good antidote to the pressures of business'. Not that their presence would have suited everyone. For whenever he had to go out to visit authors or publishers, someone was delegated to look after them. Usually it befell his secretary Juliet, a task she remembers today. One of the first was a Siamese kitten called Charles, who demanded and received, a lot of attention by the staff. Not only because he was cherished by one of the directors, but because, presumably he made much of his voice: a loud discordant bellow which Michael once described as being similar to a seagull mewing in distress crossed with the full cry of a human baby. His cries were so alien to those of a normal office that there wasn't a soul in the building who could ignore him.

Cats apart, Michael involved Juliet in his other love, horse racing. A few years earlier, Michael had been introduced to horse racing by his uncle, Godfrey Joseph. He was an expert, knowing all the wrinkles, and he took Michael to many races. Michael was soon well and truly bitten by the racing bug and began placing bets regularly each week, albeit they were small, for his wages at Hutchinsons did not leave much to spare. There Michael was soon regarded as an authority on the sport and went to many race meetings with Walter Hutchinson. Their friendship continued even after Michael left Hutchinsons to join Curtis Brown, though it was Laurence Pollinger who then became his regular companion. He often found it difficult to leave the office to place bets, so it became a regular task for Juliet. This meant a trip to King and Lewis, the nearest bookmaker, sometimes twice a day if he was lucky. As I have said he never won vast sums, but he did enjoy the gamble.

One practice at Curtis Brown, the reference to colleagues by their initials, was years later, to be adopted by Michael, and very successfully too. Normally, used for internal notes, Michael's company used it for humorous advertising. Advertisements would appear in the trade press as memoranda from one director to another commenting on sales and achievements.

Curtis Brown had offices in Leipzig and New York. Their *News Sheet,* a modest four-page production, extolled their successes, especially those of their London Office. Incidentally, it was printed by Unwin Brothers at Woking, then known for their massive output of novels and who were to become one of Michael Joseph Ltd's main printers before they joined the Illustrated Papers Group. It is interesting to see that the Editor, commenting upon the English Section, makes the point that they do not have enough room to list all the authors of 'first novels'. The number was significantly higher than usual. (Could this be Michael's effect?) Amongst the authors listed though, are some evocative names, Hector Bolitho, Cicely Hamilton, Lloyd George, Ethel Mannin, Edith

Sitwell and Major Yeats-Brown; in all some forty-eight authors were listed.

Every office and occupation has its fringe benefits. Curtis Brown was no exception. Their authors and publishers were scattered all over the world and daily, letters and packages would arrive bearing philatelic gifts. Michael began to collect them, at first haphazardly and later with skill. His friends were duly asked to send him first day covers and his collection expanded rapidly, becoming a mirror of his contacts. Looking through them now there are some noteworthy envelopes, in the philatelic sense, including:

Pan American Airways – First Day Cover: Canada to Eire 1924
Brazil to London – by a Zeppelin Flight in 1931
Southern Rhodesia – bearing 'Passed by Censor' 1944
Tokyo to London – via Trans Siberian Railway 1937
(This last was from Hessell Tiltman)

Though practically every country is represented, the process of placing them in the two large Ideal albums ceases after 1935; being a publisher kept him far too busy. When I looked into the collection, it was in some chaos: stamps were everywhere but in the right places; little envelopes filled to overflowing from his visits all over the world. A philatelist's dream!

Working in a literary agency meant that Michael was faced with many speculative manuscripts, all of which had to be read, a task which consumed much of his time. One of his major talents was in encouraging new authors by constructive editing of their work; and because he knew how to write, and was successful, he could persuade them to accept criticism and to make changes without hurting their egos. In the majority of cases, the first few pages were the most important in exposing the author's talent or weakness. Sometimes, though, spotting talent was a good deal easier. Whilst at Curtis Brown, he had been introduced to Daphne du Maurier and it was through his encouragement that she began to write books instead of short stories. Her grandfather George du Maurier had written two best-selling novels, *Peter Ibbetson* and *Trilby*. His talent, it seemed, ran throughout the family. Michael placed her first book, *The Loving Spirit* with Heinemann and in the process, became a friend of the family. But it wasn't easy getting her to write a book as I shall reveal. He also believed that her sister Angela had inherited her grandfather's talent and when in later years he had his own firm, he became Angela's publisher. Always a man with an eye to the future!

Daphne did need encouragment and Michael found the ideal opportunity when he took his family on holiday. They all went to stay at Fowey, in Cornwall, which conveniently, was right on the du Mauriers' doorstep. He took the whole family – including the newly-acquired Siamese kitten, Charles, to stay at the Fowey Hotel in the summer of 1930. The hotel provided a welcome break from the pressures of London, and the magnificent views overlooking the estuary and harbour formed ideal subjects for Michael to capture on film. Michael invited Daphne to join him and his family at the hotel on several occasions, and one of these visits is recorded on 16mm silent film. She appears to enjoy being filmed and very happy to be with Michael. He took the opportunity to discuss and advise her on her book, and when he returned from holiday, he was confident that she was once more fired with enthusiasm again. He hoped it wouldn't be too long before he saw some results of his labours.

When Christmas came, and Michael still hadn't heard from Daphne, he sent her a copy of his book *Short Story Writing for Profit.* As 'a hint' it worked, for the draft manuscript of *The Loving Spirit* was completed by the end of January. Michael read it and then wrote to her commenting that he liked it and had sent it off to Heinemann. Their reply was – Yes, they would like to publish her book, but the text was too long and needed cutting. This was where Michael excelled, for he was not just an agent.

One of the first things I did when I returned was to go along to Michael Joseph's house and meet his wife and children, and then we set to work on *The Loving Spirit* typescript. He showed me how to cut, and I understood fully the reason for it, taking it back home to finish in the garage-room. No sentimentality about this job. I was ruthless, and crossed out passages that had given me exquisite pleasure to write. But it teaches me a hell of a lot, and does me no end of good for the future.

As her relationship with Michael built up, she very quickly made a lasting impression. Michael once described his office in this way, 'The walls of my room are covered with photographs, mostly of authors. In one corner is a picture which always attracts attention – a photograph of Daphne du Maurier. It does her less than justice; the piquant beauty of her head, like a fragment of Dresden china, is merely suggested. The fair hair does not gleam in the light. But it is a magnetic portrait. She is a du Maurier.' Yes, Michael could express himself fully on paper, especially when inspired by his young lady authors.

If ever the is a job in the publishing world which provides the best platform for meeting the most famous and talented people, it is the role of a literary agent. The opportunites are far greater than just being a publisher as the literary agent, unlike the publisher, is not confined to the 'house authors'. So Michael, working for Curtis Brown, was now able to make many new friends, both at work and socially. Not a man to miss any opportunity to write, he turned his hand to journalism for an overseas newspaper. That he was asked to become a correspondent reflects the wide respect for his judgement and acceptance of his abilities. Michael, who had had only ten years to build up this reputation, had clearly made his mark.

It was in the early thirties, that Michael began to write a regular contribution for the American newspaper, *New York American* under the banner *Gossip from Overseas*. He was promoted, with this description. 'No one knows the English literary world of today better than this former captain of machine gunners who was an author and journalist with famous English authors and publishers.' The paper initially included a full page of 'Gossip' on what they termed 'The Page Opposite', but the majority of the contributions made only a column of about 600 words. I do not believe that these were ghosted for him as the columns contained no American phrases, and further, the news items in these columns are not to be found in other of Michael's press cuttings.

Michael had the pleasant task of projecting the ambience and news of the literary scenes taking place in England. What the articles also demonstrate is the wide range of friends he made in the course of writing. For a nation that yearned for culture, and still does for that matter, this was a golden opportunity for Michael to report on pleasant and varied meetings with the literary famous. Once he wrote about the 'Malvern Festival' where George Bernard Shaw's new play *Too True to be Good* was being put on for the first time. Before the first night, the critics had been flown up to Malvern especially for the event and it appears that they were upset by the flight. The reviews were unanimous in condemnation – even those critics who were normally polite to Shaw joined in the chorus.

Shaw's reply to his critics, as Michael described, was: 'I have read very few of the notices and so far found nothing extraordinary. I expect that, as usual, the great majority of the critics have not been equal to the occasion. I cannot help being about fifty years ahead of them.'

Mr Shaw was evidently the star turn of the Festival and dressed accordingly for the event. He was to be seen, rigged out in knickerbockers and a Victorian cyclist's hat; he cut an impressive figure. One brave reporter asked him if he wore these for effect or comfort. His reply – 'Neither, I wear them to annoy you.'

One of Michael's friends was Cecil Scott Forester, who had already written several books, including *The Gun*. Some English critics were already aware of his talents and Hugh Walpole, one well known critic of the period, compared him to Tolstoy. No wonder Michael was delighted, later, to have Forester amongst his first list of authors when he became a publisher. Reading the 'Gossip' column of July 1933, it is clear that he knew Forester very well. For he wrote an article describing Forester's life in geat detail – and this was two years before the start of Michael's great publishing adventure. Describing his school days to Michael, Forester said, 'Undistinguished, except for my consistent naughtiness. I must have been easily the most wicked child ever born.'

> The truth is that he excelled at boxing and cricket and, despite his record of evil, contrived to achieve some remarkable scholastic successes. [And as an aside, Michael added:] it is refreshing, incidentally, to meet an author who was not invariably at the bottom of the class.

He included many well known authors in his column and one was 'Bill' Hessell Tiltman. His family had owned shipyards in Kent, and he had consequently been able to travel the world as a youngster. He grew up to become a great opponent of political tyranny and wrote a book entitled *The Terror in Europe,* in which he attacked those who denied free speech in the USSR, Italy, and Poland since the World War. The majority of the readers though, would not have known that he and Michael were also great friends.

Commenting on Rudyard Kipling, though, to his American audience, Michael disclosed that this famous author lived in Kent, and on the flight path which the 'giant airliners' took to get to Paris. They flew low over his house which was used as a landmark, and he used to complain about the horrible noise of their engines. Meeting one of the pilots one day, Kipling was surprised to find out that the pilot knew him. Not personally of course, but topographically. Kipling was 'six tall chimneys, a round pond and a square pond'.

The 'Gossip' was not always centred on the English literary world and Michael occasionally allowed his brief to take him overseas. Writing about events in Dublin, the Irish Sweepstake caught his eye of course, and he also noted for the American readers that the *Irish Official Gazette* listed some prominent English authors' books which had been banned by the Irish censor. As I have related earlier, censorship of books in this country was then a subject for discussion rather than for action. With *Lady Chatterley's Lover* being pirated and printed in the States, the subject obviously seemed appropriate to comment upon. He goes on to list some eleven titles, among which was Miss Panter-Downes's *My Husband Simon.* The American edition was known as *Nothing in Common but Sex* and Michael postulated that the Irish authorities had banned the book simply on the strength of the American title! He went on:

> The State incinerator in Dublin used for the destruction of books seized under the Irish censorship had a busy time. Its past victims

include books by D H Lawrence, George Bernard Shaw, Michael Arlen, Edgar Wallace and Sherwood Anderson. Even plays by Shakespeare have been burned. I hear that books by Sinclair Lewis, John van Druten, William Gerhardi, and – need I say? – Dr Marie Stopes, are destroyed on sight.

Such is the state of Ireland in this year of grace 1932.

I don't suppose the Irish were too happy about these revelations.

Then there was Edgar Wallace. The last time Michael met him was at the Press Stand at Goodwood. (The horses again! It just goes to prove that taking time off from the office to go socialising makes good business sense, despite what the taxman says.) Wallace, who had an intimate knowledge of racing was so engrossed in these events that Michael found it difficult to accept that Wallace could write a novel or play – or both – in a weekend. It was his one absorbing hobby – it was hardly a relaxation to him as he was determined to win. Not only did he play the bookies, but he owned horses as well, determined to win a race under his own colours. According to Michael, he was also an appallingly bad tipster! Wallace's death in February 1932 came as a shock to everyone because it was so unexpected. He left a legacy of 150 novels and many plays and articles.

In another article, Michael directed the reader's attention to Lloyd George's *Reparations and War Debt* which had been selling at about 400 copies a day and this was May 1932. However, Michael on this occasion took a swipe at authors in general, when he commented upon Lloyd George's writing, remarking that he wrote the book with a short stumpy pencil, sharpened occasionally with his nails. His manuscripts were *really* hard to read. Michael incidentally, used a conventional fountain pen even for his first draft.

Naturally, at work he met many well known, as well as aspirant authors. Biographies were one type of book often handled by Michael at Curtis Brown. Amongst the better known were those of Lord Oxford, John Evelyn, Noël Coward and the then Queen of Roumania.

Other well known authors included, Michael Arlen, Francis Yeats-Brown, R. C. Sherriff, Winston Churchill, Bertrand Russell and Sir Philip Gibbs. Quite a roll of honour, and the best part of all, is that he interviewed them all, if that is the right phrase, in an informal way. And many were later to have their books published by him.

Michael was once sent a manuscript by John G. Brandon, an Australian who had travelled the world and thought he would turn his hand to writing. The story, entitled *The Big Heart* impressed Michael and he 'placed' it with Methuen, who managed to sell some 7,500 copies as soon

Michael at Fowey Hotel with Charles

Daphne du Maurier with Edna

as it had been published. What good judgement and effective publishing. The point though is that he had again used his expertise to edit the manuscript into a style that would be publishable.

*　　　*　　　*

Up to this time, Michael had been an editor and author. Now, he was an established Director and General Manager of an international literary agency, and he was convinced that the role of the agent was important. He believed that one advantage of an author using an agent was that the author did not have to devote his time to the sometimes sordid study of the complicated and ever-changing market. When he was once questioned by an interviewer on the benefits of an agent, he showed him the *Christopher Robin* handkerchiefs, explaining that A. A. Milne had authorised the designs and received a royalty on the sales of them. And he cited other examples, such as *Winnie the Pooh* garden statues and pencil boxes, proving that the agent could do more than just ensure that the author's book was actually published.

Whenever a sale is made at a spectacularly high price, history is made. This certainly was the case in 1934 with Charles Dickens' *Life of Christ* (later published as *Life of Our Lord*). The sale was naturally one of the largest the company had then handled.

The world rights to this religious work realised £40,000, equal to half the entire fortune that Dickens left at his death. Monica Dickens, his great-grand-daughter, recalls that he did not want the story published as he had written it for his children, and further, he thought it was not even worth publishing. Sixty years after his death, the price paid by the *Daily Mail* to Hempsons, the firm of solicitors acting on behalf of the Dickens family, was quite extraordinary, especially when the entire manuscript consisted of only 14,000 words. It is hard to realise that only eight years before, the General Strike had occurred and the weekly wage for a labourer was then about £2.12.0d. Today the price paid for the story would be equivalent to around £1,400,000.

The strain of the setting up this deal, with nearly everyone at Curtis Brown being involved, caused Michael's ulcer to play up again and he had to take a few days off work to recover. To that end he decided to combine business with convalescence and visit colleagues and friends in Glasgow. As it was May, he took Edna with him, for the scenery then was at its best. He managed to visit a number of publishers, not without totally losing his way in their complicated traffic system. His sense of direction was never very good. They drove up to see Loch Gair before travelling north up the Argyllshire coast to Oban.

£40,000 for The Life of Christ

Curtis Brown

*   *   *

Michael had had a promising career ahead of him with Hutchinsons – so why did he want to move into the role of 'literary agent'? An activity which was still quite new for the publishing world. Agents became a necessity, for authors, as for years publishers in general had treated them very shabbily. They were not liked at first – publishers considered agents to be 'a fifth wheel' in their working lives, but soon realised that they minimised wasted time by reading and rejecting unsuitable manuscripts for them. To authors, they represented someone who could offer advice, and could also market their ideas into various products as well as selling the film rights. Maybe it was the fact that agents were becoming an effective and exciting part of publishing that Michael decided to consider joining their ranks.

He had had his first book published and was working on the second, when the opportunity presented itself to Michael. His appetite for broadening his experiences was, I think, the driving force behind him. Intellectually bright, as his school days proved, he was never one to take the easy path which had been trodden by many before. He wanted the challenge. Through friends and contacts, he was introduced in 1923 to Mr Curtis Brown, who thought Michael might well be an able agent. For one of the main abilities required by agents then, was to have a command of the English language, an understanding of publishers' needs, and the ability to edit the prospective manuscript before the publisher had sight of it. Hence, when a submission was made to a publisher, by an agent, the publisher would know that he would not be wasting his or his reader's time.

Once Michael was embroiled in his role, he naturally expounded the benefits to any reader who sought advice. He gave lectures and wrote numerous articles too. One notable speech was given to members of the London Branch of The Associated Booksellers of Great Britain and Ireland and was later carried in an abridged version in *The Bookseller* for April 1935.

Reading through the notes used when he gave the lecture, I concluded he wanted to stress various points. Not the least was that the literary agent was a comparative newcomer. The professional agent was becoming more important owing to the growing complication and importance of literary property.

Later that year though, he wrote a very cynical article about the role of a literary agent in *World Press News*. In this article, Michael portrays the role of the literary agent as a nightmare. This is his story.

There are few people privileged, if I may misuse the word, to see and hear authors in the raw. In the presence of editors and publishers an author dissembles naturally. He usually has the good sense to smile and smirk and listen cordially, even if unwillingly, to the publisher's jokes.

Who, then is the real victim? (of the nightmare). Not the public, before whom the author has trained himself to appear as a most engaging personality, excelling the shy violet in modesty. Not even the author's family. They soon learn to tell him where he gets off. Some families disown their writing members on principle, and a good thing, too – for the families. An intimidated wife or husband may suffer here and there, but he deserves no sympathy. After all divorce is easy.

The one victim who cannot escape is the author's literary agent. It is to his agent that the author runs, eager to pour out his troubles, grievances, maledictions, grouches, and general dissatisfaction with the world around him. And the unhappy agent must listen and assume appropriate expressions and say, 'Isn't it too bad,' – and, – 'We'll have to put that right,' in the proper places. For the author pays the agent. An agent cannot live without authors, and the author knows it.

An agent is at the mercy of all authors, big and little, old timers and this-is-my-first-effort novices. He dare not dismiss any of them summarily. When a publisher lets a fish slip through his net, it is an unfortunate error of judgement; when an agent does so, it is a disgrace. A publisher is forgiven for deciding not to risk his time. And the wretched agent must pore over MSS. Worse still, he must involve himself in correspondence with authors and be available for interviews. The author who is turned down by a publisher has a scornful but tolerant smile for the publisher's fallibility. To be turned down by the agent is ignominious, and makes an enemy of the author for life.

On the whole, however, women are worse. Their acid smiles and hints are more difficult to cope with than any outbursts or complaints. Gaily they flutter in, with 'I'm not going to keep you more than *two* minutes; I know how busy you are,' and I groan inwardly, knowing this means an hour at least. There is no limit to their exasperating tactics.

The number of authors and would-be authors who demand appointments or call without one (I do not know which is the worse) in the expectation of free advice is incredible. What most of them really want is not advice but an opportunity to talk about themselves and their work. Occasionally they ask a question, just for the sake of appearances. Very early in my career as an agent, I discovered the meaning of abstracted expression, which invariably shows on their faces while I am trying to reply. They are not listening at all, they are concentrating on what they are going to say next.

The greatest pest of all is the amateur who comes armed with a letter of introduction. Those 'influential' letters! The perverse genius who discovered that the easiest way to get rid of a bore is to pass him on to someone else with an insincere letter of recommendation deserves a special inferno.

For every author who gains admittance in person, there are at least a hundred who, from necessity, mail their manuscripts. The fact that they are unknown to you does not prevent them from asking for free advice and criticism and prompt attention. What they really want, of course, is flattery, preferably by return mail, followed by substantial sums of money. What they get is merely an honest opinion, usually and deservedly adverse. Authors whose MSS are not read at once are usually loud in their complaints at neglect, but, if their MSS are read and returned promptly, they invariably complain that they cannot possibly have received proper consideration. Which all helps to make life pleasant for the agent.

The best sellers are, if anything, more vain and jealous than the rest. The fact that their success is founded on large sales does not prevent them from despising the public. They become conscious of their 'art', truculent with publishers, and insulting to strangers.

The common pose among authors that they are poor men of business is another manifestation of their insincerity. Most of them have no need of an agent at all. Why they employ one and pay him commission is, however, easily explained, they want someone else to do the dirty work. The sordid details of their business are beneath their dignity. Their 'art' is incompatible with commerce.

These cynical views are strongly expressed for someone so intimately involved as a literary agent. This article was repeated, but with embellishments, in other magazines, so it can be assumed that several editors thought the contents were suitable material for their 'literary' readers. In parts, Michael expresses contempt for the charade that has to be enacted in order to keep everyone happy. Well, life has taught me that when people become contemptuous, or overtly critical of their job, it indicates that he or she had another source of employment ready to go to and human nature being what it is, they behave accordingly. So it was with Michael.

The articles written in the middle of 1935 were published when there were rumours of his own company being formed. If anyone was going to summarise the role of the literary agent, then Michael had a word or two to say.

Reflecting on literary agents in general, they had found a niche for practising the art of editing manuscripts, unlike many today. Michael's undoubted successes were the result of his empathy and understanding of publishers' styles and needs. He also understood how to treat authors and get the very best out of them. Any criticisms he made of the author's work were readily accepted, for they knew him not only to be an author highly regarded in literary circles, but a man who himself understood and appreciated the requirements of the book market. Even in 1935, the varied abilities of agents led Michael to say:

> There are too many literary agents in this country, in my opinion. Some, I regret to say, have little or no qualifications for their job. We may one day see the agent elevated to a professional status, with safeguards against unqualified practitioners. *(Bookseller 11.4.35)*

When the press announced that Michael was about to become a publisher in a deal with Gollancz, those in the literary world muttered amongst themselves, and with just cause. For here was an agent with contacts in almost every well-known publishing house. He could possibly take some of their best authors. There were several cold shivers in certain publishing houses that summer. They were fully justified.

Dorothy Whipple had become one such author that Michael wanted. Her book *Young Anne* had been published by Cape a few years before, and they rejected her next title, *High Wages,* which was published by John Murray. *Greenbanks* was Dorothy's first best seller and with *They Knew Mr Knight* she achieved a reading world wide. She records in her autobiography *Random Commentary* that David Higham of Curtis Brown had become her agent. Doubtless steering her to success.

Early in 1935, Michael went to visit Dorothy and she recalls the startling news he brought with him:

> At home, at night, he staggered me by telling me that he was going to set up as a publisher and wanted me to write a book – an autobiography – for him to publish before the end of the year. I kept on saying I couldn't do it, but he kept on saying I could. We argued about it long after midnight.

He was a persuasive man and determined to become her publisher. Eventually she agreed, and in April began to write *The Other Day,* an autobiography covering her 'first twelve years'. A task that she found somewhat difficult, at times too difficult and wrote to Michael saying that she just couldn't do it. When he had seen the few pages that she had written, he wrote back encouraging her to continue, which she did. In the meantime she sent two short stories to him. His comments on reading *Dora Smith* and *The Killing:* 'exquisite, hold the very essence of childhood – mustn't be touched, are perfect.'

This led Dorothy to note: Michael is the sort of editor – publisher – to work for! I take criticism from him as happily as I take praise, because I know he "knows".'

She was right, because after all, he 'was' an author in his own right – having had nine titles published before he became a publisher himself – clearly his empathy would be complete. He understood his authors and their whims and egos.

In between all the pressures of business, Michael found time to write the odd article. He did, I think, pen the following ode, which expresses a wry sense of humour derived from his years of experience as a literary agent and the many publishers with whom he had associations.

Ten little publishers sitting in a row
Heinemann looked at it and promptly answered 'No!'

Nine little publishers on a summer day,
Chatto said to Windus 'Chuck the thing away!'

Eight little publishers sitting in their study,
Benn picked his teeth and murmured 'That's pretty bloody!'

Seven little publishers all looking unwillin'
Constable rejected it and so did Macmillan.

Six little publishers never in a hurry
From 1910 to '28 it sat around chez Murray

Five little publishers piling up their money,
Herbert Jenkins giggled 'Send us something funny!'

Four little publishers, nice and red and warm,
Cassell said 'We've lots to do re-printing Lesley Storm

Three little publishers, and I began to weep,
For Hodder looked at Stoughton, and Stoughton was asleep.

Two little publishers, and Jonathan Cape
Said 'You aren't quite convincing on seduction or on rape!'

One little publisher and then the book was dead
And buried, for a monument, beneath the Bodley Head.

I cannot trace the exact date that this was written or indeed if it was ever published. Perhaps this is not the first time it has appeared, if so I hope it doesn't cause anyone to say, 'Oh, not again!' but instead – 'how delightful to see it once more!' To me, the ode encapsulates in a humorous way, his deep knowledge of the publishing world.

When Michael announced that he was leaving to set up as a publisher, two of his colleagues believed that *they* could do better by starting their own literary agency. David Higham and Laurence Pollinger did leave to set up on their own account, and not without a good deal of drama and ill feeling which became public knowledge. Michael's departure from the company was not tainted by their actions. Curtis Brown saw to that by making it quite clear in a letter published in *The Bookseller,* explaining when Michael was leaving and who was going to handle his work in future. Curtis Brown wished him well.

Juliet also had serious thoughts about joining Michael in his new venture, even to the point of submitting her resignation. But she had doubts about the future and she changed her mind at the last moment, which was a great pity, for as a team Michael and Juliet worked extremely well together. Had she joined the new venture, she would doubtless have been as good a publisher in her own right, as the agent she did become.

Juliet continued at Curtis Brown, working in various departments, but without the same job satisfaction. She persevered and found herself as war broke out working in the American Department. This wasn't very pleasant either; however, Juliet put up with her troubles, thinking that she would eventually be called up. When no 'call up' papers arrived she made discreet enquiries through a friend, and discovered that 'the authorities' thought that by remaining there she could do a better job for Anglo–American relations than anywhere else!

Chapter 6

Publishing
The Early Years
1935-39

'Every generation produces good books which, later on,
are almost completely forgotten, or, at least, unduly
neglected.'
Michael Joseph, Bookseller 1936

Michael Joseph should never have been a publisher at all, but why, and how, did he become a publisher in the first place? Contemporaries will nod sagely and murmur something about 'being started by Gollancz and then breaking away to become independent'. Whilst these remarks are true, they camouflage a drama that was hidden from the press and indeed, many of his friends. But why did he become a publisher? He once commented that he derived intense satisfaction by achieving a blend of idealism with commercial considerations and he liked to express through the medium of books he published, his admiration for good writing. But I'm jumping ahead, for the motives which drove him to become a publisher started many years before.

One spring morning in 1935, Michael, I imagine, sat quietly at his large partners desk at Messrs Curtis Brown, the literary agents, with numerous manuscripts piled around him. He was deep in thought. Maybe it was the fresh breath of spring air that cleared the atmosphere in his smoky office, maybe it was the number of rejections on his desk, but today he felt decidedly different. A habitual and heavy smoker, he opened another packet of his favourite cigarettes, du Maurier; he had that April morning received several rejected manuscripts. A normal situation he mused, but on this occasion the number gave rise to muted frustration for he believed that they were far too good for rejection. Having spent so many hours editing and encouraging authors to rewrite parts of their books, he of all people should know, or so he believed. He felt these rejections were a slight on his literary judgement. He lit another cigarette and reflected on his career.

After the First World War, he remembered how he had returned to civilian life and joined the ranks of editors, working on one of the many magazines specialising in publishing short stories. He flinched. It had not been a happy period and in 1920 he had joined Hutchinsons as advertising manager. Once again, this work had not inspired him, (though the experience was later to prove invaluable) and he still yearned for a broader editorial responsibility, and with this aim in mind he had applied for a post in Hutchinson's editorial department to work on their three fortnightly part-works. No one was more delighted than he when he learned that he had been selected for the job.

He had left Hutchinsons in 1924 to join Messrs Curtis Brown where he had found that the work was much more to his liking. His experiences had brought him into contact with both new and experienced authors. Above all, these contacts provided him with the ideal platform to carry out his market research, although the term was not a common one then. He knew what authors were earning and therefore what he should be offering for novels.

During the early 1920s, Michael had outlined how publishers' and authors' aspirations could be achieved, if both were to succeed and make money. His books on these subjects had been extremely successful and sold more copies than he had ever anticipated. He had, he mused, become an authority on publishing, without having actually published a single title.

It is now clear from the notes that he made, and the copious press-cuttings, that he had been thinking about becoming a publisher for some years. Every aspect of the business was covered, including authors' earnings, the problems of libel, authors' taxation, production costs, distribution problems and trends in book sales. He must have spent hours deliberating before he reached his decision to enter publishing. Apart from what he felt about the rights and wrongs of what should be published, how would his colleagues feel? He was in a privileged position as a literary agent and had very many useful contacts which he could turn to his advantage before declaring his hand.

A few weeks later in 1935 before the formation of the company, Cecil Forester was visiting Michael's office. He had been sent by a bookseller in Cecil Court on the recommendation of James Hadley-Chase. (The author of a once notorious book, *No Orchids for Miss Blandish.*) Cecil was not in a good mood, and over tea, he began to bemoan the treatment he had recently received from his publishers, Heinemann. Michael, who had enjoyed reading his *African Queen,* took the opportunity to tell Forester that he was himself thinking about setting up as a publisher. A golden opportunity was presenting itself. Forester explained that at a recent reception at Heinemann's, Charles Evans their chairman had not recognised him, still less stopped to speak to him. He felt snubbed. Forester felt that he would rather be 'a big fish in a small pond than a little fish in a big pond'. So if Michael really was going to become a publisher, would he like to take him on as an author?

Michael gladly let Cecil telephone his agent A. D. Peters, and he derived much pleasure from hearing Forester tell Peters to send his next manuscript to Joseph, the new publisher. Naturally, it was not to Peters' liking but Forester insisted for he was on close terms with him, being one of the few to address him as 'Gus'. The manuscript duly arrived and this was the sort of luck that Michael needed, for here was *The General*. The move was also hugely successful to Forester, for under Michael's care he went on to achieve real fame with the *Hornblower* series.

But, although his knowledge of authors and publishing was extensive, if he was going to become a successful publisher he had one serious problem: the lack of sufficient capital to set up his own company, but he had been working on that problem for some time.

*   *   *

One of the brighter and more successful publishers at the time was Victor Gollancz. He had demonstrated over the years that success could be achieved in those difficult times, and quickly too. His offices were also in Henrietta Street. Michael approached him over capital, for he knew that Victor had started his firm with capital contributed by friends. I doubt if there was any link other than agent and publisher between them prior to his approach; it seems that Michael simply saw Victor as someone who knew the trade and had the necessary capital to help him set up his own company. There was certainly no close bond of friendship, for they were so different in character. Victor was an extrovert, and at times arrogant and domineering, whilst Michael, like the cats he loved, was composed and cautious, yet had that innate ability to charm his way persuasively. Their politics were different, as was their approach to publishing, with Victor supporting the Left, and Michael the Right. Of course, Victor saw in Michael a very successful literary agent, a knowledgeable author, and must have thought that he stood a very good chance of succeeding as a publisher. Victor needed little persuasion to back him, for Michael had brought him many profitable books and he thought it would be better to have Michael with him than in competition. But in agreeing to do so, Victor added a number of caveats.

In Sheila Hodges' book, *Gollancz – The Story of a Publishing House*, Victor is described not only as being autocratic, but having 'phenomenal drive and energy, and the ability to work about six times as hard as the normal person'. He was a man who renounced convention and was always eager to experiment. It is quite understandable that others around him did not find him easy to get on with and amongst those was Victor's last employer, Ernest Benn. He was like Victor, a man of strong and positive character, but he disliked Victor's publishing ways, and did not approve of his style of entertaining. Victor would be quite liberal with drink and this was quite offensive to Benn, who was a strict teetotaller. So inevitably came a parting of the ways after six years, during which Victor had been an increasingly successful publisher, a period in which he had taken the firm from magazine publishing into the realms of books, and in so doing had developed an appreciation for the market. What is more, he too must have thought that he could do better.

He left Benns to start up his own firm with no capital. However, he was supported by his many friends who contributed the capital by paying £12,000 for 40,000 £1 shares. I mention this because in the summer of 1935 when Victor was arranging the capital for Michael to set himself up in business, a much smaller amount was involved, though the same profitable trading results were expected.

The publishing firm of Michael Joseph was registered as a limited company on 5 September 1935, the directors being Victor Gollancz, Norman Collins and Michael as managing director. As Victor was putting up the capital, he was in effect spawning a subsidiary.

To the trade the announcement was stale news, for on 29 May that year the press had carried announcements of the company's impending formation. As I have said, Michael's previous career as a literary agent had provided him with the vital contacts, and with a large number of sound (and some now famous) authors. *The Bookseller* commented on 29 May 1935:

> Many of them [authors] were far from famous when they first came into contact with Mr Joseph, for if there is one thing for which he is better known than any other, it is the discovery of fresh talent, and the kindly care and unremitting energy with which he has nursed this talent to fame and prosperity . . .
>
> The new company will have financial resources adequate to enable it to operate on the full modern scale, for Mr Joseph holds the view that, however regrettable it may be, the inexorable logic of modern economic developments has rendered the small publishing house obsolete. He plans to publish about a hundred books during the first year; but all of them will be books which, in his view, *should* be published, and none of them will be issued merely to add to the existing number of books on the market.

The news provoked a spate of letters to the trade press, and amongst those printed in *The Bookseller* for 13 June, were some fairly caustic ones. One, from Mr Harold Forrester of Edinburgh exudes sarcasm:

> The brightest gem is that sentence which tells us that Mr Joseph is to publish one hundred books during his first year – which SHOULD be published. Is it not rich? Isn't the arrogance superb? What a world we have been living in!
>
> We have long been under the impression that when a publisher issued a book it was because he thought it should be published. How we have been deceived! Apparently such eminent firms as Macmillan, Methuen and Murray have been publishing books without regard to their merits or sales, but merely to add to the grand total for the year. How good of them to be so regardless of profit! Yet, how bad of them to spoil the chances of really wanted books!

Clearly, Mr Forrester missed the significant earlier paragraph, as Michael was referring to new authors, whose work he felt should indeed be published, for often it was of better literary standard than some of the 'safe' authors, whom publishers preferred for obvious commercial reasons.

Another correspondent was Charles Evans of Heinemanns who wrote, 'I should like to thank Mr Harold Forrester for his vigorous and brilliant letter concerning Michael Joseph, Ltd.' – no doubt piqued at losing C. S. Forester to Michael.

The Bookseller confirmed that other well known authors would be published by the new firm, namely: Sir Philip Gibbs, Dorothy Whipple, Clemence Dane, Eric Linklater, Lady Cynthia Asquith, Ethel Mannin and Michael Arlen. No wonder a ripple of apprehension ran through publishing houses that year. The agitation was further enhanced by the association with Victor Gollancz, whom the trade recognised as a powerful and effective publisher.

One of the main reasons why Michael had been boastful about the number of books he was going to publish was that Victor had 'commanded' that, if he was not to lose any money, Michael must achieve a turnover of £40,000 in his first year. So when announcing his intentions, he *had* to say that his firm would publish a hundred titles if he was to achieve the required turnover in the sluggish trading conditions of that time. For the effects of the Depression were still lingering and it was difficult for any new business to make a start, let alone achieve profits. When the press broadcast the news of the company's formation, no official agreement actually existed between Michael and Victor. In fact, there wasn't an agreement until September, though Victor and his fellow directors had agreed amongst themselves that the investment could proceed in July 1935.

Despite the autocratic conditions in the agreement with Victor, Michael went ahead and the formal tenancy, servicing and subscription documents were signed on 27 September 1935; one day after his 38th birthday. He then set about recruiting staff. The first was Bob Lusty who came from Selwyn and Blount, a Hutchinson imprint.

He had at one time asked Michael, if he should ever hear of an opening in another small company, to let him know. Lusty was broadly hinting at his disenchantment. Michael's response was vague, replying that if he heard of a suitable opening he would, of course, let him know. Hardly surprising, then, that Michael invited him to lunch at the Savage Club shortly afterwards to tell him that he had decided to become a publisher himself. If Bob would like to join him then he would go down to see Walter Hutchinson to negotiate his release. He did not think there would be any problem as formal contracts were few and far between in those days and a weekend visit to the Hutchinson home in the country was always attractive.

The company was to start from several unpretentious rooms in the Gollancz offices in Henrietta Street. They would meet there next. Michael had already secured a new secretary and Peter Hebdon as the office boy, but Peter stayed with the firm, eventually becoming managing director.

Bob's first introduction to the company was to be shown his office which was a room totally devoid of furniture, with five undistinguished manuscripts on the floor. Not even a carpet! Michael suggested that he might like to furnish the office himself but without spending too much on the furniture. In his book, *Bound To Be Read,* Bob extolled the prospect of a £500 a year salary in his new position. A princely sum, he thought. What would he have said if he had known that Michael was allowed under the terms drafted for his agreement with Gollancz, to draw £2,000 and expenses.

Another recruit was Charles Pick, whose appointment as a salesman was announced in the trade press on 11 December. Michael was, of course, technically still employed by Curtis Brown until the 31 December, so the publishing company started on 1 January 1936. Charles's appointment which also included the announcement of UK and Overseas agents, carried the colophon of the mermaid for the first time. The mermaid, though, did not embellish any books until 20 April 1936 when the first title appeared. The choice of a mermaid came about almost by accident. Allen Lane's launch of the penguin had captured the public's imagination and naturally, Michael's thoughts had been drawn to the marine world for a similar subject. He had roughs drawn up that autumn by Philip

Youngman-Carter who went on to produce the final artwork. Philip had produced many jackets for Bob when he was at Hutchinsons; he was the husband of Margery Allingham whose novel the company later published.

Many years later, Bob Lusty was to level a friendly (at times acrimonious) criticism at Charles Pick when he claimed to have been a Founder Member of Michael Joseph Ltd. In the literal sense, of course, the Founders were Victor Gollancz, Norman Collins and Michael. Charles cannot rank amongst them, but, in the generic sense, as he was employed before January 1936 and the company did not publish any books until later that spring, my view is that all members of the company, employed when the company started selling books, were 'founder members'.

At the outset there were only three directors, Michael, Victor, and Norman Collins, also of Gollancz Limited. A two to one boardroom imbalance which meant that Michael could never win a major boardroom vote. At that time this aspect didn't seem to matter, and as Victor was putting up all the money, Michael could hardly argue.

The agreement with Gollancz for the tenancy of the offices at 14 Henrietta Street commanded a rent of some £300 per year plus of course all rates and other taxes. But when it came to the agreement covering the investment of capital, the clauses were much more stringent. Although the original signed documents have not been found, Michael's personal records indicate that up to £10,000 share capital could be subscribed and that this was to form the company's backbone, but Victor attached many caveats to his investment. Initially only £4,000 was subscribed, whereas some £12,000 was raised when Gollancz first started his business in 1928.

Victor also insisted that Michael had a separate service agreement with Michael Joseph Limited which formed another investment caveat. If Michael Joseph Limited's accounts showed a trading loss of some £2,500 at the end of the year, in any year other than the first, then Victor could exercise various rights, such as the dismissal of the managing director. Further, if the losses amounted to £3,000 in any three consecutive years then Victor had the right to terminate the agreement and withdraw the capital. On stocks there was a constraint that they should not exceed two per cent of the turnover for the first year, and never more than 4.55 per cent. If you consider the vast difference in the value of the pound today, this last restriction hardly seemed fair. Finally, there was a clause in the agreement between the two firms which precluded Michael from publishing any book which might clash with the political, economic and sociological subjects that Victor was publishing. Very tough terms!

In the early months of trading Victor questioned the value of Michael's advertising campaign. Although there were no constraints in the agreements on this matter, when the trading results began to show steady losses, Victor brought pressure upon him to cut out advertising which Michael found quite untenable.

As I mentioned earlier, Michael had pronounced that he intended to publish 'about a hundred books during his first year'. The spring list announced only twenty titles, leaving a large number to be published in the autumn. The die was cast, for it would be well nigh impossible for him to achieve a turnover of £40,000 on a reduced number of titles.

The first book list was not only unique but innovative. For the first time, a publisher's book list carried coloured illustrations. These, drawn by Audrey Wynne, were described in the trade as 'Irrelevant and sometimes Irreverent'. Some reviewers correctly anticipated that other publishers would follow this new style of book list. Another feature of his book lists was that they were to be issued at half-yearly intervals.

The lists included authors who were to remain with Michael Joseph for some years: names such as Dorothy Whipple, C. S. Forester, and Max Saltmarsh. The autumn list announced twenty-nine titles, but as Victor Gollancz was pressurising Michael about turnover a supplementary autumn list was issued announcing a further seven titles. It included two authors whose books he thought would sell well: *Which Way to Peace* by Bertrand Russell and *The Abyssinian Tragedy* by Haile Selassie. Two other writers on that list who were to remain firmly with the new company were Clemence Dane and Eleanor Farjeon.

Fifty-five titles was far short of the hundred that Michael had announced to the press and the total sales were not likely to reach Victor's suggested target. He should have published fifty-six, but one title, *Goring's First Case,* failed to make its debut in the spring and was repeated in the autumn list. Sales were insufficient and the £40,000 was becoming more difficult to achieve as time passed.

The spring and autumn lists had been chosen with great care, not only for their literary merit, but for their sales potential: commerce dictated that no book should remain in stock for too long. Perhaps this is why, of the twenty authors in the spring list, thirteen had been published before; he needed to begin with some proven writers. It was luck more than anything else that had brought him one of the first, C. S. Forester. His book *The General,* a title which became a best seller, prompted a letter from H. G. Wells who confessed he had never heard of C. S. Forester, but of the book he wrote:

> *The General* is a magnificent piece of work and a portrait for all time of an individual in his period, and in a way a history and elucidation of the British aspect of the Great War. I take my hat off — belatedly,

I regret to say, because I see he has done half a score of books – to C. S. Forester.

To receive a letter from such a man must surely have underlined the degree of Michael's good fortune in acquiring Forester as an author. The letter also provided a useful piece of publicity material, which Michael sent off to *The Bookseller* and they later published this extract.

At the same time as attracting established authors he had set about attracting new ones. Earlier in 1935, Michael had visited Dorothy Whipple and persuaded her to write an autobiography. She started writing *The Other Day,* which covered her 'first twelve years'. When Michael was about to publish her book, they met again.

I lunched with Michael Joseph at the Isola Bella. He brought violets for me and two large white-headed pins for me to fix them to my fur. (Just like him. Other men might provide flowers, but not the pins to wear them!) He says *The Other Day* is far the best thing I have done yet. He says I don't know what a good book I have written. I glowed with sherry and happiness. The Book Jacket arrived at our table by special messenger – so good . . .

What a flattering gesture, but it was simply his way of making his authors feel important. Cynics might say about the jacket that it was just the printer cutting matters fine!

A good example of Michael's ability for spotting talent came when he heard Herbert Hodge's broadcast on the BBC about his experiences. Listening to his talk, Michael realised that if he could persuade him to write, here was an author who could capture the public's interest. Hodge had worked as a lumberjack in Canada, in various garages, and more recently, as a London taxi driver. Throughout his life, he had enjoyed life's rich experiences which, when related with enthusiasm, were very entertaining. Michael went out of his way to meet Hodge and succeeded in encouraging him to write. His autobiography *It's Draughty in Front* sold well; enough to warrant a second title the following year, *Cab Sir,* and a reprint in a 'cheap edition', of his first book.

When the autumn book list was published, Michael was asked to review it for *The Bookseller.* Perhaps he engineered the opportunity, who knows? In the article, published on 7 October 1936, he comments that he received a letter from Sir Philip Gibbs. In it, Gibbs 'congratulates Michael on a first-rate list'. Michael modestly didn't think it was so, but that it was an 'improvement on our first list, both in quality and quantity'.

Michael was certainly lucky with his first choice of authors and, flushed with a little success, he launched into 'packaging', but not in the sense that the trade refers to today. He produced a set of Christmas cards on the theme of peace, which were dramatically drawn by Arthur Wragg in pen and ink.

Two years before, Bob Lusty had, whilst at Selwyn and Blount, published Arthur Wragg's book *Psalms for Modern Life* which had been a very successful title. This was followed by *And Jesus Wept* which left a lasting impression on Bob Lusty's mind for it brought him 'great joy and pleasure'. So enthusiastic was Bob that he wrote to *The Bookseller* in November 1934, extolling the book's literary and religious merits. The result was an article covering half a page which was excellent free publicity. This led him to encourage Michael to package a collection of Wragg's illustrations which would make, he thought, excellent Christmas cards and, on the basis of the illustrator's book sales, an attractive financial proposition. The idea became reality. In launching the package in the autumn list, Michael had this to say about the 'Wragg' Christmas cards:

> Our experiment in publishing Arthur Wragg Christmas Cards (twelve in a specially designed box for 5s.) looks like coming off – in the book and not in the theatrical sense. I have a firm conviction that there are a good many people who want Christmas cards that are neither pretty-pretty nor conventional. Arthur Wragg's message is Peace: what could be more appropriate for Christmas?

On a commercial note it must be said that the company was not always the best payer of royalties, for Wragg sent Michael a very pointed, and personally drawn Christmas card. The message was clearly written at the foot:

> I know it strains our loyalties,
> But where the hell are royalties?

The Workers Bookshop believed these cards were excellent and ordered 500 sets, but alas, they did not sell too well and they asked Michael to take back some of their stock. He refused, and they then lobbied Victor with whom they had a close relationship for they sold many of Gollancz's books. To retain this relationship and possibly for political preferences, he agreed with them. He wrote to Michael suggesting that he and Norman 'would be in favour' of accepting about half of their stock back. In other words he was saying, if you were to put this to a formal board meeting, you would lose the vote. But Michael took a strong stance, for the sales meant profits, and consulted his solicitor, Graham Smith. Graham's advice was heeded; Michael remained adamant and refused to take them back, but he somehow avoided a head-on confrontation at the next board meeting. The Christmas card venture was not a great success, for, apart from the Workers Bookshop agreement, both Victor and Norman Collins felt Michael should not have committed himself to such an extravagance. Suffice it to record that this contributed to a very unhappy period for Michael; his efforts in striving to set up a viable company made him a heavy smoker and this further exacerbated his 'tummy' problem.

Relations between Michael and his two fellow directors were becoming strained and, apart from the 'Wragg Christmas Cards', another incident contributed to the deterioration. *Silver Tongues* was a collection of famous speeches edited by John Hayward which Michael wished to publish. Although it was not an overtly political book there was the chance that it might be made a choice of Foyle's Right Book Club. Victor took a dim view of this and put his foot very firmly down on the opportunity, one that would have brought in a tidy sum, which was galling for Michael at a time when he needed every penny to improve the new company's position.

In an effort to stimulate sales Michael issued a 'Newsletter' to those interested in the forthcoming titles. Unlike the trade booklist, this was available direct and free to the public. They were started early in 1938 and at least five were produced during the year. Circulation was not very high, about 500 copies, and the extent never exceeded eight pages. The venture was not destined to be a permanent feature and soon died. Many years later he tried again with a proposed Mermaid newsletter, but this too failed to be anything more than just an idea.

By the end of October 1936 there was an impending loss of over £2,000, causing Victor to become more concerned – he considered that Michael was spending too much on advertising and again questioned the expenses. Michael argued that of twenty-nine books in the autumn list, thirteen had less than £10 spent on them and of these, four had no advertising at all.

To put this into perspective, the titles being sold that year were priced at 7/6d to 12/6d (37 to 65p today). It seems inconceivable that any publisher would try to market a book, whether by a new or established author without any advertising at all. To spend £10 at that time on any title equates with say the sales value of about thirty copies, not much to shout about.

Michael wrote to Victor at the time, that authors were beginning to say that he (Michael) didn't advertise, and agents, the trade and reviewers would react accordingly. If he could not advertise in sufficient volume – which would at least give a boost to the sales, then he viewed the future with distinct alarm. The concern which Michael had about advertising had started earlier in the year and although he had sought advice from

Victor, help had not been forthcoming. Not surprisingly for Victor, who being, a very successful and dynamic publisher was taking the attitude of 'do as I say, not as I do'; his company was spending heavily on advertising, especially in the Sunday papers.

Frank Swinnerton mentioned Victor Gollancz's attitude in a piece about the new firm's appearance as a publisher and the Gollancz involvement, in *The Publishers' Weekly*.

> Some publishers used to believe that if a book was going to sell, it sold; and that if it was not going to sell nothing could be done about it. They did nothing about it. The new system, not invented by Mr Gollancz, but speeded up by him, took it for granted that the publisher's business was to sell books, and not merely to have them bought ... Having made up his mind that the Sunday newspapers offer, in the case of his fiction and general books (not those later political ventures), the best field for publicity, he concentrated upon them ...

In at least two surveys, again from *The Bookseller,* in August and November 1936, Gollancz Ltd was one of the top spending companies. He took 394 single column inches in August, making his company the largest spender and 520 single column inches in November when he was beaten by Hutchinsons with 966 single column inches of space! No wonder Michael was frustrated by Victor's double standards!

In retrospect, another major reason for the poor trading results was that sixteen months' expenses had to be shown against the sales income of the first twelve months. However, the high quality of authors and the books appearing in the first book list indicated that the company had a fair chance of succeeding. But it seemed that the lack of sufficient funding by Gollancz and his prevention of the necessary advertising were contributing to the poor results. Michael could not win. Something had to be done.

It seemed to Michael that if he was ever to make money, it would have to be without Gollancz. He started negotiations to sever the company as early as December 1936. At that time, both sides thought it might have been possible within three months. But this was not to be, and the company continued to be supported by Victor throughout the following year.

A point of much friction was Victor's attitude on promotion generally, which Michael found disquieting, and he remonstrated with him on the subject. He patently had not appreciated the markets to which Michael's books were aimed. And there were other rows too, sometimes over what now appears to be trifling matters.

During the year there had been inter-office rumblings which now indicate that members of the existing Gollancz staff must have resented the new company. There were complaints about a ventilator in the rooms that Michael had rented, which when in operation allowed draughts to whistle through to Gollancz's other offices and to which his staff objected most strongly. A minor irritation, but it seems it could not be resolved by the people concerned and had to be sorted out by the principals themselves. And by memoranda. In another incident, Michael in a 'tit for tat' action complained about the noise of the other offices and that frequent use of the duplicator was upsetting his staff. A sure sign of tension.

Bob Lusty recalls that – as it was reported back to him – that Victor had said on one occasion to Michael 'That Robert Lusty's not the man for you, he makes too much noise in his office'. Victor used to have a short nap after lunch and Bob's office was directly above! You can just imagine the thump, thump of heavy footsteps after a good lunch!

By December, it became clear to all concerned that the joint company was untenable and consequently Michael had immediately to set about finding the necessary capital to buy himself out. This was not an easy task; had this been so, he would have already set himself up. The atmosphere had progressively grown more tense, and Michael consulted his personal solicitor, Graham Smith, who was later to become a close and good friend as well as a family solicitor. He was often taken into Michael's confidence and his help had been greatly appreciated on the earlier 'cause célèbre' of the Wragg Christmas Cards.

The publishing world had been going through a tough time for the past four years, and publishers were still finding it hard to sell their books. One of the problems in the pre World War II years, was the sudden onset of inflation. Production costs were rising. In a report which appeared in the *London Mercury* in 1937, Geoffrey Faber comments 'Esparto paper is already up by 33 per cent, wood paper by 40 to 50 per cent ... binding costs are already up by more than 2½ per cent'. All this suggests that Michael may well have miscalculated some of his costs, whilst under the pressure of making a profit for Gollancz.

Gollancz's accountant forecast a further loss for the second year of about £3,000. He therefore pressed Michael to resolve the situation, but it must be said that the approach was in a friendly manner as he didn't want to be seen 'kicking someone when they were down'. Michael responded politely but insisted on a confirmation that if the losses were below the £2,500 level which Victor had considered the base, he would still allow Michael to buy the firm. That assurance was given, leaving the way clear for Michael to proceed. In the meantime, books still had to be published.

By the autumn Michael had moved out of Gollancz's offices to premises over a wholesale fruiterer, next door but one, at 17/18 Henrietta Street. There he issued his list for autumn 1937 which carried the following quotation from *The Publisher's Circular* about the new company's publishing record:

Elinor Mordaunt's novel *Royal's Free,* chosen this week as the *Daily Mail* Book of the Month for March, is the fifth major choice awarded to Michael Joseph in less than twelve months publishing. The other books were *The General,* by C. S. Forester, and *The Rocket,* by Jeffery Marston (both *Evening Standard* choices), *City for Conquest,* by Aben Kandel (Book Guild choice). In addition Michael Joseph have had two Allied Newspaper choices and five Book Society recommendations. This is not bad going, out of a total of 54 books published.

Those *aficionados* of rare books will be quick to spot that there are only a few of Michael Joseph Ltd titles with the address as 17/18 Henrietta Street for the move was only a stop-gap and the firm moved again to 26 Bloomsbury Street. The first editions of those titles published in the autumn of 1937 will be rare indeed.

These early publications were a great success and once more vindicated Michael's faith in his own judgement. This faith went a long way to strengthen his resolve in his disagreements with Gollancz.

One of the better prospects for 1938 was Sir Philip Gibbs' *Across the Frontiers.* The entry in Michael's spring catalogue anticipated the political nature of the contents. When Victor read the description he became concerned, for the author seemed to suggest that 'Hitler himself may be the architect of this new peace in Europe'. As Victor had recently directed his efforts towards alerting the population to the dangers ahead, he saw this publication as one in possible conflict with his own list, though at the time no final manuscript had been delivered, and without it all was conjecture. But Victor was aroused and a ferocious correspondence took place, culminating in a Board Meeting in February 1938. Michael's attitude was that Victor, having agreed to publish the book, could not renege, especially as Sir Philip Gibbs was a well known author whose previous book *Ordeal over England* was not in conflict with Gollancz's views.

With two representatives of Gollancz on the board it was hardly surprising that Michael felt he was in a tight corner and there was no room for manoeuvre. Everyone became tetchy. His agreement with Gollancz clearly stated that a book of this nature would have to be submitted to Gollancz for editorial approval but there had never been any suggestion that Michael would be refused permission to publish. But the inference was there and it was bitterly resented.

The row was all the more sensitive as Michael had known Philip Gibbs for some ten years, and breaking the contract played heavily on his conscience. For it was Gibbs who had written a foreword to one of Michael's own books, *Journalism for Profit* published in 1925. History records that *Across the Frontiers* was published, but after the split from Gollancz.

*   *   *

Michael, often an impulsively generous man, demonstrated this when a man called Osbourne came to see him. He had an idea for a book which he expounded in great detail. Unfortunately it was not worthwhile and Michael turned it down. Osbourne was naturally disappointed and went on to explain that he was very hard pressed for money and needed at least £5 to keep him going. Michael immediately offered to lend the money, but Osbourne a man of pride, refused as he could never repay him. As he stood up to leave he said, 'If you really want to help, go and have your photograph taken by Howard Coster' (a renowned portrait photographer). 'If you do, at least I will get a pound for the introduction.' Previous to this, Edna, Michael's wife, had been chivvying him to have his photograph taken, and it was this that finally persuaded him to comply.

Reluctantly, he went along at the appointed hour and had no idea that out of this meeting would come an introduction to one of the firm's best-selling authors, whose sales would go far to secure the company's rocky finances: Richard Llewellyn.

Many years later, in an address to members of the British Council on 'The Selection of Manuscripts', Michael spoke about it:

> While I was clamped in a chair under bright lights the photographer suddenly said: 'You're a publisher aren't you? Well I know a young man who's a genius.'
>
> I'd heard that sort of thing before and my heart sank. The photographer went on to tell me that this young man was trying to write a novel and needed encouragement. I feebly said 'Better ask him to come and see me' and promptly forgot all about it.
>
> But a few days later the young author presented himself at my office. I luckily remembered his name. He didn't look like a genius; he was quiet, rather pale, and his hair was properly cut. He had a slim piece of typescript with him – the first two chapters of his novel. I read them – and this is where I was really lucky – decided to offer him a contract on the strength of those two chapters. It is the only time I have ever commissioned a first novel ...

The payment of the commission, which Victor considered excessive, produced a fresh outburst from Victor Gollancz as Sheila Hodges in her history *Gollancz: The Story of a Publishing House 1928-78* recalls.

Nothing was heard for over two years and the title was taken out of the forthcoming lists. Then the colourful, eccentric Llewellyn turned up with the manuscript. It was nearly 900 pages long and Michael set about editing it at once. He worked through three days and two nights, taking out the strong Welsh idiom and inserting a bastardised version which would be more acceptable to a wider readership. Even then it needed finishing, with Michael telling him how to complete the book. Without Michael's background and training, the story might well have been very different; the title that Llewellyn had chosen did not seem quite right to Michael and he persuaded him to change it from 'The Land of my Fathers' to *How Green Was My Valley,* his argument being that this had a more nostalgic and biblical connotation.

To return to 1937, Michael, up against the daily petty wrangles, started to write to all his friends and contacts in search of capital. He was in need of at least £5,000 to sever the ties with Gollancz and another £5,000 to provide further working capital. Even so, this would mean keeping a tight rein on finances for some time ahead.

Neither the family coffers, nor the assets were sufficient to raise the capital required. Michael remembered his longstanding friend, 'Bill' Hessell Tiltman and he wrote off to him, but unfortunately he was many miles away, in China. His reply, in a letter dated 14 November, 1937 stirs the emotions and illustrates their relationship:

Tientsin, China

My Dear Mitch,

Your long letter, written from Acacia Road on October 26th, has just caught me here, a few hours before I set out on the long trek to Henrietta Street. I'm more than glad to have your news, even though I don't altogether like it. There are periods or phases when life seems to have a 'down' on one, but I suppose it remains true that the solution is to hang on grimly through the bad bit until another good bit comes along . . .

Events at Henrietta Street do not altogether surprise me. What it boils down to is the fact that you were being used as long as that seemed the most profitable course; directly an alternative appears on the horizon (in the shape of contracts and goodwill which you must leave behind) you are thrown out with the bathwater. One does not expect philanthropy in business – even Left Wing business! But the idea that one will at least get decent backing up to a point, encouragement, and a modicum of loyalty in the face of inevitable setbacks dies hard. We go on expecting to find it in the face of all evidence to the contrary. Maybe I've grown too cynical with the years and the miles, but I cannot see that V.G. has extended to you, in return for all your work and your brain power, one halfpenny, one gesture, one pat on the back just to back up a colleague. In other words, he's handed you a raw deal, and the only good thing about it – up to date – is that M.J. has demonstrated to the world that he is a publisher of quality who can make the grade, and one of the best judges of a worthwhile book extant. The most encouraging thing I can write, Mitch — and I mean it — is that whatever transpires and whether you are able to raise the capital or not – the last two years must have strengthened tremendously your standing . . .

You obviously do not need any advice from me on your course of action if you can't get the capital, and it comes to a fight. If the gloves come off, my last twenty sen [sic] piece is on Mitch – more especially having regard to the details re postponed books, and the loss of profit due to political interference set out in your letter. And the further fact the junior partner in the firm of Mitch and Bill is hurrying back to London to spur you on . . .

One obvious fact does seem to me to stick out: against losses in two years of ————, [Michael had to fill in this figure] set contracts non-existent in 1935 and today worth say only £10,000. Plus goodwill worth, say, £5,000. Work it out, and where does the loss come in – even if another year's overheads are taken into account? V. G. is apparently trying to argue on profits in the bank, and ignoring the profits invested in the business. I cannot imagine the Left Wing Messiah relishing the idea of working out that little sum under cross-examination in public, though he is quite likely to bluff in private.

In other words, and again, stick to your guns . . .

Bill returned safely to England to help Michael in his time of need. Surely that is what true friendship is all about.

Another friend who had faith in Michael was May Edginton. She agreed to buy 2,000 shares in the restructured company, putting Michael well on the way to independence. And to complete the financial package, Bob Lusty added funds as did the company's accountant, A. S. Craven who was, years later, to leave the company rather abruptly.

It was with some satisfaction that Michael announced to his colleagues that the capital could be raised and the company would be bought out from Gollancz Ltd, a fact that Victor already knew about, but formalities had to be observed at the next Board Meeting. The public announcements would be made later and so events transpired. On 14 March 1938 the draft was signed by Gollancz and the news appeared in that week's *Bookseller*. In the announcement the editor commented that it had not come as a surprise to him as Gollancz was more preoccupied with politics, which clearly had not appealed to Michael. The editor seemed to stress the point, as a picture appeared adjacent to the announcement showing Victor in the middle of a demonstrating crowd jostling with the police and trying to deliver a letter of protest to the German Embassy.

So ended the first chapter of the company's history, leaving Michael considerably wiser. Severing the company imposed decisions of loyalty on members of staff who had been loaned to Michael by Victor. Prior to this upheaval Michael had had the support of Gollancz's staff for accounting and administration, and when the two companies actually split, a number of Gollancz's employees were to join Michael Joseph Ltd. Amongst the first was Miss Greenfield, who handled the invoicing, and Miss Bird, who was later enticed back to handle the Wages and Bought Ledger. Miss Greenfield, later Mrs Hebdon, joined the firm in the middle of the great row and the company's move to 17/18 Henrietta Street. She remembers earning the princely sum of £5.0.0 per week, which was a good wage at that time. Miss Bird, known to her many friends as 'Dickie', and Miss Greenfield were not alone in their respect and affection for Michael. For when Gollancz took his company, at the outset of war, from London to a country house in the village of Brimpton, Berkshire, Miss Bird became unsettled. It didn't take much persuasion for her to return to London and work for Michael. She will always be remembered by the many authors and staff, for her charming personality and the excellence of her calligraphic handwriting.

The thought of permanent offices at 17/18 Henrietta Street, which were over a fruiterer prompted Peter Hebdon, Charles Pick and Bob to keep their eyes open for more suitable offices though it is doubtful that anyone told Michael about their ideas until they had found a place. By chance, Bob Lusty and Peter Hebdon came across 26 Bloomsbury Street which was to let. At first sight the premises seemed ideal, though much too large. When they described these new offices in Bloomsbury, Michael was far from enthusiastic for once settled, even in temporary accommodation, he did not like change. They persuaded him to view the premises and he had to agree that they were indeed more suitable. The rent – £350 a year – was a sum at which Michael flinched when he heard. They couldn't stand that sort of commitment, but Charles Pick thought he could find someone to rent the two top floors. This he did, much to everyone's delight; and the someone turned out to be a firm called Imperia, the London offices of a continental company. Michael had, fortuititously, allowed Charles to act for them in addition to his role as salesman.

Wragg's own Christmas Card

March 14th, 1938.

Messrs. Victor Gollancz Limited and Messrs.
Michael Joseph Limited announce that the connection
existing between the two firms is by mutual arrangement discontinued from the present date. As part
of this arrangement, Mr. Victor Gollancz and Mr. Normen
Collins leave the Board of Directors, and their places
are taken by Arthur Stanley Craven and Hubert Hessell
Tiltman (with Mr. Michael Joseph continuing as Chairman
and Managing Director). Messrs. Victor Gollancz Limited
have now no financial or other interest in the company of
Messrs. Michael Joseph Limited.

Draft announcement of Michael's break from Gollancz

Once they had moved in, Michael felt very comfortable in his room at the rear away from the noise of the traffic. It overlooked a small and very dilapidated garden, one which estate agents would describe as 'a mature garden'. There was rubbish everywhere, very little grass, and a mulberry tree presiding forlornly over a patch of earth supporting only a few straggly weeds. Certainly not much to look at, but the rooms adequately accommodated everyone and staff could work in an atmosphere conducive to publishing.

*   *   *

During the two years with Victor, Michael had had his fair share of luck. One instance was when Charles Pick happened to meet the great-grand-daughter of Charles Dickens at a party. Monica Dickens was then working as a domestic servant and maybe it was the ambience of the evening, but having chatted to her he suggested that she ought to write about her experiences and she agreed to try. Her book *One Pair of Hands* became a great success and was the forerunner of many more titles. Although the credit goes to Charles Pick who discovered her, it was Michael who beguiled her with his charm and persuaded her that she could write, for he had the ability to show her how, and gave encouragement when the task became too difficult. She was completely captivated by the excitement he generated. After the war, Michael and Anthea, his third wife, went to see her in Boston; she recalls: '. . . he was so charming and sort of – electrical still, it gave me nostalgia for the days when I was this dopey girl of 22, suddenly growing up into reality, and he was so utterly charming and fascinating, and of course I was "in love" with him in a hero worshipping way, and he made me feel he was quite intrigued with me. Playing a game, he was, but it *was* fun.'

Ursula Bloom also knew Michael well. She was a dedicated and hard-working author who had been writing from the age of seven, devoting some six to eight hours a day to her work. When she had the time she would frequently be found at the Joseph home accompanied occasionally by her son, who had joined the navy. His visits were an added bonus because he had become the idol of Michael's daughter Shirley. At the tender age of four, Shirley had 'fallen in love' with this hero with the gold braid on his uniform.

Another authoress to visit the family was Angela du Maurier. Like her sister Daphne, Angela received much encouragement and help from Michael. In her most recent book, *Old Maids Remembered,* she wrote:

The late Michael Joseph who published my first four books was wonderful to me. He believed in me, and this was what helped to boost my morale more than anything. He was no yes-man, indeed he was utterly ruthless with each manuscript of mine, and how I got through writing without tears I do not know, but I used to go to his house and he would go through the damn thing until I had wondered why I had written it and why he was going to publish it, and he said, 'Because I think that one day you will write something good'.

In producing her first book, Michael asked her artistic and equally talented sister Jeanne, to design the dust jacket for *The Perplexed Heart,* Jeanne willingly obliged. The reviews were stimulating: 'The du Maurier family gives us another brilliant writer ... Not only astonishingly good but amazingly mature ... illumined by something very near genius' (Philip Page, *Daily Mail*) 'It will make Angela famous overnight' (Dennis Wheatley, *Sunday Graphic*)

The book, published in the spring of 1939, began, much to everyone's delight, to sell well and justified Michael's intuition. By that autumn it was in its third impression.

Angela went on to write another three books, *The Spinning Wheel (1940), The Little Less (1941) and Treveryan (1942)*. Because her first book sold well, agreeing to publish these were relatively easy decisions despite a severe restriction of paper, for, during the war, books of quality were in great demand.

In ordinary life the ability to read, write and converse are sufficient in themselves. Authors and publishers – especially publishers however, consider the ability to spell an essential feature of their lives. The educated author, and publisher, will always feel slightly superior to those who blatantly cannot spell even the most common words.

In the late thirties, the Americans developed a craze of 'Spelling Bees', which were games all about the art of spelling words correctly. In society, high-brow hostesses found that this type of game was a great ice-breaker for parties. The BBC helped this craze along too. So it comes as no surprise to the reader that the publishing world and authors rose to the challenge thrown down by Christina Foyle at one of their famous 'luncheons'.

On the occasion of the Ninetieth Foyle's Literary Luncheon, held at Grosvenor House in May 1938 one such 'Spelling Bee' competition replaced the usual speeches. Lined up against the Publishers, were Lady Cynthia Asquith, Naomi Jacob, Russell Thorndyke, Pamela Frankau, Ursula Bloom and Dennis Wheatley. Defending the Publishers' reputations were Hamish Hamilton, W. P. Crane, *Rich and Cowan,* Lovat Dickson, Gerard Hopkins, *Oxford University Press,* Edmond Segrave, Editor of *The Bookseller* and they were captained by Michael Joseph.

In the Chair was Mr S. P. B. Mais, standing in for 'Freddie' Grisewood who could not get away from the BBC. The tension and expectation before the game must have been high as the attendance had swelled to some 1,000 for lunch!

It seems that events did not go well for either the publishers or authors. Mr Crane misspelt *heifer* as heffer, and found *mucilage, liaison, idiosyncrasy* too difficult. Mr Hamilton confused *hebdomadal* with *abdominal,* and forgot the second *s* in *reconnaissance.* Mr Segrave and Mr Hopkins were stumped by *mesembryanthemum, depilatory, veterinary, reconciliatory* and *flannelette.*

But the authors fared even worse. Lady Asquith misspelt *esurient, bissextile* and *malassimilation.* Miss Jacob failed with *phthisis* and *committee.* The authors, led by Cynthia Asquith claimed to have to spell the more difficult words, complaining that the publishers' side were being given 'kindergarten' words to spell!

Whereas both Michael and Lovat Dickson correctly spelt all their words including *hyalitis, perambulator, manoeuvre, somnambulism, rodomontade, abhorrence* and *fogey. The Times* aptly described the event next day, using the headline 'AUTHORS AS POOR SPELLERS – PUBLISHERS NOT MUCH BETTER'. I hate to think how some of us would fare today!

Michael must have felt fairly pleased with himself for he came out of the affair with aplomb and his pride intact. Doubtless, they all parted friends but many years later, he was to have a major public row with Edmond Segrave. The event had also been a marvellous opportunity to score a point or two against his authors, Ursula Bloom and Cynthia Asquith. Not least, it was an opportunity for boosting the sales of dictionaries. Foyle's had previously announced that sales had already increased by some thirty per cent in the preceding weeks, and holding a 'spelling bee' luncheon would enhance the figures further.

One of the company's more unusual titles, which they published in the spring of 1938 was *Portrait of a Windscreen* by Gawen Brownrigg. This title had been accepted the year before by another publishing house, which had had the book printed and bound. Then one of the directors read it through and thought it unsuitable for publishing and ordered the whole lot destroyed. One of the few 'file' copies that escaped destruction found its way into Michael's hands via Mrs Alfred Knopf. He read it and agreed that the title was worth publishing. It was never a best seller but sales were reasonable, justifying the publication. Selecting the right manuscripts, though, was often a case of luck and though Michael seemed to have just the right knack, it was not always the case. Sometimes the luck was thrust in front of him.

The following year Michael planned to go to New York and he timed his visit with the maiden voyage of the *Mauretania*. Richard Llewellyn's manuscript of *How Green was my Valley* accompanied Michael to New York on this voyage which began at Liverpool on 17 June 1939. I mention the date as the voyage was to be the beginning of many overseas sales trips. Amongst those on board were Blanche and Alfred Knopf, the American publishers. Michael made a point of meeting them – the stimulating voyage providing the opportunity to establish a firm friendship. Their association was later to prove very useful to Michael. And in later years Bob Lusty was to make the same leisurely voyage, for this was the romantic era of the big ocean going liners, which provided the epitome of luxury travel in a relaxed lifestyle, and which engendered opportunities to make friends.

The voyage to New York was, according to the records, 'favoured with cool breezes' but on his arrival he found the weather was extremely hot and muggy. By midday he was glad to take advantage of the air-conditioning of a nearby restaurant. After lunching he set out to see the city and hailed one of that city's ubiquitous *Yellow Cabs*. By a chance in a million the owner, an extrovert of many faces, befriended Michael. Leon, with his lean looks and flamboyant red tie struck a chord in Michael's memory. Later, it came to him, he was a complete look-alike for George Gershwin. Although the man drove fast and skilfully, he kept up a running commentary without causing his passenger the slightest concern. He knew New York intimately, every street, every alley and building, or so he claimed.

That evening, Michael left his hotel to seek a quiet spot for dinner, and there to his surprise and delight was Leon again. 'Take me somewhere cool and quiet', requested Michael. 'Leave it to me' replied Leon, making Michael's evening, for he was only too delighted to deliver himself into such capable hands and lean back and relax.

Leon was as good as his word. They travelled for some miles downtown or so it seemed, until he pulled up outside a mundane and unpreposessing restaurant. Setting Michael down he said 'I'll call for you later.' 'Where will you be eating', asked Michael? 'Why don't you join me?' Considerably taken aback, he hesitated; it was most unorthodox but he succumbed. Over dinner they exchanged personal details and a friendship began. One thing Leon insisted upon was that while he was taxiing Michael on business he would accept payment, but while on pleasure there would be no charge whatsoever. An agreement which Michael had, reluctantly, to accept. So began a unique visit, memories of which he drafted for publication but to my knowledge have never been published.

'Mike, what's the first thing you do when you get to a new place?' Without giving me time to make the non-committal reply he obviously expected he went on, 'You know what every good American does when he finds himself alone?' I thought it tactful to consider this in silence. 'Well Mike, you know how it is. We all want the same thing, don't we? You come from England, but it's the same there, isn't it? You just say the word and I'll fix it up. We're friends, aren't we?'

He misinterpreted my silence. 'Just leave it to me. I know places – Mike, I know all New York. And everyone knows me. There's a wonderful place up on 63rd Street. It's got everything. White girls, coloured girls, Chinese, and they're all ladies. It's a beautiful place, Mike. Valuable furniture, real carpets and everything clean. Clean as the inside of this cab. I know the Madam, and she'll do everything for a friend of mine. Champagne at cost price. She'll cut the other price, too. If you are a stranger, you wouldn't get out under twenty-five or thirty bucks, but you could have the whole works, Mike, for' – he made a rapid mental calculation – 'for about ten. Maybe less'.

I hated to disappoint him but explained as best I could that I wasn't much interested in valuable furniture and luxurious carpets and that I didn't care overmuch for champagne. Even at cut prices. Leon was puzzled, and I fear he formed a poor opinion of European virility. But he brightened up when I suggested that we might perhaps spend one evening in feminine company. I was determined that in Leon's eyes at least my peculiarities should be limited to outlandish habits with knives and forks and an English accent.

The following evening he asked whether I would like to make the acquaintance of his wife and family. He had, he said, told her about me and, thinking it would help to keep us both out of mischief and put things onto a proper footing, I accepted the invitation at once. I took with me a copy of Clemence Dane's *A Hundred Enchanted Tales* as a present for Leon's little daughter. Leon examined the book with what I can only describe as reverence. What impressed him was my name in print on the spine: a refreshing experience for any book publisher . . .

Leon's daughter evidently inherited her father's high spirits. She was four years old, small for her age, but with a bubbling good humour which radiated through the small dark apartment. She made it abundantly clear that she had never seen anything like me before. When I said something she insisted on me repeating it, and gurgled with laughter at the strangeness of my accent . . .

Leon's ideas of entertainment were catholic enough. When a Canadian publishing colleague turned up unexpectedly at my hotel, Leon took charge. 'What, never been to a burlesque show?' he said. 'I'll take you tomorrow.' The three of us spent most of that night

Picture above is of Miss Ursula Bloom, Mr. Michael Joseph
and Mr. Dennis Wheatley at Foyles "Spelling Bee" Luncheon.

Foyle's Literary Luncheon,
(Spelling Bee competition)

26 Bloomsbury Street

The Mauretania reaches New York, with MJ somewhere aboard

smoking and drinking. I had a busy morning and by the time we met Leon I was pretty tired.

It was still very hot when we took our seats in the theatre on Broadway. The audience was wholly masculine and noisy. A team of knockabout comedians provided the first turn, and there was much clamouring for the strip tease dancer who was to follow. I have forgotten her name but she was, I believe, the current sensation on Broadway. By the time she appeared my seat had become more and more comfortable. I have a vague recollection of a lady pirouetting somewhat languidly from one side of the stage to the other, with some discarding of outer garments. I was awakened by tumultuous applause and catcalls and Leon's voice saying, 'Well, would'ya believe it? He's asleep!'

In between the bright lights Michael managed, amongst other things, to meet Harold Latham of *Macmillan Company,* who he thought would buy *How Green Was My Valley.* Just how important this meeting was, is to be judged by the fact that they did indeed publish the book, paying a substantial sum, just when it was most needed.

Michael returned to England aboard *RMS Aquitania* in July, taking part in such shipboard activities as 'mixed bathing', 'Keno Lotto' and visiting the cinema to see *Within the Law,* featuring Ruth Hussey and Paul Cavanagh. Somehow, though, I don't think he took part in the advertised 'Swedish Drill' at 8.30 in the morning. But he might have, if he had realised that war was shortly to be declared on Germany.

Chapter 7

Publishing
In Time of War
1939–48

*'A publisher can recognize a good book when he reads
the manuscript, but it is impossible for him to predict
whether the book will be a success.'*
Michael Joseph 1928

Publishing during the Second World War and the immediate post
war period, was not quite so hazardous as had been anticipated by
managements at the outset of war. Events were to take place which
played a major part in making Michael's firm and many other publishers
successful. In Michael's case it was not just because the bombs missed
the offices in Bloomsbury Street, but because the war created market
conditions which favoured the surviving publishers. So many books were
destroyed and for many, there was little to do in their bomb shelters
other than to read. It became a sellers' market for publishers. Books sold
without the need for expensive advertising.

Looking through Michael's correspondence covering those formative
years, it seems that there were at least three occasions when the firm's
future was put in jeopardy. The first was the split between Michael and
Gollancz, the second when the financial stability was threatened and the
third time when Michael volunteered to serve again in the armed forces.

In 1938 the company had only just begun to settle down after the
break from Gollancz in March. Then came the further disruption caused
by the move to 26 Bloomsbury Street in the summer which exacerbated
matters, but Michael, in addition to keeping the fledgling company going
had time to concentrate on the autumn List. This was the largest to date
with over forty new titles. These included books from Walter Allen,
Frank Tilsey, Owen Rutter and C. S. Forester, and works from several
new authors.

He returned home from America in 1939, before, as the saying went,
'the balloon went up'. For months, Hitler's threats to the Jews, to

Germany's neighbouring countries and to England were highlighted by the enlightened, Gollancz being one of them. Then came that infamous piece of paper from Chamberlain, proclaiming *peace in our time.*

Michael like so many others, had anticipated the coming of war as inevitable but he had much more to lose than most. Weighing up the odds he soon realised that if it came to a fight and England succeeded in defending herself then there was a reasonable future; but equally, if England lost there would be little hope for the company, let alone himself. He thought about the staff and assumed that many would be called up for service when the time came. Two probable exceptions were Bob Lusty and Peter Hebdon whose physical state would preclude them, Bob being deaf in one ear and Peter being an epileptic. (As events transpired, they were never asked to serve.) With war imminent and Michael's decision to take an active part again, his immediate problem was how to ensure that the company survived, which meant that he had to continue to read and select manuscripts for publication wherever he happened to be. It seems now that he felt if he could keep an eye on the acquisition and editing of new titles, then the company could perhaps continue to publish new books successfully. He was counting on the support of Bob and Peter whose rejection from service was going to be very much to the company's benefit.

When Michael broke the news to the staff that he was itching to rejoin, naturally they, like his family, were dismayed. War had not yet been declared they argued, and what was the point of seeking an active role? He was almost too old for active duty, married, with family responsibilities, and publishing was at least beginning to provide him with a modest standard of prosperity.

Michael started to weedle his way back into the services, but as in the last Great War it did take time. War with Germany was declared on 3 September 1939 and despite his efforts, he heard nothing until that November when he was asked to attend an interview. Fortunately, this delay, allowed Michael time to consider and plan the company's immediate future.

On the positive side, he had Bob Lusty, Peter Hebdon, Charles Pick and a reliable staff. The firm did, after all, have a number of good authors who, if they continued to write good books, would ensure a safe future, though many feared the worst if war came. Michael saw in Bob a man of many talents, not least of which was his ability to organise production and administration. He had installed a comprehensive production chart that encompassed the complete history of each book. Matters had run smoothly in the initial years, supporting Michael's view that Bob could easily manage to run the company on a day-to-day basis. He believed that if major problems arose, he could help make critical decisions at arm's length; he had in mind, for example, the choice of which books to be published; and perhaps, with Bob's co-operation, he could still make the major policy decisions, sure in the knowledge that they would be enacted. It was a harmonious relationship that worked well, and as events turned out, he did give the task of running the company whilst he was away to Bob Lusty. Of everyone there, he knew that Bob could always be counted upon to get books printed, bound and distributed. Bob remembers the period well in his book *Bound To Be Read*.

> But there was a gaiety of spirit, a certain excitement in the air around us which is always necessary, but seldom nowadays in evidence, if editorial initiative and urgency is to flourish in any abundance. We were a happy ship, with Michael a little remote from the rest of us on the bridge and I operating as his chief officer. The burden of every day was shouldered by Peter Hebdon, Charles Pick and myself. This was the way I liked it; and Michael Joseph, satisfying himself that overall it worked, left us wonderfully free to get on with things.

However, during the short time that Michael was to be away on duty, he was sent many manuscripts to read. He found these a good antidote to the renewed pressures of active service and helped him to keep a finger on the pulse of the firm. On some he gave his opinion and editorial judgement. Once Michael was away on active duty from the firm, Bob Lusty wrote regularly, keeping him informed of the successes and troubles. Peter Hebdon also wrote to Michael, giving other news which he welcomed. During that time, Bob wrote many a letter, sometimes even two a day. In the main, and as the Manager, it fell to him to do the bulk of the writing, keeping Michael informed of sales figures and events. Questions of policy and choice of manuscripts would sometimes be lengthily discussed and in this unusual manner a conclusion was reached.

It was a happy state of affairs, as members of staff were to record. John Banbury, a reader, was seconded to the Army Pay Corps but before he left he wrote to Michael to let him know that he had nominated him should references be required. He went on:

> I shall be very sad to leave Bloomsbury Street and I should like to take this opportunity of thanking you not only for all you've taught me, but also for the fact that I've enjoyed working with you quite enormously. Even if I were never to see the inside of a publisher's office again, I could not regret the eighteen months I've been here; they've been far too pleasant for that. In the meantime I can only say thank you very much and hope that I may be able, in the comparatively near future, to return and participate again in the triumphal progress of MJ Ltd.
>
> Yours ever, John Banbury

Return he eventually did, and he played his part in maintaining the company's success, for he is credited by Bob Lusty as the man who thought up a new title for a manuscript by a Doctor Richard Ostlere with the uninteresting title of *Merrily Merrily* to *Doctor in the House*. This was the start of that famous series of the *Doctor* books written under the well known alias Richard Gordon.

That November Charles Pick also left to join the Army Pay Corps, his first posting being at Reading. Later on, in the Royal Artillery, his tours of duty took him to India, Ceylon and Singapore. He never forgot that, back home, the firm would need information on overseas markets and in the latter days of the war, when Michael was convalescing, Charles posted a long letter outlining the state of book sales in Bombay and Calcutta. This extract underlines his loyal thoughts.

> There is, of course, an increasing demand for new books in India and the booksellers complain bitterly of their supplies. This demand will undoubtably increase as the number of Europeans in the bases like Calcutta and Bombay increase. Also, more and more Indians are reading English books – particularly novels. The prospects for the continued demand are good.
>
> Paper rationing [in India] has been introduced and no new licenses are granted for those not publishing before June 1944.

He goes on to outline how one publisher, Jackson Marshall, had succeeded in distributing many of Collins titles and because books generally were in short supply, for paper rationing was having the same effect there as in Britain, they captured a major share of the market. He introduced Charles to another company, Thackers, who, he said, might well be in a position to print and publish some of Michael Joseph's titles. Charles's opinion continued: 'My own opinion, based mainly on Marshall's estimation, is that Rumer Godden would sell at least 3,000, Forester 5,000, Hornblower R. N. 10,000, Joyce Cary 3,000 . . .'

The letter had been addressed to Bob Lusty who doubtless had it copied and sent to Michael at Copyhold Farm.

*   *   *

Back home, the war did not make dealing with authors any easier. The company had published Caryl Brahms and S. J. Simon's *A Bullet in the Ballet* and when they next came to see Bob with their following manuscript. He obviously found them difficult to deal with – for in his book, he describes them as 'a lunatic couple'; their behaviour to Bob seems, at times, to have been patronising. Miss Brahms, who normally referred to

Bob as, 'Trusty Lusty', once flattered him with 'Let me call you Angel-Face Mr Lusty, because you *are* such an angel, you know.'

Later, Bob wrote a letter to Michael remarking on his frustrations of dealing with her, as she had become as big a nuisance, as the Paper Controller, printers and binders combined. What made the relationship between Bob and Michael a little sensitive later on, was that their second book *Don't Mr Disraeli* began selling very well – being reprinted at least twice in its first year of publication!

Working for the company during those wartime conditions placed a greater stress on the staff whose loyalty and hard work ensured that books were produced. Salaries were only just adequate to provide the basics, and balancing the home budget was always tricky, especially the problems caused by the shortages and ration books. The constant bombing raids over London brought an added tension to life – forcibly brought home to the staff when, on their way to work, they saw familiar buildings completely destroyed and people passing by bandaged up from the wounds sustained in the previous night's raid, no doubt thinking 'there but for the grace of God go I'. Many streets were blocked by fallen buildings and fire, the smell of smoke and dust pervaded whatever the weather.

The effect of the bombing raids also hit book production. In one period producing books was well nigh impossible, but where there's a will, there's a way, and Bob Lusty with the help of all the remaining staff, kept production going. In October 1940, James Burn and Brendons in Plymouth (the company's binders and printers) were hit and much of the company's printed stock was destroyed. It was not until the following May that Bob was able to persuade the Paper Controller to replace the seven tons of paper. At one point he reported to Michael: 'Poor old Burns were blown up for the third time on Saturday night and so were our blockmakers. It makes things very complicated, but one gets curiously used to it. A year or so ago the idea of losing our printers, binders and blockmakers within three weeks would have worried us out of our lives.'

But life went on, bringing out the best in the British people. In the autumn of 1940, Peter Hebdon and Miss Wendy Greenfield, who also worked in the company, had decided to get married. Chivalry and pride prompted Peter to ask for a raise, not just to enable him to support her but because she was earning more than he at the time. He approached Bob Lusty on the matter, who referred his request to Michael, thus passing this sensitive subject over to him. He got his increase, and they duly married shortly afterwards.

The Autumn List included Dorothy Black's third novel, *Never Leave Me,* and in August Bob Lusty wrote to Michael asking for advice.

Although her books had been selling quite well, Bob reported that the company was not making much profit. They had a contract for three titles and he had learnt that there was a fourth in the pipeline. Her agent, Pollinger, thought that the company might not want to take on a fourth title in such a short time and wondered if he ought to take her next book to another publisher.

Bob thought it wasn't necessary to keep her and recommended that they should let her go. In his view, she did not fit the company's lists and if four titles were published in a year then her sales were bound to suffer. Michael agreed:

> On the whole I think you are right. We can't do four titles a year the only thing is, it seems a pity to let anyone go if we are assured of a regular output and a regular if modest profit. It all helps turnover, and the making up of a list. We've had so many one-book people – just look through our past lists! – that we can do with a few regulars. They help to stabilize our lists with the trade and when cheap editions come back again I suppose we shall need authors like Dorothy Black.
>
> Perhaps it would be worthwhile suggesting to Pollinger that she publishes part of her output under a pseudonym in another list? But if that won't do I agree that we can't publish the lot. Three books a year is the absolute maximum for us, and you may think that this is too many.
>
> If we have to let her go be sure to write her direct (sending Pollinger a copy of the letter) expressing our regret at losing her. I have known her for years, as you may remember, and it's as well to keep on good terms.

But whatever the solution arrived at, her next title, *Burmese Picnic*, appeared in the Autumn List the following year so bridges were not burnt after all.

There is no doubt though, that the element of luck played an important part in the company's success. For during the war, several factors were to help them. Not only a large cheque from Macmillans in New York for *How Green was My Valley*, but the scarcity of paper and the consequent rationing placed restrictions on advertising, and the shortage of books meant that it was easy to sell books. Before the war, publishers increasingly spent more on promotion. Many overspent and this made the publisher's existence a very risky one indeed. Michael had argued with Gollancz that in the formative years of the company, a certain amount of advertising was essential, but once a company was established it was only too easy to overspend. It was also too easy to put out an optimistic number of titles, hoping that they would sell, and when they didn't, the company's future became precarious. The war brought rationing and the national press were not exempt. Issues carried fewer pages, denying publishers the option of expensive advertising. This reduced the overheads for selling books which meant greater profits. Stocks of books in publishers' warehouses were being destroyed by bombs, which resulted in books becoming scarce.

The shortage of paper also created a great opportunity for publishers to be original with reasons for rejecting a manuscript from an author. 'Can't get the paper' was a response that no author could easily argue with, and many publishers were said to have used this convenient reason. It is not clear whether the company ever used this reason but Curtis Brown once advised Bob that if any publisher used this reason to his agency, they were taken off their lists for the time being.

No sooner had Michael been invalided out of the Army in May 1941, than Bob Lusty wrote to him concerning the major problem of acquiring paper. For back at the office, publishing books had slowed, not just because manuscripts were in short supply, but because paper shortages had delayed operations. The Government had seen fit to limit the amount of paper that could be used for printing books, which in itself seemed reasonable. However, the Ministry of Supply employed 'Paper Controllers', who had taken, as the basis of the rationing, the period from 31 August 1938 to 31 August 1939; a period in which Michael Joseph Ltd had become independent from Gollancz and had not published many titles. Rationing was based on the tonnage used in that period, which made matters worse for the company, as they had reduced the standard weight of papers they used by 30 per cent once they were independent. The Controller who looked after MJ's supplies was based at the Great Western Hotel, Reading – and, Bob who had tried to negotiate a better deal, now thought that Michael might have the time to travel over to Reading to argue their case!

Bob had prepared a lengthy and detailed report of the fifty-three books published to date, the total weight 550 hundredweights (about twenty-eight tonnes). The autumn list required much more paper, about one hundred and twenty-three tonnes and the ration at 60 per cent. And there was worse to come as this percentage was soon to be reduced to 50 per cent. Whether Michael's efforts had any effect, cannot easily be traced, but the majority were published in the end. Bob was given a great deal of leeway to manage the business, but when matters got tough, he usually referred the problem to Michael, for by then it was a real challenge just to stay in business.

One of the traits of the publishing world was the friendship and the gentlemanly manner in which business was done. As Manager of the company, Bob Lusty had maintained this attitude, and this led to a surprise opportunity passed on to him by the company's paper supplier, Dickinsons. The account of events is recorded in Bob Lusty's book *Bound to be Read*. Suffice it here to say that he was able to acquire up to forty tons of allocated paper under the rationing scheme. The only caveat, that he had to have the books produced by the printer to whom the paper was originally allocated. This, then, was a major piece of luck. The benefactor was Wilfred Harvey and the printer, Purnells, who did indeed subsequently print many titles for the company.

Sales figures for the middle of the war reveal just how well the company was faring. The company's best sellers in those days were of course, the much-acclaimed *How Green was My Valley* by Richard Llewellyn, which sold over 90,000 copies in the first two years of its publication. *Captain Hornblower,* a trilogy by C. S. Forester achieved over 15,000 sales, but another of his titles, *Captain from Connecticut,* sold twice this number. *The Oaken Heart* by Margery Allingham, about which Bob Lusty was very enthusiastic, sold over 13,000 copies. Perhaps more significantly, the company managed to achieve sales for most of their titles of over 3,000 copies.

In a series of letters and notes, the growth of these sales can be traced. Bob had always been chasing that elusive £40,000 turnover which had been the target set by Gollancz at the start of the firm's life. This would have meant a monthly sales exceeding £3,300 and in a letter to Michael in March 1941, Bob exuded delight at £3,575 for February (against £1,930 for the previous February, though quite why this was so low I'm not sure, for January's figure had reached £8,683). This had been a notable month, for Michael's efforts in selling the rights of *How Green was my Valley* to Macmillan in America just before the outset of war, had come home to roost. The sales for that month included a huge royalty cheque for £6,595! An immense sum, that went a long way to fund the company in those difficult days. With ups and downs, sales continued to be encouraging. In the first six months, sales had exceeded £24,000, and he was now confident the company would pass the elusive £40,000 that year. This doesn't seem much today, but salaries, for example, were about £260 a year for a senior executive and the cost of producing an average novel was around £300.

But it was a time when almost every publisher whose books were readable, was successful. The population, fearing air-raids, would rush to their Anderson shelters and sit it out. There was not much to do – other than to lose themselves in a good book. The bookbinding trade also reflects the growth. Burns had 250,000 books to bind in July 1940 and this rose to 450,000 by September that year. Peaking at 2,500,000 books in 1942, the figures prove that if ever there was a period when publishers simply could not go wrong, this was it.

On Monday 20 April 1942, Michael Joseph Limited released a curious press announcement, 'Adolf Hitler and Michael Joseph Ltd both celebrated anniversaries. The company's sixth year of trading and Hitler's fifty-third birthday.' Half the company's publishing life had been under conditions of war but notwithstanding these, twenty-eight books of theirs had been recommended by the *Book Society* and the *James Tait Black Memorial Prize* had been won twice. First with Forester's *Captain Hornblower* and then by Joyce Cary's *The House of Children*. This was a very successful time for the company for the announcement went on to state that of the last thirty-seven new titles, twenty-two had been reprinted to meet the demand.

This growth presented Bob with the extra problem of finding a second printer when Brendons became full. In June 1941, he wrote to Michael confirming that he had been successful in finding Unwin Brothers of Woking to print the company's non-fiction books for the autumn. Unwins were as reasonable in price as anyone he could find, and they had the advantage of being near Burns of Esher. Transport was so slow that this was really a great advantage.

*   *   *

Immediately Michael was 'relegated to the unemployed' at the end of May 1941, he rented a cottage in Little Witcombe, near Gloucester, aptly named Peace Cottage. From here, he sought a larger house and settled on Copyhold Farm at Curridge, near Newbury, but he wasn't able to move in until June. In many ways this was to be an idyllic home, close to Newbury for access to London and the office, not to mention the racecourse. Yet far enough away from the sensitive areas which could be targets for the German bombers. There were fields for his daughter's horses and splendid copses which appealed to Michael for there he could make good use of his shotgun.

Under orders, but doctor's orders this time, to take life easy for a time, he returned to writing, and it was not long before he started to turn his notes of recent army experiences into a book. For the first time he used, for original writing, a typewriter, which he had asked to be sent down to him from London. This was to be the first title he had published under his own imprint. It is not difficult to find the reason for this, paper rationing being strict, he wanted to make sure that his work actually got published and if his own firm took it on, then he could also exercise some control over it. Therefore in November, he wrote to Bob:

I think I have found a title for my own book – *The Sword in the Scabbard*. It is perhaps a bit pretentious, but it has the suggestion I want, and since I didn't do any fighting it fits the book. You might let me know what you think of it. I have now done 60,000 words, and the book should be finished before the end of the month. When you have had a look at it – and I shall welcome your criticisms and any suggestions – I hope it will be possible, assuming you want to add it to our list, to put it in hand without delay. I know how difficult things are now, but I am anxious to get a set of proofs to my late Colonel. It would be damned awkward if he were suddenly sent abroad. And if, as is quite probable, the M. of I. [Ministry of Information] insist on alterations that will mean further delay, which I want to avoid, for if the war situation suddenly changes the book will lose most of its interest. I think I mentioned that galleys will be essential in view of the probability of considerable cuts. And no corrections clause in the agreement for the same reason!

Bob, having read the book, sent Michael a congratulatory telegram – he was obviously much impressed. Later, at Michael's request, he sent a draft blurb for the jacket. Michael's reaction? In his memo to Bob he wrote: 'When I read your draft blurb I was appalled (!) but without making any comment I gave it to my family to read. They entirely approved, so I read it again and, reluctantly, have come to the conclusion that (with slight amendments) it should be used.'

No sooner had Bob received a specimen page of typesetting from Unwin Brothers, than the Ministry of Supply introduced new regulations concerning the size and extent of books that publishers could produce. *The Sword in the Scabbard* was planned as a 224 page book but it seemed to Bob that as the author was also the publisher, the book should certainly comply with these new regulations. Any bending of the rules might have meant incurring the wrath of the Paper Controller. He immediately advised Michael that they comply, and informed him that he had asked for alternative specimen pages of type to be set. The new conditions meant that the book would have to be reduced to 192 pages which would not have had the same sales appeal for the price. Michael argued that because the typesetting had started before these new regulations had been announced, he could escape their constraints. Despite Bob's protests, the book was published as originally planned, in fact making 228 pages, but the *War Economy Standard* took effect thereafter.

Once this was published he turned his hand to writing the now famous cat book *Charles – The Story of a Friendship*. (The story of this book is covered more extensively in Chapter 8.) It was for Michael, very much a labour of love but he still had time on his hands. He was growing stronger, though, despite attacks of lumbago and 'flu.

Well away from the pressures of the office, he was easily distracted from thinking about publishing problems. He enjoyed the friendships that the time and the place allowed him to build up. It was here while he was convalescing that he met and became great friends with the artist, H. M. Bateman. 'H. M.' or 'Mayo' as Michael knew him, would call in on most Sundays, to swap stories and generally gossip about the war. However, when Michael was steeped in writing, his visits were not welcome as they interrupted his concentration. But Bateman did not seem to notice and their relationship deteriorated one weekend to a point when Michael lost his patience and, in the theatrical sense, threw him out. However, once the book *(The Sword in the Scabbard)* was finished, the schism did not last long. In a gesture of reconciliation H.M. offered to sketch him playing the piano, something that he knew Michael liked to do and thought would be a suitable peace offering.

Michael had his moments playing the practical joker. Brenda Bateman and Shirley went to visit a near neighbour, who offered them each some extra meat, pigs livers and trotters – something that was severely rationed. The Government had also by then decreed that anyone who reared animals for home consumption could not donate to friends and inspectors toured the countryside to enforce this rule.

Edna was delighted when Shirley walked in bearing these gifts, but Michael with a glint in his eye, picked up the phone and disguising his voice, rang the Batemans pretending to be from the local Inspector's Office. It was all very well contrived for in the background was someone busy typing (this was Shirley, who was in on the joke) – 'I've just been informed that you have received some extra meat and this is just a friendly call to remind you of the rules, and to inform you that an Inspector will be calling this afternoon.'

Brenda Bateman did not recognise the 'voice' and spent a very worrying few hours. She turned to H. M. for help, but he declined – 'You did the deed, you get out of it.' Brenda argued that 'he really ought to help her – after all, he'd eaten some that lunchtime'. In the end she telephoned Edna to confide her fears, only to be told that – with hysterical laughter in the background – 'she may have to wait a long time!'. The joke then dawned on her, at which point she cheerfully called Michael all the names she could think of, and some of them would have to be 'bleeped' out of any account!

Some time later, Brenda got her own back by appealing to Michael's liking for young ladies. She phoned him, impersonating the Matron from the local American Hospital, and commanded that he should provide accommodation for two members of their staff. He immediately began to object but changed his mind instantly when he was told that they were young nurses! 'Can't take two, but would be happy to take one', he told her, to which 'the Matron' agreed. 'She'll be arriving this evening.' The thought of a young, and no doubt pretty young girl in the house appealed to his ego and imagination.

Michael went in to tell Edna 'bloody nuisance – just been told that we have got to take in a young American nurse. There's hardly enough room here as it is.' But he set about making the box-room available for the nurse and moved the furniture around, which Edna considered an unusually helpful thing for him to do. Well, the appointed hour came and went. Night fell, and still no nurse. Michael became quite impatient. Where was the damned girl.

Meanwhile Edna, returning a phone call to Brenda, mentioned in passing the billeting arrangements that had been made and could not understand why she had not turned up. A gleeful 'Well, you might have to wait quite some time' made Edna instantly realise what was happening and decided to keep Michael in the dark, but she could not keep the pretence up for long! He was suitably chastened, realising that his 'Achilles' heel' had been severely bruised.

Not only did he allow H. M. to sketch him, he also had a small portrait done in oils. (This is shown on the bookjacket). Once taken with the idea he had a full size portrait of Edna painted by Cecil Jameson. Today these are both prized family possessions. As he regained his health slowly he was able to take a more active role in the company, though it was not until 1949 that he could attend the office full time.

Many years before, in June 1935, Michael had attended a party thrown by Christopher Sandford of The Golden Press, Kensington. There he met H. E. Bates, who had already become a well known author. Now here was someone whose work Michael had admired and was possibly ready for poaching. He confided to him that he was intending to set up as a publisher and tried convincing him that he might do better if he joined forces. However, Bates expressed himself to be quite happy with Capes.

"... then we'll forget the matter. But if ever you [Bates] should change your mind will you remember that, of all our young authors, it is you that I would like to publish most?"

There and then, genuinely and not with that mere politeness that parties so often generate, I said that if ever at any time I was forced to consider a change, I would go to him. M. J. in fact, had already outlined several ideas about publishing that much appealed to me. He thought, quite rightly, that in those days far too many books were being published, a great many of them indiscriminately, with the result that each book got far too little individual attention and in consequence authors were poorly served. This struck me as sound

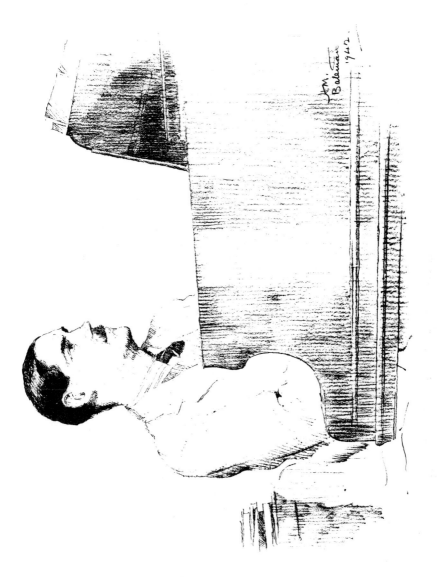

Playing his tune, Michael by H.M. Bateman

sense. What I also liked was that his new publishing house was largely to be based on fiction, of which M. J. had considerable knowledge, and this of course was my field.

Some nine years were to elapse, during which time Bates had served in the Public Relations section of the Air Ministry. This took him to many parts of the country and in due course to Oakington, where he met a Captain of a Wellington Bomber, who had been shot down over France and had successfully made his way back to England. The story he had to tell was to form the embryo for another book, one which was to mark the turning-point of Bates' career.

When he had finished what was to become known as *Fair Stood the Wind for France,* he showed it to his old service friend Fletcher Allen, who served with him in the Public Relations section, a good friend and mentor. He thought that Bates should have his business handled by an agent, and had introduced him to Laurence Pollinger during his Curtis Brown days.

Independently, another friend at the Air Ministry, James Hadley-Chase who had written *No Orchids for Miss Blandish,* mentioned to Charles Pick, when he was home on leave, that Bates seemed unhappy with Jonathan Cape. When Pollinger approached him, he agreed to the move.

Up to that time, Cape who had published nearly all of his books had apparently been rather presumptious about securing this manuscript and had omitted to attend to the materialistic gestures that normally are extended to authors. Laurence Pollinger believed that he deserved better and suggested other publishers to Bates. His reaction was spontaneous:

> Without hesitation my mind went back to my first meeting, nearly ten years before, with Michael Joseph. M. J., I declared, was to be my man.

Michael used to say that luck plays a very important part in a publisher's successes. Being in the right place at the right time, and saying the right things, especially when you believe in yourself, attracts the element of luck. *Fair Stood The Wind For France,* published in 1944, became a best-seller.

Michael and H. E. became close friends and shared a common interest in football. Before the war Michael used to support Clapton Orient, whose home ground was at Lea Bridge Road. Orient, now known as Leyton Orient, then competed in the Third Division South, but despite this they played very exciting football. During the First World War, Michael had played football himself but was never very adept. He enjoyed brief fame amongst his friends when the Army, mistaking him for a player with the same name, selected him for an official Army XI! Apart from football, they shared a love for fiction and he enjoyed H. E.'s friendship without any argument or rancour throughout their lives.

The success of Michael's publishing company cannot be judged by the fortuitous *luck* that he so often quoted. And it wasn't just the success of one author either. Just after the war, The National Book League asked readers to suggest lists of ten outstanding and significant books published during the war which, in their opinion 'would be of general interest to prisoners of war and service men and women returning home'. The list which Wilson Midgley, for The National Book League, adjudged to be the best, included not one, but three of Michael's books. These were *One Pair of Feet* by Monica Dickens, *The Way of a Countryman* by Sir William Beach Thomas and *Fair Stood the Wind for France*. Three out of ten for one publisher was quite an achievement but Michael was brave enough to publish an advertisement in *The Bookseller* proclaiming these titles *and* the six remaining by other publishers. Not a practice adopted today, but perhaps it was the high standard of literary merit that all these titles represented.

Christmas that year witnessed a party at Bloomsbury Street. One of the mementoes from that evening was a special issue of the company's *Book News*. The author of this is unknown but it names all the personalities of the period, Tom Couper, E. M. Bird, Frank Raper, Charles Pick and Peter Hebdon.

*   *   *

Regaining his health, Michael took a greater interest in the activities of the business and of course, from a distance he could take a view of how publishing was progressing generally. It was to the company's advantage that he was able to do so, not being involved in the mundane activities of administration. It was a case of actually being able to 'see the wood for the trees'. The market was clearly changing, for once the war restrictions on paper supplies were relaxed, companies would spend more on advertising and promotion again, and publishing would become much riskier – even for a company like Michael Joseph Ltd. After much deliberation, he decided to issue a memorandum to other directors which I reproduce below, for it aptly summarises how he felt at the time.

It also foreshadowed the impending row with Bob Lusty and the great division that had started to build up between them, though there was little evidence of this during the war. With peace now declared, life and businesses began to return to normality. However, some years were to elapse before all the restrictions of wartime disappeared. Michael wrote;

I think the time has come to take stock of our position.

The abnormal prosperity which all publishers have enjoyed is coming rapidly to an end if it has not already ended. We have had more than our share of this prosperity partly (I like to think) because of our own good judgement and the efficiency of our office team. But it would be foolish to pretend that we do not owe much of our success to sheer good luck.

We have indeed enjoyed one of those prolonged runs of luck which come the way of some publishers and our present position is perhaps comparable with that of Heinemann twenty years ago. I think it is especially true in publishing that nothing succeeds like success: and there is no doubt in my mind that such outstanding early authors as C. S. Forester, Richard Llewellyn and Monica Dickens laid the foundation for our success with such later authors as Vicki Baum and H. E. Bates. Bates is of course a conspicuous example of the good luck I have mentioned; we all know how many good books he had written before *Fair Stood the Wind for France,* and how poorly they sold.

For some time past I have increasingly felt that we are all inclined to be too complacent and too ready to believe that our run of luck will continue. We have received a great deal of praise from the trade and I recognize that our Sales Department has earned it by its tact and efficiency during difficult years. But it remains true that our good reputation in the trade is founded on *successful books;* and we shall lose popularity if our books become less profitable to handle. There is in my opinion a real danger that this may happen. Some our our leading authors show unmistakable signs of deterioration. There is furthermore a risk that with the advent of more competitive conditions and falling sales some of our valuable authors may be enticed away by other publishers. This danger has not yet been experienced to any extent by anyone in the office except myself, but it is a very real danger, especially as we have been openly envied for a long time by other publishers some of whom, I am sure, would not hesitate to snatch away our authors if they could. This is where we are especially vulnerable, for it is the nature of authors to blame not conditions and certainly not themselves for their declining fortunes, but their publishers.

For all these reasons I think we should stiffen our policy. In the trade we must be always on our guard against overselling the market. It is far better to be frank with buyers about our books and our expectations: in the long run this policy will pay good dividends. On the editorial side we must keep a careful eye on contract renewals and be more attentive to authors. No opportunity should be lost of keeping

26 BLOOMSBURY STREET,
27th June 1950.
LONDON, ...19........
W.C. 1.

C.30.   IN ACCOUNT WITH   **MICHAEL JOSEPH, LTD.**
ROYALTY STATEMENT FOR HALF-YEAR ENDED 25th March 1950. 19......

DATE OF PUBLICATION	TITLE OF BOOK	PRICE	NUMBER SOLD	RATE				
30/8/43.			12 11	20% on 5/. =	60 11 .			
	CHARLES. 5/-.		353.	Overseas. Proceeds £52. 5. 6 10% =	5. 4. 6			
					£65. 15. 6			

E. & O. E.

M I C H A E L 🧜 J O S E P H L™
26 Bloomsbury St. | London, W.C.1

DIRECTORS
Michael Joseph
Robert Lusty
Shirley Savage
Anthea Joseph
Joan Lusty

Telephone Museum 2545
Telegrams "Empybuks, Westcent,
London
Cables "Empybuks, London"

18th September 1953

Dear M.J.
Here is the requested cheque
for £14 -0 -0, which I am sending
EXPRESS post, to reach you early tomorrow
morning. I do hope the awful cold
is much much better, and that you
and Anthea are enjoying a lovely
week-end.
Affectionate wishes to
you both.
Dickie

The memorable calligraphic handwriting of Miss Dickie Bird.
Now Mrs B Walsh

them happy and, more important, of keeping in close and regular touch with them. Inside the office itself there must be much closer co-operation and co-ordination. In the past there has been a lamentable reluctance to pass on information which ought to be shared. This sort of water-tight handling of the firm's affairs can be disastrous and I therefore propose to tighten up office organization in this respect.

To sum up, war-time conditions – and I add the first three post-war years to this period – have inevitably had an unhealthy effect. We have had too much praise and not enough criticism. Publishing is a highly competitive business and competitive conditions are fast returning. We must not be smug about our past success and we must not assume it will continue.

This note clearly signalled his anxiety for the firm's future. He meant business. No doubt it had a salutary effect on one and all. Bob had written to Mr Wyatt of Wyatt & Watts (Pty) Ltd in Melbourne seeking to establish a publishing agency instead of just an importing agency. Michael had also been in correspondence with M Darling (Pty) in Cape Town and it seemed from their responses that only a visit from Michael would achieve any results. His plans for the immediate future included these overseas sales trips, but many months were to elapse before they came to fruition. In the meantime sales were becoming harder to maintain.

Michael's predictions were uncannily right – for the market became steadily inundated with more books than the public would buy. Now that the nation had other things to do, reading became a habit of the few. In the late forties and early fifties publishers again found commerce difficult, but his company's luck held, with new, and successful, authors joining the ranks. Amongst them were James Baldwin, Rumer Godden, John Masters, A. G. Street, Max Murray, The Duchess of Windsor, David Low, Joyce Cary, Dora Saint and Richard Gordon.

The publishing world is always, it is said, in a state of crisis. The late forties were no exception and Michael wrote a review of the publishing scene for *The New Statesman and Nation* entitled 'Publishing Slump?'. Reading it again today, it is easy to understand why the industry feels it is always in a crisis. Too many titles were being published again, printing and publishing costs were increasing but it was almost impossible to increase the price of books. The influx of American books, the advent of Penguin's cheap paperback books and remainders all contributed to the problem. Michael was for him a little outrageous in his summation of remedies.

In the difficult times ahead there are ways of salvation open to publishers, although none, I fear, will replace the necessity for a general price increase. The first is increased co-ordination between publishers, to reduce their working expenses by pooling their purely administrative departments . . . Secondly, the abolition of remainders, which have for many years been a curse in the book trade, just as the accumulation of second-hand cars bedevilled the motor-car industry before the war. If I had my way, all books would be compulsorily pulped two years after publication unless a stipulated number of copies had been sold by the publisher within the preceding twelve months . . . Thirdly, the Government should be given no peace until the publishers' problems, especially overseas, are dealt with more sympathetically and intelligently.

As he had stated in his memorandum to staff, he found that communications between directors and staff had become lax. He was often unaware of people's actions. Once, Bob had sent flowers to Mrs Joyce Cary, a gesture that Michael usually undertook and Michael only discovered that Bob had sent them in time to stop duplication. This caused Michael to write:

I don't want to be tiresome on the subject, but it really is important that you should let me know when you are sending such things as congratulatory telegrams and flowers. I might easily have duplicated the flowers to Mrs Joyce Cary. Although Joyce Cary's letter suggests otherwise I hope they were sent from the office or from us both?

There have been several similar instances recently which might so easily give the impression that the left hand knoweth not what the right hand doeth. It is moreover embarrassing to me if I am excluded, even inadvertently.

This was one small, and in itself, an insignificant problem of communications but it does illustrate how easy it is to cause others to feel affronted, even colleagues.

The relationship between Michael and Bob Lusty had become strained in the early fifties. Michael was in absolutely no doubt that Bob had done a sterling job whilst he had been away at war, keeping the mundane and production operations of the company working and ensuring that books were actually produced. Producing books must, at times, have seemed an impossible task, for as I have described earlier, this was sometimes done in extremely difficult circumstances; can you imagine the horrors of having your major printer, and bookbinder, being taken out of production almost simultaneously by bombs? But these superhuman achievements were now very much a past matter, and Michael's appreciation of the difficult markets had, perhaps, made him more sensitive to the trivial.

As I recorded earlier, Michael was one publisher who knew the worth of authors. By his standards a successful author would have an output of one title a year; this would at least enable the author to spread his costs over several years, and make the most of the income. Every author yearned for the best-seller, but when it came, the income tax arrangements were such that they lost most of their increased income in tax. Michael feared for authors' futures and went out of his way to go to their aid. Reading through his notes of the period, he took a very active role in arguing the case for a fairer taxation. He started to correspond with other publishers in the late forties, but everything was to come to a head in the early fifties.

Michael moved to London after Edna died and based himself at the little flat in Gower Mews. From then on he was able to dedicate himself full-time to running the firm. The publishing business was not always a tense affair. There were happier moments. For example, when the company was ten years old, a reception was held for some sixty people at Claridges to mark the occasion. The evening saw a plethora of famous authors and personalities whose books Michael had published. The party must have been successful for receptions were to be held again in later years to mark other occasions.

At this time he was living at the flat in Gower Mews Mansions with Anthea Hodson. Anthea was not only an extremely efficient secretary, but she had a very sound judgment for good authors. And after Michael's death, it was she who spotted James Herriot and encouraged Dick Francis to continue writing his extraordinarily successful novels. The combined publications contributing enormously to the company's financial and public standing in later years.

Chapter 8

You can't race cats 1923–58

'To win and hold a cat's affection a process of never-ending courtship is necessary. Cats, like women, will not be taken for granted. They must be admired, petted, coaxed into good humour, played with when they are playful, left to themselves when, as often happens, they prefer to be alone. Nothing is more destructive of friendship than attempts to force a cat into something contrary to his mood.'
Michael Joseph, Cats Company

Michael was well known for his love of cats and he was renowned internationally for his affections. But he was much more than a cat lover, for he believed there to be a big difference between a 'cat lover' and someone who is just devoted to them. The latter will only express their affection in limited doses and when they have had enough, go away to do other things. To them, for example, there are limits to where the animals are allowed to go or sit, and if they don't come back at night then, the doors are locked and they are left to fend for themselves.

Michael was different. He was the epitome of a cat lover or ailurophile. His long and close relationship had started when he was very young with Zulu, but it was not until he married Hermione Gingold that he became seriously involved. After a long day at the office or travelling, he would arrive home to be greeted not just by his wife and family, but by all his feline friends too. He enjoyed an intimate empathy with his feline friends which at times stretched Hermione's, and later, Edna's patience to the limit, for when Michael sat at the table for a meal, it was quite common for one of them to join him. Minna Minna Mowbray, Binks or Charles would sit on the table top and patiently await a tasty morsel that he would share with them. Binks turned his nose up at roast chicken and even sniffed at fish. His favourite was rabbit so the first thing that Michael had to do on return from London was to go out and shoot one. He was like that, cat mad. Neither Binks or Charles would steal from his plate – they would simply sit quietly purring and enjoy the frequent soft caresses of their master. Some might say that this was simply the result of good training, but in fact there was never any formal training as such. It was simply a normal thing for them to do when Michael was around.

Michael would go to extreme lengths to provide fun and enjoyment for them, frequently creating toys and games, for these would amuse them whilst he was away. He lived for their enjoyment. He not only wrote books about them, but also short stories, and made radio broadcasts of his experiences, too. One which is perhaps the best known of them all is the life story of *Charles O'Malley,* in a full length-book. Reading it now, it is easy to understand that Michael was in communion with Charles, a relationship which spanned twelve years and survived a world war; and one which endured travel by car, train and boat and several temporary homes and flats. These forced Charles to fend for himself in widely differing circumstances. He had to adapt first to life in central London, then the remote parts of the Berkshire countryside. Charles was not his first Siamese cat, and at the time, he was not particularily eager to have another, but perhaps Michael ought to recount the story, as he did in 1944, for a Children's Hour broadcast in August by the BBC.

I don't suppose anyone ever wanted a Siamese kitten for such an unworthy reason. I already had a cat, a pretty tortoise-shell tabby called Minna Minna Mowbray; and anyone knowing Minna Minna Mowbray might reasonably have supposed that she was enough for one household. Minna herself had no doubt on this point. She was the acknowledged mistress of the house, and kept us all in our place. For so small and innocent-looking a cat she had a majestic opinion of herself, treating all of us, except her own kittens, with the most regal condescension.

That was why I decided to get a Siamese cat. I said to myself, Minna must be taught a lesson. And, from all I had heard and read, if there was one sort of cat that would *not* be over awed by Minna, it was a Siamese.

And so, one summers's day many years ago, I chose a Siamese kitten. Or rather, the kitten chose me. There were six of them with their mother, most enchanting to look at, but so far as I could see, all exactly alike. As you may know, Siamese cats when very young are a sort of dusty cream colour, with smudges of brown on their faces and ears and paws and tails, and bright china-blue eyes. All kittens are pretty, but I think Siamese kittens are the prettiest of them all. Well, as I was wondering which to have, one of the kittens detached itself from the rest and trotted bravely towards me. That settled it. "This", I said, "is my little cat . . ."

. . . Even an 8-weeks-old Siamese has a very powerful voice; and people who hear it for the first time may well wonder whether it is a hungry seagull or a human baby with a pin sticking in him. You get used to it after a time, and even like it – at least true cat lovers do – but I admit it is rather an unusual noise.

That summer my family were at the seaside, in Cornwall, and for a few days the Siamese kitten shared a flat in London with me. I didn't decide on his name in a hurry. The naming of cats calls, I think for careful consideration. In the end I decided to give him not an Oriental name but something more dashing – for he was a most adventurous kitten. I called him Charles O'Malley, after the famous Irish dragoon.

Those early days were great fun. Charles settled down in no time, and when he wasn't asleep or eating he hurled himself around the flat; scrambling up the curtains, trying to jump impossible heights, knocking things over, hiding under the bed and pouncing on my bare feet – that was a game he played all through his life – and generally having a thoroughly good time . . .

. . . Soon the day came for our long journey to Cornwall. By this time Charles had accepted me as the master of his destiny; and I confess it was a refreshing change after Minna's capricious affection. So off we went, by taxi to Paddington and then on the long train journey. The ticket collector took Charles for a marmoset, but Charles was too sleepy to be indignant about that.

He was wide awake enough when he met Minna. The whole family assembled expecting fireworks: but when Charles made a playful rush at her, she only spat in a ladylike manner, turned her back on him and looked at me as much as to say, "We are *not* amused . . ."

. . . But Charles was different. From his earliest days he attached himself firmly to me, followed me about like a dog, insisted on regular games and conversations, and gave me that satisfying feeling of being the most important person in an animal's whole world. I had a grand time introducing him to such excitements and novelties as mirrors, piano and little fish out of the sea. He was most entertaining to watch; his discovery, for instance, that the other Siamese kitten in the looking glass wasn't real. I can see him now, cautiously approaching the mirror, watching the movements which matched his own; and I remember his comical surprise when he made a pounce on to the surface of the glass. He was determined to solve the mystery, and he did. He put his paw, very slowly, behind the mirror, and when he found nothing there he looked up at me as much as to say, "Well, that's a nice trick to have played on anyone". He was never deceived again by reflections in the mirror . . .

...His energy, however, was amazing. He would play for hours with toys I made for him, such as a feather tied on to a piece of string with a length of elastic; or with a ping-pong ball, in pursuit of which he hurled himself at all angles. In many ways he was more like a puppy than a cat. He would almost beg me to play with him, and in the evenings he used to wait for my return home, sitting on the landing and racing down stairs when he heard me opening the door ...

...And nothing pleased him better than to interrupt me when I was writing or using the typewriter. The scratchy sound of pen on paper had a great fascination for him; and when he tired of tapping my pen or the typewriter keys with an inquisitive paw, he would pretend to go to sleep on top of all my papers. The only way I could get on with my work was to make a paper ball and throw it across the room. Then he was off like a flash ...

Miss Dixon, from whom he purchased the little furry kitten all those years before, could have had no idea of the destiny that lay ahead. Today Charles's gravestone remains with the family, despite several house moves and it serves to ensure that he is always remembered.

I am not sure whether Michael acquired Charles to celebrate the publication of *Cats Company* or whether Charles was the inspiration for the book. But about this time Michael launched himself into setting up a sort of club to promote cats. His slogan for the club was 'Justice and better publicity for the Cat.' He reported to *The Star*, 'We shall start work under an influential committee and our aim will be to secure a better social and legal status for the cat. Hitherto this most individual of domestic animals has had to play second fiddle to the dog. For example, in the recent debate on the Road Traffic Bill it was disclosed that the cat was excluded from the protection afforded to dogs, pigs and poultry. We cat lovers feel that our friends should have the same Parliamentary representation that is given to the dog.'

The club, to be known as The Companionship of Cat Lovers, included well known people as founder members. Amongst them were Mr Compton Mackenzie who had eleven Siamese cats at the time, Miss Edith Sitwell and Mr Algernon Blackwood. But this was not the only effort Michael made to promote cats. He was also life President of The Siamese Cat Society of the British Empire.

Charles was registered with The Governing Council of the Cat Fancy in August 1930 and by the autumn Michael had become more and more a flag bearer for ailurophiles everywhere. Living at Regent's Park Terrace he threw numerous dinner parties. On one such occasion, in November, a society reporter from the *Daily Mail* was one of his guests and the *Looking at Life* column recorded:

At a dinner party given by Mr Joseph I met Lady Hambro (the former wife of Sir Eric Hambro), the only woman I know who regularly smokes man-sized cigars. She carries her own cigar-case, and when she smokes a cigar it looks so perfectly natural that it surprises one to realize how rare the habit is amongst women.

Mr Joseph during the dinner had a spirited argument with one of his guests [Selwyn Jepson] on the subject of the danger of cats to sleeping babies. Infants have frequently been suffocated by cats jumping up on the cots to nestle down on the warmth of the babies' faces. But it is not true that they deliberately suck in the babies' breath, as many people aver.

Michael kept a small clowder of cats at Regent's Park Terrace – and records note that every guest that evening was presented with a cat for the post dinner conversations. No doubt the felines were allowed a feast of tit-bits from the table.

Later in Charles's life, Michael took him to the Guild Hall where The Honourable Company of Cats was to be formed. This charity was formed in 1938 to raise money for three sick animal dispensaries in North London and attracted several notable personalities. The President was 'Tinker', a proud and arrogant cat belonging to Mlle Alicia Markova, the ballet dancer, whilst Charles filled the Vice-President's Chair, or should I say, basket. Other foundation cats included,'Richard Whittington', the then incumbent Mansion House cat; Beverley Nichols' three cats, Val Guielgud's 'Hugo' and together with 'Fudge' and 'Wire Room Willie' of the *Daily Sketch* they formed the nucleus of membership. The paper which supported the venture described their cats as being very tough and cynical, certainly not aristocratic, as Michael described the others. The point was made, and people joined the Company to help the dispensaries. One could join the charity with life membership then, by donating ten shillings.

I have tried to establish if this organisation still exists. Despite writing to cat associations, I have not had any confirmation. When I wrote to Grace McHattie, editor of one of the two major cat magazines, *Cat World,* she could not recall the Company, or when it ceased to exist. The only conclusion that can be drawn is that it was ephemeral.

Michael's love for cats was, and still is, well known. His articles and books led him to become an accepted authority on any subject relating to cats. In 1953, when the Royal Society of Painters put on an exhibition of 'Cats through the Ages', a show which traced the relationship between cats and humans for the past 4,000 years. Kenneth Kendall on a contempory BBC programme, *The Eye Witness,* reviewed this exhibition and Michael gave listeners a graphic description of what he saw:

It isn't an ordinary cat show, in fact there is only one real live cat to be seen, an Abyssinian cat called Chloe. If you've seen pictures of the cats of Ancient Egypt you'll have some idea of what this cat looks like, very proud and dignified, rather small, and exquisitely lovely. I hope you will forgive this description, I'm very susceptible where cats are concerned . . .

The best pictures, I think, are the work of people who obviously know cats very well; James Mason, for instance, he's a great cat lover and some of his excellent drawings are to be seen at this exhibition. I liked very much the needlework pictures which are on view, and in particular the large embroidered rug which has been worked and lent by Lady Aberconway . . .

Mason and Aberconway, may be unfamiliar names to you, but Michael always took the opportunity to mention his friends and authors when the occasion presented itself. After all, this was a golden opportunity for advertising! In complimenting them, he realised that it was a way of stroking their egos and, when and if they were to write another book, they would be certain to come to him to publish their works. Cynics will say that this was just good business sence prevailing, but Michael really did believe in what he said, especially when talking about cats.

I cannot leave the story of Charles without reprinting the short poem in his memory.

> I shall walk in the sun alone
> Whose golden light you loved:
> I shall sleep alone
> And, stirring, touch an empty place:
> I shall write uninterrupted
> (Would that your gentle paw
> Could stay my moving pen just once again!)
>
> I shall see beauty
> But none to match your living grace:
> I shall hear music
> But not so sweet as the droning song
> With which you loved me.
>
> I shall fill my days
> But I shall not, cannot forget:
> Sleep soft, dear friend,
> For while I live you shall not die.

Every time I read this, it remains as emotive to me as the first time and though Charles died in December 1942, the book about him was first published in 1943. Ailurophiles' emotions everywhere were stirred and

'My desk was part of his domain'

Michael with members of his cat family

the reprints followed. At least 50,000 copies from fifteen impressions were sold in the first six years. It was this short poem that caught the notice of Dr Ruth Gipps who included it in her cantata *The Cat*. Together with other works the cantata was performed at the Royal Festival Hall on 1 February 1957. The story of Charles is very much part of feline history.

There are many articles and stories written about cats amongst his memorabilia and I have selected one for comment. Collectively they describe more of his thoughts and views, and what can be created from an absorbing hobby. In one story, first published in *Mystery-Story*, one of the many magazines specialising in short stories in the early 20s, was entitled *The Yellow Cat*. This horror story centred on a drunken gambler whose luck had run out.

On the way home one night, so the story goes, the gambler was befriended by a strange and wild-looking cat with a yellowish coat which followed him home. His luck immediately changed once the cat had ensconced itself in his garret. His regular gambling now brought in more and more money – allowing him to move into a luxurious maisonette. On the night he brought a lady to stay, she became so terrified by this wild-looking animal that he was persuaded to take it to the nearby canal and throw it into the water, hoping that this would retain the lady's affections. His action reversed his luck and he lost everything in a few nights. He then realised that he needed the cat to bring back that luck and he went in search of it, forlornly hoping that it had survived and that he would find it near where he had left it. He did not. Days passed and without money he became weak with hunger but somehow he managed to survive. He noticed that his hands had withered, his nails had became narrow hornish strips and the backs of his hands were growing fine yellow hairs. He still sought the cat, realising that only its safe return would save him. One day he thought he saw it in the canal. He leant over the water, and there it was. He stretched out his hand, or what he could call his hand, and the cat stretched out his claws 'to enfold him in the broken mirror of the water.' He had become that cat.

I précis this story for there is by coincidence another story with the same title in *Puss in Books*. This one is entirely different and written by Elinor Mordaunt.

Michael and cats were synonymous. Even his authors had close affinities with cats. One, Eleanor Farjeon dedicated her book, *Golden Coney* to the 'Sweet Memory of Minna Minna Mowbray – by Bunny its begetter'. Her apology to Michael is also printed next to her dedication. It says more than I can about their relationship with cats.

My dear MJ.,

I had intended to dedicate this book to you. I supposed I had the author's right of choice in the matter, and could not see myself choosing any other Dedicatee. But it has been indicated to me, by the most powerful personality under my roof, that I am merely the scribe, not the author of this history. My home, as you know, carries on under a Matriarchy, and the Matriarch is Bunny. It is not enough for her that one lover of her race should set down her tale, and another publish it; she (she points out) is the author of its subject. Who then but she has the right to dedicate her child where she will? And she does not choose you.

This emotive dedication continues, but Eleanor clearly demonstrates her close affinity that she shared with cats. Michael had, however, strong views on the intelligence of cats. He was often drawn into discussions on the intelligence of cats versus dogs as domestic pets, and cats usually fared worse than dogs. Dog lovers would suggest that the dog has all the attributes to gratify his master's sense of ownership. As a domestic pet, the dog is loyal, good tempered, demonstrative and always in empathy with his owner; whereas cats are independent, finicky and disobedient, and, perhaps more significantly, they exude a sense of being in charge of their own destiny.

Michael would argue that only ailurophiles can understand the subtlety of the cat's character. One cannot judge the cat's intelligence fairly by carrying out tests in a laboratory, for it is almost impossible to teach a cat the rudimentary tricks that other animals learn. Cats are temperamentally very unsuited to training and because they are often unwilling to be trained to obey, does not mean that they are unintelligent. Your cat may follow you around and play games with you, but try to exact obedience and you will fail. Michael offered this definition of animal intelligence:

an animal's ability to reason and act for itself, in any situation which may arise in its experience, without human interference.

It was a definition born of experience and an intimate understanding of the traits of felines. Michael had during his lifetime over 100 cats – not all at the same time, he would hasten to add.

Apart from those mentioned elsewhere in the book, he recalls several in an article, which I'm not sure was ever published. One of Minna Minna Mowbray's litters produced a 'fluffy orange rascal' which he named Fowey, perhaps to remind him of the happy times he had at that Cornish sea-port. Then there was Ginnaboy, a sweet tempered cat who loved to sit on the window-sill in the hot sunlight, moving only to enjoy a good meal.

In the First World War he not only made friends with a cat called Scissors, about whom I have written in Military Matters (Chapter 4), but he adopted another when he was invalided home from France. It was against all the regulations to do so, but Lillywhite, a wistful looking tabby would miraculously disappear through the open window whenever the commanding officer came round on his tour of inspection. Michael thought that it was the sound of stray boots and spurs which prompted this action and it did not seem to matter whether Michael was there or not. His batman, Beaver, called the cat Lilly and commenting upon Lilly's agile evasion would say, 'Tha-at's a knowing ca-at' in his broad Lancashire accent. Jumping out of windows was not the only feat – Lilly was adept at extracting condensed milk out of a tin by rolling it over until the small hole was at its lowest point, sometimes with disastrous results to blankets or boots. Then Beaver would call her by names other than 'knowing ca-at'

After being 'demobbed', Michael returned to London and found a place to call home – a small, old and odd-shaped building. It was situated as he described, 'on an invisible line which separated a fashionable neighbourhood from a – well, unfashionable is a charitable description of the slum which lay to the east of the house'. It had a peculiarity, all the rooms led from one to the next in a straight line. The place was unconventional and uncomfortable but at least it was somewhere to live. Outside, the 'garden' consisted of a narrow strip of land bordered by a high brick wall precluding anything from growing. This garden strip became known as *The Strut* and though the place was uncomfortable for humans, it was ideal for cats. It was to this bailiwick that Dudley came.

He came with a pedigree as long as your arm, and as he was a gift from Michael's aunt more care than usual was lavished upon him. He was christened Dudley on account of his aristocratic manners but these misled Michael for, as events turned out, he was not a gentleman, and had to be renamed Lady Dudley much to Michael's embarrassment. As soon as she was old enough she would be seen leaping gracefully from the window-sill across the gap to the brick wall that formed the boundary of *The Strut*. She was a mute cat as was one of her kittens which Michael kept, Minna Minna Mowbray.

Of all the cats that Michael had, he grew closer to Charles O'Malley, the Siamese, than any other. Though it should be recorded that Binks came a close second. Binks, or Mr Binks to give him his full name, was an affectionate and aristocratic creature. A photograph of him appeared in the book *Charles O'Malley* but the one that appeals to me most is the one of Binks patiently sitting on the dining table, waiting with dignity but quietly purring, for his share of Michael's meal.

In later years, when he was living at Browns Farm, Michael owned another Siamese, a chocolate-pointed Siamese called Pepino. A short-haired cat, like so many others that he preferred, Pepino was typical of his breed and managed playfully to knock decorations off mantelpieces and window-sills. Much to Anthea's chagrin, he wrecked many a valuable piece of china, but being one of Michael's cats guaranteed his escape from retribution.

Michael never considered cats to be true domestic pets like dogs, which is quite surprising when one considers how much love and care he lavished upon them. He wrote, as I have said, numerous articles and stories about them and once ruefully commented:

> I must admit that the cat is only a pet when in the humour. Nothing is more shattering to human vanity than the perverse indifference of your favourite cat. One minute he will lie purring contentedly on your knee; the next, for no apparent reason, he will desert you for a less comfortable spot or an aimless perambulation. Coax him as you will, all you get is an indifferent glance and a careless switch of a shamelessly graceful tail. In the presence of your friends, the cat is at his worst. Your blandishments are completely ignored. If by any chance one of your guests happens to be a cat-hater, your cat will make straight for him and exhibit every sign of brazen affection. Is it just cussedness, I wonder, or an ironical sense of humour?

His opinion was that the cat would never make himself useful to his human patrons by fetching and carrying, or by pulling loads or running races in order to keep the bookmaking industry going. Racehorses, on the other hand, were a release for Michael's gambling habit. He could never bring himself to enter cat shows though he was a judge on many occasions. Horse racing was different.

*　　　　*　　　　*

Michael's romance with horse racing began in the early twenties, but once adept with his cine camera, he recorded one complete reel of the races at Goodwood in 1931, which understandably includes some unusual, and now even rare, sights. Apart from the numerous small wagers that he indulged in during his time with Curtis Brown, his relationship with the horses never developed any further except when on one occasion his brother-in-law, Ralph Russell, encouraged him to go out for a ride. Perhaps it was only done for the cine camera, nevertheless he looked quite a dapper sight. Eventually, being in the right place at the right time allowed circumstances and his friends to change his ideas.

One such friend was John Hislop, then General Manager of *The British Racehorse*. He was also an accomplished jockey in his own right but he was then and is today best known as an authority on bloodstock and as a breeder of some of the finest racehorses. He was destined to own Brigadier Gerard, one of he all-time greats, who beat Mill Reef on the only occasion they ever met in the 1971 Two Thousand Guineas.

Another was Ken Cundell, a trainer at Compton in Berkshire. Introduced through John, he became a very close friend indeed, as the history of Michael's affairs show. With these two mentors, Michael really burst into the horse racing world in 1951 and though he had never anticipated ever owning racehorses, now with a successful firm and a good income, the possibilty of becoming an owner became a reality. Ken Cundell may well have suggested that he started by taking a half share in one to minimise the risk, but Michael decided that he should own one outright. His horse would then *have* to be one with a good record. His decision to purchase one was made easier because Anthea, whom he had married the previous year, went out of her way to encourage him.

I remember my father telling me, when I was eleven years old, that one of his reasons for taking to owning racehorses was to advertise his authors or books by naming horses after them. Some of the costs could then be allowed by the tax authorities, to be set against the profits, making racehorse owning a much more attractive idea. The prospect of ownership filled Michael with excitement and in May 1951 he embarked on a search for the right horse. John Hislop suggested two, Kingdom and Roman Motto; either would have been a suitable start, but on further information Michael turned these down. Then John wrote again suggesting one called Irish Hop. With the same careful and thorough investigation Michael had carried out before becoming a publisher, he studied the horse's breeding and achievements, for there were many pitfalls and risks in owning a racehorse. This particular colt, owned by Tommy Carey, was in good form, for during the previous year he was placed in eight races, and won once at Salisbury. Irish Hop was a horse John Hislop knew well for he had ridden him to win at Salisbury. He gave Michael a detailed and personal recommendation, which finally decided the issue for Michael, and he bought the horse.

Once Irish Hop had gone to Compton, Michael sought to have the colt registered with the name of his own choice. Michael had wanted to promote one of C. S. Forester's books, and his first choice had been Captain Hornblower. He was denied this, as there was a horse registered by that name in France, and he settled for Midshipman Hornblower instead. He was an expensive horse – setting Michael back £1,000 – and he was immediately entered for a series of races. His first was at Kempton Park on 25 July 1951. It was a day to savour, full of excitement

Michael and Mr Binks at lunch

and new experiences. One extra privilege for owners is to watch the runners walk round and to have a few words with the jockey before the race in the parade ring. The omens were good, the horse was on form, and the jockey was the fifteen year old and extremely talented Lester Piggott. (Three years later he was to ride his first Derby winner.) All conspired to pump extra adrenalin into Michael's bloodstream, and for both him and Anthea it was a moment of great suspense. They watched Lester mount up and ride Midshipman Hornblower down to the start where the nine other runners were gathering. At the finish, he was beaten into fourth place, leaving Michael a little disappointed but undismayed. He went home still believing that of all racehorses to own, he had one which should at least retain its value and could, just possibly, win a race or two. The next race in August was at Newbury and again with Piggott riding he came in fourth, but his third race at Kempton was different, justifying all the hard work and training. He won.

This was a race that the family still talk about. The press cuttings Michael kept merely show that Midshipman Hornblower won him £386.12.0 in The Sirena Stakes, a handsome purse. This was a useful sum, especially when it cost at that time about £40.0.0 a month to keep a horse stabled and in training. Perhaps the most significant fact was that Piggott was not available to race that day so an opportunity materialised for one of Cundell's apprentices, Alan Harvey. He was not the sort of jockey who would 'squeeze' the horse during a race, (a term indicating that the jockey forces the pace) and Cundell had the feeling that Midshipman Hornblower might well be the kind of colt that did not need that sort of help from the saddle. He was right, but a change in the jockey resulted in longer odds being offered by the bookmakers, 20/1. That was a richly rewarding day, both financially and emotionally.

Michael's personal winnings were swelled by scooping the entire Tote Double. He had managed this amazing piece of luck by buying tickets on all the horses in the second race for the double with his own little-fancied Hornblower. I was there and recall the electric excitement of seeing the horse pass the winning post. And I also remember running up to meet my father and Anthea in the members' stand and stating proudly that 'I must have been his lucky manuscript' – meaning, mascot (this points to the atmosphere I was brought up in). My embarrassment thank goodness, was covered by everyone's laughter and the thought of my winnings also helped. This was the race that most of the family had a pound or two on, including Leslie up in Scotland.

By this time Michael believed that he was ahead of the game, and his money was indeed well invested, but with a short and successful season behind him he decided to sell, hoping for a small profit. Midshipman Hornblower was entered for the Teddington Selling Stakes at Hurst

Frank Chapman riding Lord Hornblower to second place
in the Newtown Maiden Stakes, Newbury 1952

Park that October. Again I was lucky enough to be there, for my father had written earlier to the headmaster of The Wells House, Alan Darvall, asking if I could be allowed home on the Friday afternoon so that he could collect me and be able to set off early enough to be there by the first race, in which the horse was running. Midshipman Hornblower finished second, nevertheless Michael's racing account was credited with £632.10.0. Financially, Midshipman was by far his most successful horse.

Michael had now been caught up in the sport in the grand manner. First he opened an account with William Hill and then the Tote. Curiously, the Tote only allowed him a credit limit of £50 but William Hill permitted £250.

Now established as an owner, Michael fancied another horse but was in no hurry to acquire one. Again John Hislop wrote, this time recommending Winterbourne as a possible purchase. He had both ridden him in training and raced him, and again he could claim to know the horse well. He had won on him at Salisbury and really was convinced that Winterbourne was a better horse than his form indicated. In Hislop's opinion, Winterbourne needed a strong jockey to succeed, rather than apprentices who had ridden him to date: they were too small and light to do him justice. John thought that on his pedigree Winterbourne should only just be coming to his best as a jumper, and would be very surprised if he did not perform considerably better next year. Michael took the matter further and called for the veterinary surgeon's report. This finally convinced him. The four-year-old bay colt, Winterbourne, set Michael back a thousand guineas (£1,050) and, like his predecessor, was taken as quickly as possible to Cundell's stables for further training. George Todd, the previous trainer, implored to be allowed to continue with him as he also believed that Winterbourne was just coming to his peak but Michael was unmoved and adamant that Cundell should take over the training. Once Winterbourne was Michael's he had the horse's name changed and re-registered as Lord Hornblower to promote another of C. S. Forester's titles.

Michael, of course, had his own colours for jockeys to wear but a new set was needed for racing Lord Hornblower as he was a hurdler. Michael ordered these, Ken advising woollen ones, from T. Frost of Bawtry. The race programmes described them as 'Navy blue, silver cross-belts and sleeves, striped cap'. They duly arrived in time for Frank Chapman to wear on his first outing at Newbury. The two-mile event, the Newtown Maiden Stakes, attracted a field of nineteen runners but Lord Hornblower managed only second place, delighting Michael nevertheless. Prize money amounted to £60 but with odds of 100 to 8 it was a great start, for on this occasion he had backed him each way. A flurry of races followed but only at the Thursby Amateur Riders Cup did he finish in the frame again. He was third, beaten by Pronounced, whose jockey ironically was John Hislop, who had ridden Hornblower to win at the very same event the previous year. That's racing, but Michael was trying to win on the flat, with good competition, which was not in Hislop's mind when he recommended the horse. And clearly local knowledge is important.

Hornblower was in the frame again in July, this time at Salisbury, where he finished third in the Carnarvon Challenge. John Hislop rode Fair Oration who had an easy win and it is co-incidental but nevertheless curious that he suggested to Michael that it might be a good idea to sell his horse whilst in form and in training. Michael decided to continue racing Hornblower, and in August he ran him again, this time at Newton Abbot. A race which marked the turn of Michael's luck.

*   *   *

There was nothing very ominous about this particular meeting, except perhaps that on this occasion Ken Cundell could not attend. He had delegated the responsibility for declaring the horse as a runner, saddling him up and planning the race to one of his jockeys, Dick Francis. It was quite natural that Ken should ask him to ride Hornblower because during the week one of Dick's less exciting chores had been the schooling of Ken's horses over jumps. Anthea had just given birth to her daughter Charlotte and could not face the long journey to the West Country. Michael stayed at a hotel in Teignmouth, where he invited Dick and his wife Mary, to join him for dinner where they could finalize plans. On present form, he should have a good race, with the tipsters quoting him a likely winner.

On the day of the race, Michael arrived at the course in good time and busied himself trying to select the winners of the earlier races. As the events unfolded and his modest winning accrued, he became mildly confident before the fifth race, though he had once again tried for the Tote Double but without success. The start of the two-mile event did not take place until late in the afternoon and as the race time approached he went to the paddock to see Dick and provide whatever help might be needed.

It was a disastrous race, for Hornblower severely ripped a tendon in his rear fetlock in the closing stages and despite finishing fifth, his racing days were over. Michael returned home terribly upset and determined to see what could be achieved with rest and veterinary treatment. It was not the sort of finish that Dick would have wanted either but both realised that this sort of thing did happen and it was just one of those risks that owners' took.

The next day Michael organised his old friend, Bryan Cartland to go down to Compton to see what he thought, as an experienced veterinary surgeon. Then he spoke to his mentor John Hislop who conferred with Cundell and agreed that the best course was to rest the horse though, other friends recommended that he should be put down as the chances of a full recovery were remote.

With this slim hope, he had Hornblower moved to his daughter's farm in Framlingham, Suffolk. The discovery of her father's horse certainly came as a surprise as she and her husband Michael, had been on holiday in Spain when the accident occurred and knew nothing about the move. There he remained, and meanwhile Michael tried to claim on an insurance policy covering what he thought was this type of risk, but he had not fully understood the implication of the clauses in the small print. In normal circumstances horses who suffered this type of injury would be put down as a matter of course, so he believed that he had some basis for a claim. But that was not to be and sad to relate, Hornblower ended his days as a hack.

This sort of experience has been known to put most people off the sport, but in the following year he bought another horse. This time he named the filly after one of his appreciative and successful authors, Monica Dickens. She was greatly flattered by this gesture, though the horse was never as successful as his earlier ones. She was only narrowly beaten into fourth place on her first outing at Warwick by what is termed 'a short head'. Sold in 1954 after only a few months, the horse provided her namesake with many happy memories and Ken had dearly wanted her to win, for he knew just how much Michael admired the author. Michael's next horse was one whose name he did not change, Make Smoke. He won the Henwick Handicap at Worcester that year, making a useful £280; though Michael was not in the sport for financial gain, this certainly helped deaden the pain of the losses incurred earlier.

There were brighter moments though. Like most men who backed horses Michael relied occasionally on intuition. Derby Day 1954 had started badly for him with one of his favourite cats being knocked down by a passing car, an often fatal event that had occurred to other cats at Browns Farm. The 'vet' arrived to deliver the bad news that there was no alternative but to put this cat out of his misery too. Hardly had he finished speaking when the cat stirred, and quickly regained composure. So impressive was his miraculous recovery that his death sentence was annulled.

That afternoon Lester Piggott, who three years earlier had not worked his magic with Midshipman Hornblower, was to ride an outsider, Never Say Die, in the Derby. To Michael, this horse seemed to be the only one to back. Never Say Die was Piggott's first Derby win, and at odds of 25 to 1 rewarded Michael with a handsome sum; only he knew why he had backed a winner.

By now Michael had allowed his interest in wagers to get the better of him and he was placing bets of £10 to £25 a race. When he could not get to the course, he would ask Ken to suggest and place his bets. With such help, and from someone who knew racing intimately, he could hardly go wrong all the time. Over the years his winnings just about balanced his losses, but nevertheless, it was immense fun all the same.

He then went halves with Ken in two horses, Neophyte and Deerfoot, but success eluded them both. In another effort to secure a winner, in January 1957 he bought a half share in Queen's Combat from Major George Troy for £500. I mention the purchase price only because he sold him six months later for £600 and, despite Michael only owning half, the profit went a long way towards the horse's keep.

Combat was Michael's last horse.

Chapter 9

Publishing
The Latter Years
1949–58

'From the beginning I have aimed at a 'quality' list and
a limited output.'
Michael Joseph, 1954

Cats featured largely in Michael's life and when he had the opportunity, and the right author came along, he naturally published about them. As he moved in 'cat' circles, he met many other ailurophiles who had thought at one time or another of recording the story of their own favourite feline. One such was Lady Aberconway. Her book was in a class of its own, containing numerous adulatory cat stories. For the question that was posed to her was 'Why do some people love cats and others hate them?' The result was an in-depth study of the writings of famous cat-lovers, to see if there were conclusions to be drawn from them. What is probably not known, is that she wrote to Winston Churchill (later Sir Winston Churchill) to ask if he had drawn any illustrations of cats that could be included. Alas, he had none, but he volunteered to let one of Sir William Nicholson's studies of his yellow cat in black and white be used to illustrate her book, *A Dictionary of Cat Lovers,* which Michael published in 1949. Churchill declined in his own charming way to help any further. Nevertheless, the book sold very well.

Another of Michael's authors on cats, was the well known film-star, James Mason, though his book *The Cats in our Lives* was jointly written with his wife, Pamela. My memory prompts me to record that for years Michael had a coloured family tree of the Mason's cats framed, and hung in the flat in Gower Mews Mansions. The book, illustrated by James, includes accounts of experiences with the numerous and much loved cats that accompanied them on their travels both here and in the States.

To digress for a moment but still on the subject of books about cats, I'm moved to comment that after Michael had died, his collection of these and other books, were disposed of, or dispersed, some returning to the company's archives whilst the rest were given away. This has driven me to try and re-establish the library, though this is by now an almost impossible task. In the process, though, I have found that antiquarian and second-hand booksellers are now asking an ever-increasing price for some of Michael's books. A pointer perhaps for the future?

Maybe one of the reasons for this, is that Michael's reputation for publishing books of quality was fully justified and collectors recognise the values. One of those which still has a certain cachet about it, is the late Duchess of Windsor's autobiography *The Heart has its Reasons.* When Edward VIII announced in 1936 that he intended to marry an American divorcée, Mrs Wallis Simpson, the entire country was shocked. The emotional scenes following his broadcast and later his departure to France, where they were to spend the rest of their lives in seclusion, were indelibly engraved on Michael's mind. He remembered the time he spent writing the script for the film about the Duke's working life and, having been a little closer than most, shared his deep disappointment. He had all but forgotten about his meetings until 1955, when he heard a rumour that set his nerves tingling. It mooted that the Duchess of Windsor, as she was now called, was writing an autobiography and was looking for a publisher. Reading various reference sources today, I think that he must have heard about this from an old acquaintance Derek Verschoyle, who had at one time been in the The Foreign Office. He knew a large number of people in the publishing world and had worked for the *Spectator*. Michael had fortuitously brought him into the firm on the editorial side.

Verschoyle brought the prospect of publishing her book to Michael, which they believed, was sure to be another best seller. When the book was well into production, Charles Pick requested a meeting with her, but all the arrangements had first to be cleared with Buckingham Palace. This granted, he travelled to Paris with the hope that he could persuade her to agree to sign books at two Paris bookshops. He arrived at his modest Paris hotel, to find a telegram from her saying that she 'would be delighted to see him. Come to lunch . . .'

When he arrived at their home in the Bois de Boulogne, she was sitting on a chaise-longue reading the day's newspapers. Pictures of Sophia Loren were on several front pages, and she asked Pick 'who is her agent? It doesn't seem fair – I used to be all over the pages – now it is a film actress.' Then they discussed the possibility of her signing books. 'You'll have to talk to the Duke over lunch about this; we'll need police protection, you know, and the Palace may not like it. We'll have to check.'

After lunch, they chatted about this and that, and Charles announced that he would have to return shortly to his hotel. The Duke implored him to stay a while longer and split a bottle of brandy. This they did,

4, ROUTE DU CHAMP D'ENTRAINEMENT

BOIS DE BOULOGNE · PARIS, 16e

☏ SABLONS 86-51 · ☏ WINFIELD

July 20th 1956.

Dear Mr. Joseph,

Mr. Pick called upon us here the other afternoon to
lay before The Duchess your suggestion that she autographs
copies of her memoirs at W.H. Smith's and Brentano's book
stores in Paris, on the day of publication of "A Heart has
its Reasons" in London.

The Duchess and I told Mr. Pick that we would like a
little more time to consider your suggestion. We know that
it is not a new form of sales promotion for authors to sign
copies of their works in book stores, It is in fact, one of
the most effective ways of bringing new books to the notice
of the reading public.

However, now after further reflection and consultation
with one of two old and trusted friends, whose advice we
value highly, The Duchess and I have reluctantly come to
the conclusion that having due regard to her position, it
would not be dignified for her to indulge in this form of
promotion in the case of her memoirs.

I asked Mr. Pick to tell you how much I have enjoyed
reading "Bugles and a Tiger", John Master's latest book you
were kind enough to send me. This former officer of the
Gurkhas certainly has a gift for vivid discription combined
with an easy and readable style.

Having known India in what many of my generation refer
to as "the good old days", John Master has revived nostalgic
memories - good and bad - of the two hundred centuries of
the British Raj in Hindostan. Mr. Pick said he thought I
would be interested in reading Master's previous writings, I
would indeed appreciate having them.

The Duchess and I greatly enjoyed your's and Mrs. Joseph's
visit to us here and were glad to have an opportunity of dis-
cussing certain outstanding points in connection with her
memoirs with you and Ken Rawson.

With our kind regards to you both,

Sincerely your's,

Edward

Michael Joseph Esq.
26, Bloombury Street
London,   W.C.1

Letter from Edward, Duke of Windsor

and the Duke recounted the whole story of his abdication. It was, as Charles recalls, an extremely moving account – of his sadness, loneliness, insecurity and frustration. Above all, throughout the war years, he had had to rely on his friends telling him what was happening. He had been taken off the lists of circulated documents and papers and rarely received any visitors. To brighten the conversation, Charles talked about his time in India during the war, and of John Masters' *Bugles and a Tiger,* of which Michael had previously sent him a copy. The Duke was so enthusiastic that Charles naturally promised to send him other titles when they were published.

The Duke told Charles of one of his proudest moments, when he was out in India. The Regiment had been on manoeuvres for three days and at the end, he was asked by the Colonel-in-Chief to join them at their celebratory Mess Dinner. When he arrived for the occasion, he was surprised not to find the Indian officers there too. He was told that they were not asked to these Mess nights. 'Well', said the Duke, 'if you don't ask them, you don't get me' – and turned around and walked away to dine elsewhere. His inherent empathy with the people had made him feel that it was all wrong, and this, decades before Race Relations became a formal subject of controversy.

The Duchess's book, *The Heart has its Reasons* was avidly read on publication. Michael worked endlessly on this one, for he realised that it would rank for essential reading material for historians. Not only had the facts to be right, but he wanted the book to convey her true feelings. He expected the book to sell well, but nevertheless, it would need to be heavily advertised and to this end the company spent £15,000 on promotion.

Michael was very particular about the books he took on, even when they came through friends. One, written by James Hadley-Chase, surprised Charles when he read through the manuscript for it was very risqué. He did not think it suitable for publication but passed it on to Michael for his opinion. No, not for us, he agreed. So Pick took it back to James who then explained that he had written it to raise money to pay for his son's operation for appendicitis. When Michael heard about this, he agreed to write to a publisher who might just take it on; half an hour later, the letter was on its way to Cherry Kearton at Hutchinsons. The book *No Orchids for Miss Blandish* was a huge success, appealing no doubt to all those serving in the armed forces.

In 1951 he took Anthea off to South Africa, combining business with pleasure, for this was also to be a belated honeymoon. The six-week tour started in Cape Town, where they stayed for ten days, moving on to Durban by bus. From there to Johannesburg, then to the Kruger National Park, finally stopping off in Rhodesia on the homeward trip to see the

Victoria Falls. The press gave them a fair coverage at each stop, but one reporter, noting his comments on current publishing problems, printed Michael's aside, 'that there were no new authors of exceptionl promise in Britain'. He cited only one new and notably good Rhodesian author, Doris Lessing, whose novel, *The Grass is Singing*, not only received very good reviews in South Africa but had sold well for a first work. The press also included another aside, 'that whilst on tour, he was looking for new authors'; a comment that he later rued, for there was an immediate reaction and manuscripts came pouring in by the score, so that by the end of their tour they had more than they could carry!

Book production and publisher's costs were less in Britain, which meant that exports to South Africa were good, and in another interview, Michael named his more successful titles. Amongst many of the company's books selling well, were C. S. Forester's *Hornblower* series and he proudly announced that Gregory Peck would be portraying Hornblower in the film *Captain Hornblower*. He also disclosed that, contrary to popular belief, Forester actually knew very little about ships. During the war, almost every officer and rating had read *The Ship* and the Admiralty had been so impressed that they sent a cable to Forester, who was in the States at the time, offering him a post as Public Relations Officer. He cabled back, 'Sorry, know nothing about ships'. He wasn't trying to be clever, he had learned everything from the Officers and men of HMS *Penelope*, when she was in dry dock!

By the 1950s Michael had reached a point when he felt that he could criticise authors as well as applaud them. He wrote caustically about the relationship between publisher and author in *The Times Book Club Review*. 'Authors love (he said) to form little groups of their own at parties (the parties usually being provided by publishers) and discuss their own and other publishers ... They talk loftily about the inner compulsion, the creative urge, and if they have had a classical education, about *ars longa, vita brevis*. As they gulp down the publisher's cocktails and stuff themselves with olives and biscuited savouries they commiserate with each other about the avarice, stupidity and insensitiveness of publishers, particularly their own'.

This was a direct attack, one which authors would not take lying down. No less a person than Paul Gallico was to be moved to reply. It is worth citing his text and leaving it to the reader to ajudge whether it is all true today.

That Joseph happens to be *my publisher* and that he has obviously performed miracles with mediocre literary material, however, is not going to keep me from pointing out that he is leading with his chin when twice in his article he makes a point of the 'parties' thrown by publishers for their authors. If there is anything that could make a writer contemplate giving up his profession and turn to something less complex and exacting like the manufacture of hasps and staples, the repair and servicing of motor vehicles, coal mining, dry-cleaning or tending bar, it is the knowledge that each day that brings him closer to writing his finis to the work on his latest book also carries him that much nearer to the deadly jeopardy of the publisher's cocktail party.

But corner me for forty minutes at the publishers's cocktail brawl designed to celebrate the launching of my latest opus and I can look forward to at least a sixty day bout of dyspepsia, colic, colitis and the staggering pip, not to mention the prolonged mental depression that results from being exposed to close association with book reviewers, advertising men and other authors occupying the same stable.

And as far as *gulping* of the publisher's cocktail, this is a manoeuvre born of necessity. To savour these brews by letting them near the taste buds is to risk ruining their susceptibility forever, not to mention the added danger of burning all the skin off the inside of one's mouth. The only thing to do when your publisher, his eyes gleaming with sheer anticipatory malevolence, pours his evilly coloured witch's con-coction into your glass, is to fling it at the back of your throat and down it with the least possible contact between you and it. The tough lining of the stomach is much more able to cope with this kind of thing than the delicate membranes of the oral cavity.

And the article continued in this vein. Paul Gallico was certainly fired up and ready to do battle but I guess publishers forgave him and he was invited again. Michael continued to publish his books – from which one may deduce that he became immune to those cocktails or perhaps that Michael had improved the standards.

Michael had a good ear for music. His interest had, many years before, brought him into contact with the renowned Noël Coward. In his time, Michael had written accounts of Coward's earnings and had obviously come to know him very well indeed.

In his diaries, Noël Coward mentions a memorable luncheon meeting with Michael on the 11 November 1951 at the *Caprice*. The date is important as it was during lunch that Michael persuaded him to publish a collection of his songs, to be known as the *Noël Coward Song Book*. It took two years to complete but the end result was a unique collection of his songs, covering a period of forty years. Well known songs such as 'Chase me Charlie', 'Mad Dogs and Englishmen' and 'London Pride' are included.

When Michael set about putting this book together, he turned as usual to his friends to contribute. So it was no surprise to me when I found

Michael and Anthea

Anthea at Victoria Falls

Bob and Joan Lusty, Miss Dickie Bird and Anthea at Yattendon

that Clemence Dane drew the frontispiece and Gladys Calthorp the line drawings in the text. A typical Joseph production!

The subject of music was to be mentioned in one of Michael's lectures at the Royal Society of Arts. The theme was Television and Publishing – many publishers were bemoaning the effect of 'TV' and feared that the medium would be very detrimental to their sales. Michael disagreed, for he was a man with considerable foresight:

> I am not seriously alarmed as are some of my colleagues. True, you cannot watch a television screen and read a book at the same time, but the day before yesterday broadcasting was proclaimed the danger to books.
>
> It was argued that wireless would kill the sale of sheet music and gramophone records, but, in fact, it has stimulated and increased their sales. Television is still very much a novelty, and as a form of entertainment it is in its infancy.
>
> Publishers should not fight against television, but regard it as their ally. As with sound radio, there can be reviews of books, dramatized excerpts, and serial versions of novels. This is the development which every intelligent publisher will do all he can to promote.

But many said that television would finally kill the book as a mass product. This has not proved to be so.

In 1952 in an effort to maintain sales Michael introduced the Mermaid Books series. The previous year had been marked by the *Festival of Britain* which did much to restore the gaiety and colour to the nation's life after the war years. These attractive books included an introduction linking the series to this Festival and were reprints of previously successful titles. Novels by Monica Dickens, C. S. Forester, Paul Gallico, Joyce Cary and H. E. Bates were amongst the first clutch to be published. The series had an unusual style of binding, which was the inspiration of Bob Lusty. They were designed to compete in the paperback market, but they were a halfway stage between true case-bound books and paperbacks. They had a limp and flexible case instead of the conventional rigid type, with a printed paper covering in a distinctive style. The high gloss finish was achieved by a sheet of film laminated to the surface. They were, as Charles Pick used to say, 'easy to wash', but for the technically minded, these were unsewn, rounded and backed, with a laminated paper case. Selling at 5 shillings, they cost a little more than a paperback, but were far superior. And for a time, sales were good, achieving figures of 7,000 to 8,000 a week.

Michael Joseph were not the first in the field to issue cheaper versions of books, there had, of course, always been 'cheap editions', but these were an attempt to compete in the paperback market but with a superior binding. Shortly after this series had become popular, Collins launched the Fontana range of paperbacks priced at 2 shillings, 3 shillings, and 4 shillings according to length. The established paperback publishers, Pan and Penguin, continued apace but did not try to compete with the better bindings. Rather sadly, the Mermaid series failed to survive, for today they still look superior to paperbacks produced in that era. But I am biased.

It is a curious fact, though, that Michael never allowed any of the titles published by the Company to be remaindered, even up to the early fifties. At one time he and Bob Lusty had thoughts of selling the old written-down stocks through other channels, but the prospects of taxation put an effective block on the idea. Michael believed that all cheap editions, remainders and lending library facilities undermined the sale of new books. Publishers were accustomed to financing new books out of past profits, and his firm, like others, now faced harsh economic facts. If the public wanted new books to buy, then they must pay more or increase library subscriptions. He need not have worried.

Sales continued to exceed expectations and, with profits improving by leaps and bounds, he set about planning the future. He took advice from his old friends Graham Smith and Martin Dubois, who advised him of possible Estate Duty liabilities. He needed to rearrange his assets, even though there wasn't an obvious heir for the firm. There very nearly was though. It was his brother Lionel's son, Michael who had expressed aspirations in this direction. So arrangements were made for him as the first part of his induction, to spend time at Tonbridge Printers who were then the major company printer. Michael thought that his nephew should at least know how the books were produced before becoming involved in publishing. But on the very day he was due to go there, he changed his mind and aborted the venture. (He later became an accomplished author.) After this episode, and with tax liabilities in mind, Michael decided that there was nothing else to do, but sell. So early in 1954, he began the courtship with Illustrated Newspapers Ltd.

In the negotiations that led to the acquisition Michael was asked to set out his policy – this was something that he had not had to do before, but after various drafts he invited Graham Smith, the company's solicitor, to meet him for a working lunch at one of his favourite restaurants *Le Jardin des Gourmets* in Soho. That meeting still embarrasses Graham Smith for, as he recalls, fifteen minutes before he was due there, he looked at his watch only to realize that it had stopped. He rushed out to the street and leaping into a cab, mistakenly demanded to be taken, with all speed, to *Les Gourmets,* a restaurant with a very similar name. Once there he went to every table but could not find his host and what was worse, there was no booking for a Michael Joseph either. He then phoned Michael's office to be told of his error, and finally arrived at the right place forty-five minutes late. Graham was astounded to find a relaxed and smiling Michael who had not even ordered, and brushing aside Graham's excuses and embarrassment, began an in-depth discussion on the negotiations.

The following morning, a small package arrived on Graham's desk. It was from Michael and contained a handsome and expensive gold wrist watch with a note that said 'the Company could not leave their solicitor at the mercy of an unreliable watch' and he 'hoped that this one would behave better'.

After revising his thoughts he sent the following draft letter to Graham. This is worth repeating, even though it may not have been the final version.

Dear Graham Smith,

From the beginning I have aimed at a 'quality' list and a limited output. The major problem which a general publishing firm has to solve is to reconcile the need for a big enough turnover with an exclusive and literary list which will attract the best type of author. I have gone into this at some length in a book called *The Adventure of Publishing* (1949) which I wrote at the invitation of Allan Wingate Ltd.

In our early years it was necessary to publish for a number of authors more popular than literary, such as Angela du Maurier and Dorothy Black ... At the end of every year, we go carefully through the list and cut out the dead wood. Inevitably some authors do not realize their early promise or after a time show no profit and their contracts are not renewed.

We have of course been decidedly lucky in our discoveries. Among them are Monica Dickens, Richard Llewellyn, and Paul Gallico, all of whose books we have published since before the war. More recent discoveries are Ruth Park, John Masters and Richard Gordon. But while we have always gone out for new authors we have steadily added to our list writers whose work has been published elsewhere with results that did not do them justice. In this way we added to our list C. S. Forester (as long ago as 1937), H. E. Bates and Joyce Cary. Bates and Cary undoubtedly came to us because our list attracted them. Thanks to successful publication of these and other novelists, we have been offered and now publish for such authors as V. Sackville-West, Clemence Dane, Vicki Baum and A. G. Street.

I attach the greatest importance to the quality of our list. We do not seek authors merely because they are profitable. I had the first offer of *No Orchids for Miss Blandish,* and told the author it would sell a million copies and unhesitatingly turned it down. Similarly we turned down *Forever Amber* and *The Naked and the Dead.* I would never have published for Peter Cheyney and somebody else can have the current American Bestseller, *Mickey Spillane.*

You will note that nearly all the authors I have so far referred to are novelists. Fiction is generally regarded as the most precarious form of publishing but I have always believed that good novelists are the backbone of a general publishing list. Their output is regular and when they become bestsellers their sales usually remain constantly high, notwithstanding the fluctuations of book trade conditions.

We have not however neglected to build up our non-fiction which is probably stronger now than it has ever been. Since publication of *One Pair of Hands* and *One Pair of Feet* we have specialised in humorous and unusual autobiography and although we always cater for the general reader we have established a few profitable sidelines in such directions as books on cats, wine and military history; for instance *The Red Beret* and *The Green Beret.*

The size of the list is an important consideration. We try to make our profit out of a relatively small number of titles. Fifty new books a year is about as many as we care to publish. One advantage of publishing for comparatively few authors is that we can, and I think we do, successfully establish the friendliest personal relations with our authors. A small list also means easier advertising under existing conditions of limited space in the few influential papers; and a higher proportion of reviews. It is a truism of the trade that too many books are published and by concentrating on a few we are able to get the attention and possibly the goodwill of literary editors, reviewers and booksellers. On the other hand, if we were to double the size of our list I am sure we should forfeit the esteem of authors and literary agents and thus lose ground.

We do *not* go in for big speculative books such as political memoirs, which require large advances. To my mind such books are a gamble and do not generally add to a firm's literary reputation.

We do not believe in publishing by committee. Decisions are often made within a couple of days and all the leading literary agents know that they can count on an immediate reading of anything important. Although I am always willing to, and often do read MSS at short notice, we have a pretty good panel of experienced readers which includes Walter Allen, Viola Garvin, and a number of specialists. At least two others in the firm I regard as first rate readers of excellent judgement.

To sum up, our policy is to publish books of general interest and of literary quality; To keep the size of our list within manageable limits: and to publish as economically as possible. We keep down for instance, the cost of our press advertising: I have had something to say about advertising in *The Adventure of Publishing*.

I have said nothing about the administrative side but I attach the greatest importance to our sales organization, which we are constantly trying to improve. As a result of my journeys overseas we have, I think, greatly strengthened our overseas representation.

I do not claim that there is no room for improvement. The editorial side of the business will undoubtably need reinforcement to provide for the years ahead. I have some tentative plans in mind and shall be glad to outline them, at a convenient time . . .

Yours sincerely,   M J   17.1.1954

It is history now, but by July when the deal had gone through, Michael's lifestyle began to change completely. He was able to devote much more time to his horses than hitherto, and thanks to expert help from Cundell and Hislop, enjoyed being steeped in the racing world.

During these negotiations he spent hours ruminating at his flat in Gower Mews, but there were distractions. Conveniently located near the West End of London, he found it easier to attend some of the many functions to which he was invited. One such evening was Foyle's Bookshops' Fiftieth Anniversary which took place in February 1954 at the Dorchester Hotel. He was amongst very exalted company that night, company which included Lord Justice Birkett, Sir Compton MacKenzie and J. B. Priestley. Michael had also been asked to say a few words – making a welcome diversion from planning his own company's future.

Later that year, Foyle's organised the luncheon to celebrate the hundredth Oxford and Cambridge Boat Race. This was a much larger affair but nevertheless, held at the same hotel. Several hundred people thronged the hall for the event, which was chaired by The Rt Honourable Lord Brabazon of Tara. Michael was again on the top table, though he didn't have to speak this time. Next to him was Mr John Attenborough and opposite him, was Bob Lusty, though he was too far away to be able to converse!

He would often attend functions when I was on holiday from school and staying with him at the flat. During the day, we would both go to the office, for I had become the 'gardener' at 26, albeit only on a

Michael and Anthea at Foyle's 50th Anniversary 1954

temporary basis. But first, I would have to wait patiently until he had finished with the bathroom. It was for Michael a morning ritual. He would awake – make tea – and then disappear into the bathroom, first ensuring of course that Binks had some fresh milk and was entirely happy. His cats always took precedence. He would be there for what seemed hours, and when I once went in to retrieve a book, I found him to be facing the mirror, meticulously grooming his hair. Staying awhile I watched him remove the odd grey hair from his eyebrow and then delicately trim his hair to perfection. Throughout his life, he considered that appearance was of paramount importance, though from the photographs of him taken at various times throughout his life, he could never be described as a dandy. Although he wore fashionable clothes, they were rather sombre and staid; I remember that he always wore braces and that his trousers were very high waisted. He dressed to blend with others and wore what would be acceptable to society. Typically, he would go to the office in a sombre suit, with immaculately polished shoes, and topped with a trilby.

We would then set off together, to walk the four hundred yards or so, at a slow and measured pace. He never gave anyone the impression that he worked under pressure and needed to rush from one meeting to another. Walking with a slight stoop, which eased his frequent 'tummy' aches, we'd arrive at 26 after everyone else. By this time the post would usually have been put on Michael's desk and he'd begin the day by reading these letters, many of them from his overseas friends. Every now and again, he would be diverted by an interesting stamp, or a humorous item in the paper, and out would come the much-used folding scissors from a battered leather pouch. It was a little habit which greatly amused his family and friends. Now, these very cuttings and scraps reflect his interest and humour, without which much of the information in this book would not have been accessible. If there was a headline with a double meaning or one that could be confused with a member of the family, you could be sure that he would keep the cutting, only to donate it to the appropriate person. Actually, the bulk of his cuttings originated from Durrants Press Cuttings Service which he retained for most of his life.

When I stayed at the flat in earlier days, and was too young to explore the city on my own, he'd arrange for Miss Bird, (or 'Dickie' as she was affectionately called) to take me to see the sights of London. All the usual ones of course, Trafalgar Square, a trip on the Thames, museums and cinemas. She was always very kind to me, and I did enjoy those times. What I was completely unaware of, was that she still had her work to do back at the office, and after I had gone, she would remain to catch up, writing royalty cheques, checking that the petty cash was right and that the 'bought ledger' was up to date. I have many happy memories of those days. Later, when older and more confident, I would be allowed to wander around Bloomsbury and the West End on my own, visiting news cinemas or killing time until lunch, when Michael would include me with his guests.

But although I was enjoying the atmosphere of 26, Bob Lusty was not. Soon after the war had ended, Michael had, as I have described elsewhere, started to take a more active interest in the firm, and after his wife Edna died, he devoted all his energies to it. The company had certainly flourished during the war, due to market conditions and to Bob's tremendous efforts in actually getting books produced. There had never been a problem in selling them, which made it easy for the few travellers, who could count on a comfortable commission. Afterwards, when conditions returned to normality, and advertising and paper were no longer restricted, the way the company functioned became of concern to Michael. Bob felt that, as things were then, with satisfactory profits being made, he did not need to consult Michael on every mundane problem. He had, after all, managed to run the office successfully whilst Michael had been away. However, once Michael realised he was not being kept fully informed and that many, sometimes important items of information were not getting through, he began to resent the feeling of being an outsider. Perhaps Michael was envious of the company's success in his absence or Bob resented Michael's renewed interest in the firm. This was the beginning of the rift.

It was the little things that irritated Michael, but one of the more abrasive events had been Verschoyle's appointment which had greatly upset Bob; he thought that he had a say in the editorial control of the firm. After all, his title when he had joined the company was Editorial and Production Manager and Michael had appointed Verschoyle without any reference to him. This exacerbated the tension and matters continued to deteriorate. This and other minor things played on Michael's mind. He began to contemplate the future without Bob and called in Charles and Peter Hebdon to tell them of his forebodings. For obvious reasons, he held the meeting away from the office, at the flat in Gower Mews.

Michael explained to them that he thought Bob had 'grown too big for his boots'. After all, he only owned 10 per cent of the share equity whilst Michael had ninety per cent. The lack of communication and his insular attitude had become unacceptable to Michael and his future with the Company was now uncertain.

From Bob's viewpoint, he felt thoroughly ignored by the way Michael had conducted his negotiations with Illustrated Newspapers as there was no 'consultation'. But in his position, Michael may not have wanted to consider consultation anyway. Meanwhile, Bob had been attracted to Messrs Hutchinson and negotiations had been taking place. They offered an opportunity that he could not refuse, and when he left shortly after this, neither he, nor Michael, were on speaking terms.

It was at least a year before they were seen talking in public again – and that was at a W. H. Smith's party where Michael went up to him to shake him by the hand and wish him well. Bob was somewhat cool in his reaction as he thought it was pretentious, and didn't respond.

The Company continued to prosper, producing books which were to rank as 'best sellers'. Many publishers claim to have 'best sellers' on their lists and it is a much-abused term. Michael was brave enough to publicly state what he considered the qualifications to be, for one of his books to rank as a 'best seller'.

When the Company celebrated its twenty-first anniversary he issued a statement on the subject, which took the form of a trade and press advertisement – here is a section of it:

> What is the value – to the reader and author – of an imprint? What makes for success in publishing? In our view, a publisher is not to be congratulated on a massive output. There are too many books – or rather too many bad books . . .

> . . . the firm of Michael Joseph has restricted its output to an average of fewer than fifty new books a year. We have had our share of failures, but on this occasion may we perhaps mention a few books which have evidently given pleasure to readers.

> The term 'best seller' can mean anything. By our definition (a sale of over 50,000 in the original edition) we have 42 to our credit, an average of two a year. Biggest successes were *How Green Was My Valley, The Snow Goose, One Pair of Hands,* and *One Pair of Feet* and, since the war, the *Hornblower* stories, *Bhowani Junction, Doctor in the House* and Richard Gordon's other books. Our sales of these total over three million copies.

> Authors "discovered" by the firm include Monica Dickens, Paul Gallico, Richard Gordon, Richard Llewellyn, and John Masters. We also publish for H. E. Bates, Vicki Baum, Joyce Cary, Henry Cecil, Clemence Dane, C. S. Forester, Geoffrey Household, Doris Lessing, E. S. Turner, V. Sackville-West and other distinguished writers.

> We do not pursue "best sellers", although they are always welcome. We are (in one sense of the word) amateur publishers whose biggest satisfaction is the discovery of new talent and the progress, in reputation and sales, of our authors.

Forty-two best sellers of quality and literary merit in twenty-one years – a remarkable achievement indeed. I should imagine that this is a performance that has probably not been achieved by any other firm then, or since.

Of course there were many celebrations that year and the event was recorded in numerous ways. One of the opportunities that Michael had, was to write an article to appear in the *Spectator*. He was quick to acknowledge that he owed Victor Gollancz 'an unpayable debt' for the knowledge he had gained from him about publishing. Well it was now easy to say that, having made the company one of the most successful in Bloomsbury.

He took the opportunity to review the events of the past years; a pleasant and unique moment to savour. He went on to comment about the element of 'good luck'. Those envious of his successes would say that he had much too much of that thing called luck. Others commented that he had very good 'judgement'. Well, on that point he remarked, in an article for the *Spectator:*

Good judgement? I suppose that is needed, too; but, like good writing, its importance is exaggerated. Some excellent judges have failed as publishers, just as many authors have failed who can write angelically. [If you believe that successful authors *write* well, read some recent best sellers.] It is not false modesty on my part to say categorically that to make the grade a publisher needs, above all else, thumping good luck . . .

You can back your judgement by taking on authors who have so far failed. And you can look for new talent, which without the magnetism of good luck is likely to be as unrewarding as hunting needles in haystacks . . .

You may pick the right authors, but all the publishing effort in the world will not put them on the map unless they produce saleable books. Some authors do not mature for years: others dwindle to nothing. When you back a winner you can congratulate yourself – but if you have any sense you will give the credit to good timing rather than good judgement. (5.4.57)

Soon after this statement was issued, Michael's health deteriorated drastically – it was that dreaded ulcer again. Although he was never a very fit man, when he was ill, at least he had in Anthea the comfort of an exceptionally able wife. She possessed such tremendous energy; after a day's work, she would rush about, fussing over his meals, whilst ensuring that all the animals were well looked after, and yet she still found time to listen to all her friends and look after her children. She really did care for Michael and went out of her way to ensure that he had every creature comfort. Three years earlier they had enjoyed a wonderful and relaxing cruise to America on *The Queen Elizabeth,* so once he was on the road to better health she suggested that they went on another such cruise.

Michael had made a note about that earlier voyage. He and Anthea had both found their fellow-passengers on the first class deck less than interesting. Michael was not one to feel superior by travelling first class, it was simply a case of appreciating creature comforts. Straying down to the second class deck one evening, they discovered that passengers there were more entertaining, and conversationally more stimulating, so for the return voyage, they travelled second class to capitalise on their finding.

Thus, for his convalescence they travelled this way again, hoping to make many more new friends. They entered several of the ship's competitions and between them they managed to win several of the literary quiz contests. Voyages aboard *The Queen Elizabeth* were fun and their egos nicely massaged. He had time to reflect on his son Stephen who had just returned from a year at Iowa University. There, he had witnessed how effective theatre in the round had been and since he had returned, had introduced this medium to theatre-goers in England. Stephen, Michael used to say, had already become an accomplished theatre director but perhaps the achievement that he was most proud to share in, was Stephen's use of this medium to show the work of new playrights. It was a strikingly successful idea; one of the new playrights was none other than Alan Ayckbourn.

When they finally returned to Browns Farm, they were greeted by a very worried Kitty Millar, who had been looking after his cat, Binks. By this time Binks was very old and Kitty knew that he was not well. Knowing how much Michael loved him, she was terrified that he would die before Michael returned home. Binks survived his illness but old age finally overtook him and Christmas was not quite the same that year. Kitty's visit to Browns Farm was of course to bring Michael up to date with all the important things that had been happening whilst he was away. There was a huge pile of letters to answer. So the library door was shut for several hours and no interruptions were allowed. He found it difficult to concentrate – for he was still elated from the voyage. Michael broke off from the task of dictating to go and sit at the piano in the old lounge and play the popular melody of the day – *Island in the Sun,* no doubt trying to prolong the happy atmosphere of that voyage. It was such an anti-climax to be home.

Back in the swing of things again, he soon sought out his friends at the Savage Club again. Michael was always a good listener and enjoyed the jokes that were retold in the bar. One occasion which Alan Wykes, the club's secretary for twenty years, remembers Michael enjoying a mighty chuckle with Eric Robinson, the musician, who told the tale of the 'childless couple' ... 'they went to see their local doctor, blood samples were taken and they were told to return in a week, which they did. He was very solemn. "I'm afraid you'll never have any children," he told them. Then, to the man, "You've got too much sugar in your blood" – and to the woman, "And you've got too much albumen in yours." And to both, solemnly, "No, I'm afraid you'll never have children; but you could make some fabulous meringues".'

But the conversation wasn't always humorous. Alan Wykes, was deep in a lively conversation with John Pudney one evening when Michael and Macdonald Hastings joined them. All they could talk about that evening was salmon fishing, boring everyone around them in the process; no doubt telling a few typical fishing stories about the size of the ones that got away.

Alan Wykes, also a reader of manuscripts for the *Strand Magazine*, shared Michael's love of cats, and whenever they met they would immerse themselves, oblivious of others, swopping feline stories. Alan's appreciation for Siamese cats had followed the publication of *Charles*. He had been so touched by this emotive story that he yearned for a Siamese himself. His kitten came from Hazel Scott who was then secretary to Richard Usbourne, assistant editor of the *Strand Magazine*. She brought the kitten into their offices for Alan to collect and whilst she sat typing letters for Richard, the kitten contentedly fell asleep on her lap.

After lunch Michael and Macdonald Hastings, the editor, returned to conduct a lengthy meeting in Mac's office. Outside, Mac's secretary, Angela Mack, told Alan that the visitor was none other than Michael Joseph, and invited him to introduce his 'thirty bob' kitten to Michael. When their meeting broke up, she got Mac to introduce Alan who proudly showed Michael his new-found friend but the kitten was now running amok, chasing a ball of string and getting in everyone's way. Office colleagues were astonished to see these two grown men on hands and knees, playing with the kitten, and completely disturbing the business atmosphere. Mac watched patiently for a time, but eventually threw up his arms in despair and disappeared back into his office! Alan reminded Michael of this incident, when they met again after his return from America, but by this time the kitten had become a fully grown cat and a subject that Alan would bore everybody about, except Michael.

*   *   *

In previous years Michael had observed that the production costs were increasing more rapidly than retail prices. It was hardly surprising that on 3 August when *The Bookseller* published statistics showing that the average price of books had fallen, Michael took exception to the editor's presentation and conclusions. This was, incidentally, the last (and well-recorded) row that Michael had before he died.

The row began with statistics for the first six months of 1957 recording that the average price for all titles published was 16s 7½d. This compared with 17s 3½d for the previous six months and 18s 2d for the same period in the previous year. These led the editor to comment that 'The reduction in the average price, at a time when the standard general book is manifestly going up in price, is a reflection of the rapidly increasing output of inexpensive paperbacks, both new books as well as reprints.' Michael was really incensed about the confusing presentation of these figures.

The evidence of his first broadside was a letter to *The Times* following that paper's article, 'The L. s. d. of Bookbuying', pointing out that the figures in *The Bookseller* were unintentionallly deceptive, for they included every title, especially all the cheap reprints in paperback form. Michael argued that the figures would make more sense if titles selling at less than 2/6d and over 30 shilling were excluded. He knew from the records kept by his own company that cloth-bound novels were definitely increasing in price, a fact which he said benefited both the author and bookseller.

Edmond Segrave rushed into print to defend his case and *The Times* published his reply the following week, preceding his own editorial article. He pointed out that it was the significant increase in paperback titles that had influenced the average. To exclude those Michael suggested from the monthly list of titles published would result in 'scarcely more than half the titles surviving'. He then sniped 'Since – and this should hardly be a matter of surprise – the firm over which he presides publishes books only within the price limits he considers suitable for "realistic" computation, it is obviously a suitable candidate for examination.' He claimed that for the first six months of 1957 the average price of the Company's titles was 14s 4d, for the previous six months 14s 10d and 15s 4d for the same period in the previous year. Further, Michael was, he thought, only referring to novels which were hardly reflective of the overall position. (advantage, Segrave.)

Michael's reply courtesy of *The Times* and not *The Bookseller*, was to pose the question, 'What we all want to know is whether the price of new books is increasing?' He also argued that Segrave's statistics were incomplete and misleading for they excluded the output of the country's largest publisher, *Her Majesty's Stationery Office*. Having reminded the readers of this he went on to state that his company had published twenty-one titles outside his suggested parameters on price and had at least five titles selling well at 1s 3d up to 3s 6d. (advantage Michael.)

He then sent a letter to Segrave for publication, defending his citing of novels and adding that non-fiction titles had also increased in price. Whitaker's Almanack, he noted, had increased from 15s to 18s 6d in the previous three years. It was undesirable and dangerous to create the impression that books were not increasing in price. Averages need not be misleading.

He had a point, but then so did Edmond Segrave. Today the figures avoid this issue.

*   *   *

In the company's first fifty years, luck, flair and good organisation have been the basis of successful publishing. The company has not only survived, where others have perished, but it has continued to bring new authors of a high standard and published, as Michael once said, 'books that *deserve* to be published'. The traditions (for that is what they were) that he instigated and nurtured, have been upheld and even been improved upon. The reputation for publishing sound novels continues. The discerning reader can be assured that if Michael Joseph has published a book, it is well worth reading.

Epilogue

Well, should Michael be remembered as just a publisher? Clearly his name is best associated with the publishing operation, but now that you have read this book I hope that you have been surprised and delighted at his diverse talents.

One of the criticisms of this biography is that there is little emotion in it. Did I really know the man? It is a fair remark, for, dying as he did when I was only eighteen meant that I had seen comparatively little of him, having spent most of that time away at boarding schools. We all see our parents in a different light.

To me, he never seemed to have the time to enjoy the normal family fun. He was always busy doing one thing or another. However, reflecting back over those last few years of his life, he was very positive about the practical matters of finance, trusts, and taxation. During the long gestation of this book, I have often mused how different it would all have been, had he lived on past the age of sixty. Those are just my thoughts. His legacies were much more than financial. In the first place there is the company.

His widow, Anthea went on to maintain the firm as a leader in the publishing field and earning, in her own right, the accolades due to a successful publisher. She pursued her work with complete dedication and, rather like Michael, went out of her way to be helpful and encouraging to new authors: a practice learned from Michael, perhaps. History records that she was instrumental in nurturing Dick Francis, James Heriott, Stan Barstow, James Baldwin, H. E. Bates, Alun Richards and Julian Rathbone. They will forever remember her efforts, but sadly she too, died far too young.

The company went on from strength to strength, though passing from the *The Illustrated Papers Group* to *The Thomson Organisation* in 1960. For the fiftieth anniversary the company produced another special anniversary book, *At the Sign of the Mermaid,* to mark the occasion. Many well-known authors contributed but more importantly, several colleagues of Michael's and Anthea's contributed too. Their memories are a tribute to the company's achievements.

Today, Michael Joseph Limited looks forward to a new era under the ownership of *Penguin Books*. If any historian, were to trace the company's full history in detail they would find *At the Sign of the Mermaid* an invaluable source of information.

Then there is his family which for the most part, he never saw grow up. Leslie, now retired from civil engineering, lives happily up in Motherwell, Scotland. Shirley, who now prefers to be known by her other name, Diana, maintains a farm in Suffolk. Hugh has inherited his father's flair and enthusiasm for the Turf and combines this with journalism, whilst his sister, Charlotte, lives quietly in Colchester. For myself, I have been happily engaged in the printing industry for the last twenty-six years but now have publishing interests as well. The family has grown for in all, there are now ten grandchildren. Who knows, there might well be another creative publisher amongst us?

Michael was a man who, in his lifetime, played many parts – but above all, he enjoyed life to the full.

Bibliography

Unless specified by a date, the publications listed are monthly, but in some cases, only the year of publication is known.

DATE	PUBLICATION/PUBLISHER	TITLE	SERIES/COMMENT
1916	Daily Express	The M.G.C. Wall of Defence	World War I account
30 July 1916	Daily Express	The Man Behind The Gun	World War I account
July 1916	Unknown	Mametz Wood	World War I account
10 March 1919	Evening News	Spies in Many Guises	World War I account
22 November 1920	The Globe	Books & the War	
1921	Family Reading	The Rise of the Cinema	Published circa 1921
5 February 1921	John O'London's Weekly	Gilbert Frankau & his New Romance	
5 March 1921	John O'London's Weekly	The Romance of Rider Haggard	
3 May 1921	Daily Graphic	Miss Winifred Graham (Mrs Cory)	Appreciation of her work
May 1921	Popular View Weekly	Books to Read	Reviews 'Love-A-Duck' by Stacy Aumonier
1921	Daily Graphic	Col. Arthur Lynch	Review of his book, 'O'Rourke The Great'
October 1923	Hutchinson & Co	Short Story Writing for Profit	At 6 shillings (6/-)
January 1924	Smart Set	What the Smart Set is Reading	
May 1924	Nth Staffs. Labour News	The Wonders of Wembley	
June 1924	Hutchinson's Magazine	The Yellow Cat	Short story
12 October 1924	Sunday Times	Some Piquant People	Review of Lincoln Springfield's book
October 1924	Hutchinson & Co	Journalism for Profit	At 6 shillings (6/-)
December 1924	The Smart Set	Catticism	Appreciation of cats
January 1925	The Writer	IV The Dialogue	Series: How to write Short Stories
January 1925	Smart Set	The Younger De-Generation	Contemporary review of society
February 1925	The Writer	V Composition	Series: How to write Short Stories
February 1925	Hutchinson's Magazine	Joseph Conrad	
February 1925	The Writer	The Author's Friend	Series: How to write Short Stories
April 1925	The Writer	VII Climax	Series: How to write Short Stories
May 1925	The Writer	VIII Style	Series: How to write Short Stories
May 1925	Hutchinson's Magazine	Close Pals	Interview with Sir P. Gibbs & C. Hamilton

DATE	PUBLICATION/ PUBLISHER	TITLE	SERIES/COMMENT
June 1925	The Writer	IX Types of Magazine Story	Series: How to write Short Stories
June 1925	Smart Set	Our Sex Novelists	Contemporary Review
August 1925	The Writer	XI Selling the MS	Series: How to write Short Stories
17 October 1925	Pictorial Magazine	The Last Chance	About horseracing, & the Cesarewitch Race
October 1925	The Writer	I The Field for the Freelance	Series: Practical Journalism [2]
October 1925	Hutchinson & Co	The Commercial Side of Literature	At 7/6d
November 1925	The Writer	II News: The Foundation of Journalism	Series: Practical Journalism [2]
7 November 1925	T. P. & Cassell's Weekly	Hints on Craftsmanship: No 1	On Journalism
14 November 1925	T. P. & Cassell's Weekly	How to Write for Magazines	
21 November 1925	T. P. & Cassell's Weekly	What Novelists Earn	
28 November 1925	T. P. & Cassell's Weekly	Young Author's First Novel	
5 December 1925	T. P. & Cassell's Weekly	Serial Film and Play	
12 December 1925	T. P. & Cassell's Weekly	Commerce & Literature	
21 December 1925	Daily Express	The Next Best Seller	
22 December 1925	Sunday Express	Few New Novelists	Reviews contemporary novelists
23 December 1925	Pioneer Allahabad	Few New Novelists	
23 December 1925	Ceylon Observer	Serial Film and Play	
December 1925	Hutchinson & Co	How To Write a Short Story	At 3/6d
December 1925	The Writer	III The Newspaper Article	Series: Practical Journalism [2]
1925	Hutchinson's Magazine	Gilbert Frankau	Interviewed in 1925
23 January 1926	Cape Argus	The Next Best Seller	
January 1926	The Writer	IV Pictorial Journalism	Series: Practical Journalism [2]
6 February 1926	Adelaide Register	Novelist's Earnings	
February 1926	The Writer	V Publicity and Propaganda	Series: Practical Journalism [2]
April 1926	The Writer	VII Advanced Journalism (contd)	Series: Practical Journalism [2]
June 1926	The Writer	The £ s d of Journalism	Series: Practical Journalism [2]
9 August 1926	Daily Express	What Authors Earn	Referred to 'as a world expert'
26 August 1926	Daily Express	Smoonie	Short story
28 August 1926	Daily Express	Short Story	
October 1926	The Writer	I The Scope of the Serial	
October 1926	Strand Magazine	A Splash of Publicity	Short Story
26 November 1926	Cape Argus	What Authors Earn	Article
November 1926	The Writer	II The Serial Market	Series: How to write Serial Fiction [3]
December 1926	Amplion Magazine	The Effect on Dramatists	Article
1926	New Coterie	Rouge et Noir	See footnote [1]

DATE	PUBLICATION/ PUBLISHER	TITLE	SERIES/COMMENT
1926	Pictorial Magazine	The Last Chance	See footnote [1]
1926	Hutchinson's Magazine	Them Queer Chaps	See footnote [1]
1926	New Magazine	To Let	See footnote [1]
1926	Woman	The Melody of Love	See footnote [1]
15 January 1927	Woman's Weekly	Valley of Love	Music by M. Joseph, words by Draycot Dell
January 1927	The Writer	III Editorial Prejudices	Series: How to write Serial Fiction [3]
March 1927	The Writer	IV The First Instalment	Series: How to write Serial Fiction [3]
April 1927	The Writer	V The Serial & The Drama	Series: How to write Serial Fiction [3]
May 1927	The Writer	VI The First Instalment Again	Series: How to write Serial Fiction [3]
June 1927	The Writer	VII Crook, Detective & Mystery Stories	Series: How to write Serial Fiction [3]
July 1927	The Writer	VIII Studying the Woman Reader	Series: How to write Serial Fiction [3]
September 1927	The Writer	IX The Serial Writer's Market	Series: How to write Serial Fiction [3]
December 1927	The Writer	I The Melody of Love	Series: Short Stories in the Making [4]
9 December 1927	Daily Express	Too Many New Novels	Comments: average earnings are £25
10 December 1927	T. P. & Cassell's Weekly	The Neglect of Christmas	
1927	The Strand Magazine	A Splash of Publicity	See footnote [1]
1927	Royal Magazine	C'est La Guerre	See footnote [1]
1927	Pictorial Magazine	The Pigeon	See footnote [1]
1927	Mystery-Story Magazine	The Yellow Cat	See footnote [1]
1927	All-Story Magazine	Revelation	See footnote [1]
February 1928	The Writer	II The Plane Tree	(by B. Trask – in The Women's Journal) [4]
February 1928	Hutchinson & Co	How To Write Serial Fiction	Written with Marten Cumberland at 6/-d
February 1928	Hutchinson & Co	The Magazine Story	At 6/-d
March 1928	The Writer	III A Night in March	(by S. Jepson – in the London Magazine) [4]
23 March 1928	T. P. & Cassell's Weekly	Romance of Newsgetting	
7 April 1928	John O'London's Weekly	What Do Editors Want	
April 1928	The Writer	IV Flowers are so Dear	(by P Travers – in Red Magazine) [4]
9 April 1928	Good Housekeeping	Wanted – New Women Writers	
1 May 1928	Bookseller	Some Experiences of a Literary Agent	Lecture: Foyles Bookshop 7.5.28
26 May 1928	London Calling	Celebrities on Toast	About Michael Arlen
May 1928	The Writer	V Under Suspicion	(by B. L. Jacot – in the London Magazine)[4]
June 1928	The Writer	VI Kissing-Crust	(by A. G. Greenwood – in the New Magazine)[4]
June 1928	The Writer	The Magazine Story	
July 1928	The Writer	VII Temporary Insanity	(by John Talland – in Pall Mall) [4]

Bibliography

DATE	PUBLICATION/ PUBLISHER	TITLE	SERIES/COMMENT
August 1928	The Writer	VIII To Let: Furnished	(by Edward Hope – in Grand Magazine) [4]
24 September 1928	Daily Mail	Appreciation of Cats	
October 1928	The Writer	X The Cabin Party	(by Arthur Mills – in Pall Mall) [4] [5]
October 1928	The Bookman	Sydney Horler	An appreciation of a 'thriller' writer
21 October 1928	Sunday Dispatch	Book Censorship	His statement included in article
15 December 1928	Daily Express	Kittens are in Season	Article
December 1928	The Writer	XI By Accident	(by H. Cleaver – in Hutchinson's Magazine)[4]
4 January 1929	Daily Express	Minna's Husbands	Account of his cat, Minna Minna Mowbray
January 1929	The Writer	XII Sea-Change	(by E. Robertson – in Cassell's Magazine) [4]
16 February 1929	Daily Express	As Between Cat and Dog	Account of his cat Minna Minna Mowbray and Peter
February 1929	Woman	The Eye of the Lamb	Short story
February 1929	The Writer	XIII Pot-Pourri	(by D. Rogers – in Home Magazine) [4]
23 March 1929	T. P.'s & Cassell's Weekly	Romance of Newsgetting	Press censorship
March 1929	The Writer	XIV The Black Spoke	(by W. Westrup – in Red Magazine) [4]
April 1929	Hutchinson & Co	The Autobiography of a Journalist	At 7/6d
April 1929	The Writer	XV The Pet Shop	(by B. Perowne – in the Royal Magazine) [4]
May 1929	Hutchinson's Magazine	Silly, Loving, Little Molly	Short story
May 1929	The Writer	I An Introductory Survey	Series: The Changing Free-lance Market
June 1929	The Bookman	P. G. Wodehouse	an appreciation of his work
June 1929	The Writer	II The Rise of the 'Talkies'	Series: The Changing Free-lance Market
July 1929	The Writer	III The Bogey of Technique	Series: The Changing Free-lance Market
19 August 1929	Daily Express	So That is What The War was Like	Penned as 'An Ex-Soldier'
August 1929	The Writer	IV The American Market	Series: The Changing Free-lance Market
3 September 1929	Daily Dispatch	Scissors – A Memory	World War I memory
September 1929	The Writer	V The American Market (concluded)	Series: The Changing Free-lance Market
October 1929	The Writer	VI Writing for The Wireless	Series: The Changing Free-lance Market
November 1929	The Writer	VII The Future of the Magazine Story	Series: The Changing Free-lance Market
31 December 1929	Daily Express	A Cat and Dog Argument	Written with John Scott
December 1929	The Writer	VIII The 'First Novel'	Series: The Changing Free-lance Market
January 1930	Bonnier's Nouvell	Liil Foralskade Lolly	Short story in Swedish
January 1930	The Writer	IX The 'First Novel' (concluded)	Series: The Changing Free-lance Market

DATE	PUBLICATION/ PUBLISHER	TITLE	SERIES/COMMENT
13 February 1930	Daily Express	Anyhow, Cats are Safe	About cats cleanliness
February 1930	The Writer	X Syndication	Series: The Changing Free-lance Market
26 March 1930	The Queen	Turn of the Wheel	Short story
29 March 1930	Answers	They're Off	Penned as 'Goodwood'
17 April 1930	World Press News	The Author & The Lending Library	
April 1930	The Writer	XI Climbing the Free-lance Ladder	Series: The Changing Free-lance Market
7 June 1930	Pictorial Magazine	The £ s d of the Derby	Penned as 'Goodwood'
June 1930	The Writer	XII Outlining the Free-lance Policy	Series: The Changing Free-lance Market
11 August 1930	Daily Mail	The Cigarette Game	Family game
August 1930	The Writer	XIII The Novel Market	Series: The Changing Free-lance Market
September 1930	Hutchinson & Co	Complete Writing For Profit	At 10/6d. Compendium of first five books
9 October 1930	World Press News	The Free-lance Journalist	
October 1930	The Writer	XIV What Publishers Want	Series: The Changing Free-lance Market
November 1940	The Quiver	Cats I Have Known	
November 1930	The Writer	XV The Literary Agent	Series: The Changing Free-lance Market
November 1930	Geoffrey Bles	Cats Company	
6 December 1930	Pictorial Weekly	Take Care of Your Cat	'Expert advice' about domestic pets
December 1930	The Writer	XVI The Importance of Words	Series: The Changing Free-lance Market
1930	Covici Friede	Foujita – Book of Cats	Prose by Michael Joseph
26 January 1931	Evening Standard	The Cat is in Fashion	Review; M. Joseph has kept 100 cats ...
12 February 1931	Everyman	The Literary Market	
28 March 1931	Daily Express	Charles: From Siam	Refers to his own cat, Charles
March 1931	The Writer	XVII The Truth About Film Rights	Series: The Changing Free-lance Market
29 June 1931	New York American	Bob Sherriff, A. J. Cronin	Series: Gossip From Overseas[8]
5 August 1931	Evening Standard	Your Cat	Why not take your cat on holiday
28 August 1931	New York American	Bernard Shaw, D. H. Lawrence	Series: Gossip From Overseas [8]
7 September 1931	New York American	Noël Coward, Mary Webb, Thomas Moult	Series: Gossip From Overseas [8]
23 September 1931	New York American	Sir Hall Caine	Series: Gossip From Overseas [8]
5 October 1931	New York American	Bruce Marshall, Ellen Terry	Series: Gossip From Overseas [8]
October 1931	Faber & Faber	This Writing Business	
November 1931	Good Housekeeping	I'd Rather have a Cat	Sketches by J. H. Dowd
1 January 1932	Herald Examiner	Michael Arlen	Series: Gossip From Overseas [9]
18 January 1932	New York American	Shaw Desmond	Series: Gossip From Overseas [8]
6 February 1932	New York American	Ursula Bloom	Series: Gossip From Overseas [8]

DATE	PUBLICATION/ PUBLISHER	TITLE	SERIES/COMMENT
17 February 1932	Herald Examiner	Lady Duff Gordon, Ursula Bloom	Series: Gossip From Overseas [9]
18 February 1932	New York American	Mark Hambourg, Lady Dorothy Mills	Series: Gossip From Overseas [8]
7 March 1932	New York American	Edgar Wallace	Series: Gossip From Overseas [8]
14 March 1932	New York American	Hessell Tiltman	Series: Gossip From Overseas [8]
26 March 1932	Answers	Which is the Softest Job	
11 April 1932	New York American	E. Arnot Robertson	
25 April 1932	New York American	J. A. Spender, C. Asquith, Sir P. Gibbs	Series: Gossip From Overseas [8]
30 April 1932	Answers	Gambles in Horseflesh	Penned under 'Goodwood'
7 May 1932	New York American	Lloyd George, Rudyard Kipling	Series: Gossip From Overseas [8]
May 1932	Strand Magazine	The Beauty of Cats	With many photos
25 July 1932	New York American	Sir Philip Gibbs	Series: Gossip From Overseas [8]
15 August 1932	New York American	Ethel Mannin, Major Yeats-Brown	Series: Gossip From Overseas [8]
August 1932	Woman's Journal	Cats in Comedy	Drawings by Audrey Hammond
27 September 1932	New York American	Bernard Shaw, Noël Coward	Series: Gossip From Overseas [8]
September 1932	The Writer	An Article With A Moral	
10 October 1932	New York American	Edward Sackville-West	Series: Gossip From Overseas [8]
November 1932	The Writer	Your First Novel	
1932	Pearson's Magazine	Just A Matter of Flannels	Written with Selwyn Jepson
1932	Geoffrey Bles	Puss In Books	Edited with Elizabeth Drew
5 January 1933	New York American	Francis Yeats-Brown, Alec Waugh	Series: Gossip From Overseas [8] [10]
10 January 1933	New York American	Emil Ludwig, Mark Hambourg, James Joyce	Series: Gossip From Overseas [8]
17 January 1933	New York American	Cecil Roberts	Series: Gossip From Overseas [8]
24 January 1933	New York American	Daphne du Maurier	Series: Gossip From Overseas [8]
10 February 1933	Evening Standard	Rouge et Noir	Short story
13 February 1933	New York American	Dorothy Whipple	Series: Gossip From Overseas [8] [10]
February 1933	The Writer	An Author and his Work	
6 March 1933	New York American	Dr Axel Munthe, Compton MacKenzie	Series: Gossip From Overseas [8] [10]
March 1933	Jarrolds	Heads or Tails	Written with Selwyn Jepson, at 7/6d
23 March 1933	World Press News	Why Employ a Literary Agency?	From an interview

DATE	PUBLICATION/ PUBLISHER	TITLE	SERIES/COMMENT
March 1933	Jarrolds	Collection of Short Stories	Edited by Michael Joseph
April 1933	The Writer	Why Not Collaborate	
23 June 1933	New York American	Arnold Bennett, J. C. Masterman	Series: Gossip From Overseas [8]
6 June 1933	New York American	George Moore	Series: Gossip From Overseas [8] [10]
12 June 1933	New York American	Elinour Mordaunt, Evelyn Waugh	Series: Gossip From Overseas [8] [10]
13 June 1933	New York American	Karel and Josef Capek	Series: Gossip From Overseas [8]
15 June 1933	New York American	Vita Sackville-West, Guy Chapman	Series: Gossip From Overseas [8]
1 July 1933	Answers	What They are Like at Home	Arlen, Noël Coward, Bloom, Mannin, & Sherriff
8 July 1933	New York American	Sir John Barrie, Noël Coward	Series: Gossip From Overseas [8]
14 July 1933	New York American	Cecil Scott Forester	Series: Gossip From Overseas [8]
11 August 1933	New York American	Bernard Shaw, H. G. Wells, Dorothy Sayers	Series: Gossip From Overseas [8]
22 August 1933	New York American	Selwyn Jepson	Series: Gossip From Overseas [8]
30 August 1933	New York American	Hessell Tiltman	Series: Gossip From Overseas [8]
13 October 1933	New York American	Mary Lutyens, D. H. Lawrence	Series: Gossip From Overseas [8] [10]
14 October 1933	Pictorial Weekly	Peter in Pursuit	Short Story
14 October 1933	Pearson's Weekly	The Yellow Cat	Short Story
23 October 1933	New York American	Lloyd George, Lord Grey, Helen Simspon	Series: Gossip From Overseas [8] [10]
4 November 1933	New York American	John Drinkwater, Somerset Maughan	Series: Gossip From Overseas [8] [10]
4 November 1933	Pictorial Weekly	My Struggle by A. Hitler & The Gospel of Happiness by J. C. Stobbert	Series: Book Reviews by M. Joseph [7]
7 November 1933	New York American	Louis Golding	Series: Gossip From Overseas [8]
11 November 1933	Pictorial Weekly	Ivory Poaching & Cannibals in Africa by J. T. Muirhead, & A Modern Sinbad (Anon)	Series: Book Reviews by M. Joseph [7]
18 November 1933	Pictorial Weekly	Britain Holds On 1917, 1918 by C. Playne World Panorama 1918-33 by G. Seldes	Series: Book Reviews by M. Joseph [7]
18 November 1933	New York American	Winston Churchill, Rose Macaulay	Series: Gossip From Overseas [8]
25 November 1933	Pictorial Weekly	Edward Wilson of the Antarctic by G. Seaver, & Mary of Nazareth by M. Boredon	Series: Book Reviews by M. Joseph [7]

DATE	PUBLICATION/ PUBLISHER	TITLE	SERIES/COMMENT
2 December 1933	Pictorial Weekly	Moscow 1911-33 by A. Monkhouse, & Excitement by S. Horler	Series: Book Reviews by M. Joseph [7]
9 December 1933	Pictorial Weekly	The Real Detective by G. Dilnot, & Escape by F. Yeats-Brown	Series: Book Reviews by M. Joseph [7]
16 December 1933	Pictorial Weekly	The Rowland Johns Dog Book & HRH edited by E. Middleton	Series: Book Reviews by M. Joseph [7]
16 December 1933	New York American	Louis Golding, Margaret Kennedy	Series: Gossip From Overseas [8] [10]
23 December 1933	Pictorial Weekly	A Thatched Roof by B. Nichols, & The Psalms for Modern Life, with A. Wragg's illustrations	Series: Book Reviews by M. Joseph [7]
29 December 1933	New York American	John Holyroyd-Reece, Sir P. Hastings	Series: Gossip From Overseas [8]
30 December 1933	Pictorial Weekly	First Over Everest by J. Buchan, & Land of the Rainbow by V.Mason	Series: Book Reviews by M. Joseph [7]
1933	Jarrolds	Collection of Short Stories	Edited by Michael Joseph
6 January 1934	Pictorial Weekly	Christopher Stone Speaking, & By Air by Sir H. Britain. Also T. C. Bridges & H. Tiltman's A Romance of Motoring	Series: Book Reviews by M. Joseph [7]
13 January 1934	Pictorial Weekly	The Cross of Peace by Sir P. Gibbs, & Dawn of Darkness by B. Olden	Series: Book Reviews by M. Joseph [7]
20 January 1934	Pictorial Weekly	Nijinsky by Mrs R. Nijinsky, & A. Million Miles in Sail by Captain C. C. Dixon	Series: Book Reviews by M. Joseph [7]
27 January 1934	Pictorial Weekly	Fugitive From Justice	Murder Story
27 January 1934	Pictorial Weekly	Mad Mike by G. Goodchild, & All About Fish by W. S. Berridge	Series: Book Reviews by M. Joseph [7]
3 February 1934	Pictorial Weekly	Slum by H. Marshall, & A. Gallery of Women by J. W. Drawbell	Series: Book Reviews by M. Joseph [7]
10 February 1934	Pictorial Weekly	The Forest of Adventure by Dr R. L. Ditmars, & Faint Harmony by V. Ellis	Series: Book Reviews by M. Joseph [7]
24 February 1934	Pictorial Weekly	The New Spain by Sir G. Young, & T. P. O'Connor by H. Fyfe	Series: Book Reviews by M. Joseph [7]
3 March 1934	Pictorial Weekly	Spies I Knew by Mrs McKenna, & Wife for Sale by K. Norris	Series: Book Reviews by M. Joseph [7]

DATE	PUBLICATION/ PUBLISHER	TITLE	SERIES/COMMENT
10 March 1934	Pictorial Weekly	Wonderful London To-day by J. A. Jones, & A Tale of Two Robins by G. J. Renier	Series: Book Reviews by M. Joseph [7]
17 March 1934	Pictorial Weekly	Twin Bedsteads by N. Godbear, & I Was A German by E. Toller	Series: Book Reviews by M. Joseph [7]
24 March 1934	Pictorial Weekly	People Worth talking About by C. Hamilton, & Germany, Prepare for War by E. Banse	Series: Book Reviews by M. Joseph [7]
31 March 1934	Answers	No Hair – No Teeth – No Nose	Book Review Creation's Doom by D. Papp
31 March 1934	Pictorial Weekly	Express to Hollywood by V. McLaglen, & Short Stories: How to Write them by C. Hunt	Series: Book Reviews by M. Joseph [7]
11 April 1934	The Literary Digest	Sir Gerald du Maurier	A Pen Picture
7 April 1934	Pictorial Weekly	Lord Reading & His Cases by D. Walker-Smith	Series: Book Reviews by M. Joseph [7]
14 April 1934	Pictorial Weekly	Toads & Toad Life by J. Rostand, & Amateur Adventure by Gander & Irvin	Series: Book Reviews by M. Joseph [7]
21 April 1934	Pictorial Weekly	Crimes & Case of 1933 by R. Wild, The Crimson Jester by H. H. Dunn, & Bassett by Miss S. Gibbons	Series: Book Reviews by M. Joseph [7]
May 1934	The Writer	How American Copyright Affects British Writers	
May 1934	Cornhill Magazine	The Cat: A Question	Short Poem
2 June 1934	The Literary Digest	Noël Coward writing Autobiography	
16 June 1934	Pictorial Weekly	Famous Author – on 10/-a Week	Arlen, Wren, Priestly & Drinkwater
June 1934	The Writer	What Film Companies Really Want	
July 1934	Discovery	Play, published by Gollancz Ltd	
1 August 1934	Vogue	Gentleman from Siam	About Siamese cats
11 August 1934	The Literary Agent	A Pen Picture of Sir Gerald du Maurier	
August 1934	Woman's Journal	Charles from Siam	About Charles, his now famous cat
6 September 1934	World's Press News	Good Agents Give Authors that Upward Push	
26 September 1934	Daily Mail	My Aristocratic Cat	Siamese Cats
2 October 1934	Evening Standard	The Yellow Cat	Short story
4 October 1934	BBC	The Siamese Cat – Broadcast	President of the Siamese Cat Society
October 1934	The Writer	Today's Markets	

DATE	PUBLICATION/ PUBLISHER	TITLE	SERIES/COMMENT
8 December 1934	Pictorial Weekly	Has The Future Already Happened	Article
20 December 1934	News Chronicle	Schooling for Soldiers	Penned as 'A Parent'
1934	Cornhill Magazine	The Cat	Poem by M. Joseph
26 February 1935	Yorkshire Evening News	The Yellow Cat	
March 1935	The Writer	1 Too Perfect	(by L. Lee – in Storyteller) [6]
2 April 1935	Evening Standard	A Glass of Milk	Short story
3 April 1935	The Bookseller	The Literary Agent – His Place in the World of Books	
April 1935	The Writer	2 A Dinner of Herbs	(by N. Yates-Smith in Britannia) [6]
July 1935	The Writer	Short Stories of Today	Book reviews
4 December 1935	The Bystander	Policemen Aren't Human	Short Story. Illustrated by Stephen Spurrier
25 January 1936	Manchester Evening News	A Glass of Milk	Short Story
1 February 1936	Pearson's Weekly	A Splash of Publicity	Short story
19 February 1936	Leicester Evening Mail	A Glass of Milk	Short Story
10 April 1936	The Spectator	The Intelligence Of Cats	Article
4 July 1936	Cork Examiner	The Yellow Cat	Short Story
13 August 1936	Auckland Chronicle	The Yellow Cat	Short Story
1937	Weldons Ladies Journal	Women – You attract me most at . . .	He preferred the 20+ group
October 1938	Animals Magazine	Minna Minna Mowbray	His story about another of his cats
December 1938	Animals Magazine	About My Cats	
April 1939	The Writer	The Art of the Magazine Story	Review of Kennedy Williamson's book
14 March 1941	BBC	Pussycat-Pussycat	5.30pm Broadcast
1942	Michael Joseph Ltd	The Sword In The Scabbard	At 10/6d
1943	Michael Joseph Ltd	Charles – The Story of a Friendship	At 5/-
September 1946	BBC Book Publishing Today – Broadcast	Review in The Bookseller 12.9.46	
October 1946	A.B.G.B.I.	The Author and the Book	Lecture at Polytechnic Institute and reported in The Bookseller 24.10.46
January 1947	BBC Publishing In Britain Today – Broadcast European Service.		

DATE	PUBLICATION/PUBLISHER	TITLE	SERIES/COMMENT
28 February 1948	Time & Tide	Cats on Their Own	
3 April 1948	New Statesman & Nation	Writers and the Chancellor	Refers to author's taxation
25 September 1948	New Statesman & Nation	Publishing Slump?	
16 October 1948	Publisher's Weekly	Publishing Slump in Britain	
26 February 1949	Daily Mail	Hobby Horses	Rhona Churchill interviews M. Joseph
15 May 1949	The American Weekly	Cats Can Relax Him	About M. Joseph & his Cats
Summer 1949	The Dogs' Bulletin	Cats	Account of his own cats
1949	Allan Wingate	The Adventure of Publishing	At 8/6d
10 November 1951	Trade Circular	Novels Must Go Up In Price	
22 November 1952	Time & Tide	Notes on the Way	Review of the Book Trade
29 November 1952	Time & Tide	Notes on the Way	Review of the Book Trade
December 1952	Britain Today	The New Novel	A problem of publishing
4 May 1953	Royal Society of Arts	The Function of the Publisher	Others were Dennis Wheatley & Miss C. Foyle
9 May 1953	The Bookseller	The Novel: The Function of the Publisher	
October 1953	Faber & Faber	Best Cat Stories	Edited by M. Joseph, at 12/6d
26 April 1954	British Council	Selection of Manuscripts	
29 May 1954	Time and Tide	Notes on the Way	Science fiction and literature

These articles were published but I have not been able to ascertain the date.

	PUBLICATION/PUBLISHER	TITLE	SERIES/COMMENT
	The Royal Magazine	C'est la Guerre	Short Story, date unknown.
	Drawing & Design	Charming People in Dark Places	Arlen, and John Russell
	Woman	Why I Like Women Writers	Social Comment

[1] These stories were all published in book form in *The Magazine Story* and had been published in these named magazines before 1928. The precise publication date of these has not been established.

[2] Issues 3 and 6 are noted as missing from Michael Joseph's archives.

[3] Written with Marten Cumberland.

[4] Michael Joseph reviewed other authors' stories for The Writer in the series, Short Stories in the Making.

[5] The ninth article is missing from Michael Joseph's archives.

[6] Michael Joseph reviewed more short stories for The Writer in another series entitled, Short Stories of Today.

[7] Dates assigned to these book reviews which appeared in Pictorial Weekly, might be wrong – but all were published between 4.11.33 and 14.4.34.

[8] Gossip From Overseas, a fortnightly column in the New York American. M. Joseph wrote about authors and events in the British and European literary world, often with his opinions. Those names listed above were featured but there were many others also named in passing. A number of cuttings exist which are not dated and include Lloyd George, Alan Villiers, Robert Graves, Gilbert Frankau.

[9] Gossip From Overseas also appeared in the Herald Examiner, Chicago, in edited form.

[10] Date given is that of receipt of cutting, not publication date.

*   *   *

A number of typescripts were found in his memorabilia and *may* have been published.

Sky High	A thriller, written with W. P. Lipscomb
Second Sight	A thriller, written with W. P. Lipscomb
A London Vignette	Short story
Our Square	Short story
The Truth about Our Authors	Submitted 12 times from 22.10.24 to 16.1.25 but not published during this time
Mr Wyvis	Short story
Put A Sock In It, Bunny!	Article
Sorry I'm Late	Short story, written whilst at Curtis Brown
Leave it to me	Account of visit to New York
The Outlook for the English Novel	
Post War Reading taste	Possibly published in South Africa 1955
The Spit and Polish Brigade	Written about 1944
The Publisher's Imprint	
The Author and the Lending Library	
Review of the Arts	
Meet these Publishers	
A Diploma for New Books	
To Blurb – or Not To Blurb	

Acknowledgements

I extend my thanks to the numerous friends and colleagues, who knew, or worked with, my father. Amongst his publishing colleagues, I am fortunate to have been helped by Sir Robert Lusty and Charles Pick, both being involved from the beginning of Michael Joseph Ltd; and Tom Couper, who was the Company's accountant. Together with other associates, notably the unique and much loved Dickie Walsh, they have encouraged me to believe that the company history, though brief, is correct.

I owe a special debt to my wife Elizabeth, who has spent many hours patiently going through photographs and press cuttings. Without her help in making some form of order out of them, I'm not sure that this book would have ever been finished for it has had to be completed whilst in full time employment.

Anyone undertaking to write a book for the first time finds the task daunting, but in my case the task was made a good deal easier by the use of a word processor. With the frequent need to photocopy papers for verification by others, a copier became essential. I extend my grateful thanks to to Geoff O'Connell for his help.

Many people have been very helpful in my quest for information. My thanks to them all.

Walter Allen, Brenda Bateman, James Blyth, Alan Brooke, Christian Browning, Sheila Bush, Bryan Cartland, Ken Cundell, Jenny Dereham, Monica Dickens, Edmund Fisher, Dick Francis, Christina Foyle, K. S. Giniger, Hermione Gingold, Micky Goldhill, Livia Gollancz, Rosemary Gould, James Hadley-Chase, Juliet O'Hea, Geoffrey Hebdon, Charlotte Joseph, Hugh Joseph, Leslie Joseph, Lionel Joseph, Philip Joseph, (for the family tree), Cherry Kearton, City of London School, Michael Joseph Ltd, Kitty Millar, The Ministry of Defence, Victor Morrison, Gerald Pollinger, Reginald Pound, Diana Simmonds, Graham Smith, University College Library, University of London, Sally Whitaker, and Alan Wykes.

And I am most grateful to the many publishers who have allowed me to cite extracts about or by Michael for these have contributed to a much better description of events that occurred. In this aspect *The Bookseller* has been singularly helpful by allowing me to peruse their archives which faithfully recorded developments in the publishing world.

Other publishers and organisations that have helped include:-

The British Broadcasting Corporation for 'Cats through the Ages' and 'Charles'. Other extracts cited are reproduced by permission of the relevant publishers. These include, the Daily Express, and for the London Standard, and Evening Standard; The Daily Telegraph, and for the Morning Post; the Daily Mail, and for the News Chronicle; the Observer; the Spectator, the Times Newspapers Ltd, for the Sunday Times; the Western Mail; IPC Magazines Ltd, for Woman; the National Magazine Company for *Good Housekeeping* extract, W. G. Foyle Ltd, and Christina Foyle; *Bound To Be Read* by Sir Robert Lusty, Jonathan Cape 1975. *Random Commentary* by Dorothy Whipple, Michael Joseph 1966 by permission of David Higham Associates. *Old Maids Remember* by Angela du Maurier, Peter Davies 1966, by permission of A. M. Heath. *The Blossoming World* by H. E. Bates, Michael Joseph 1971; *Charles, The Story of a Friendship* by Michael Joseph, Michael Joseph 1943, *City of London School* by Douglas-Smith, Blackwell 1965; *City of London School Magazine 1911/12; Gollancz* by Sheila Hodges, Gollancz 1978; *Growing Pains* by Daphne du Maurier, Gollancz 1977; and by Doubleday & Co in the USA. *The Sword in the Scabbard* by Michael Joseph, Michael Joseph Ltd by permission of David Higham Associates Limited. *The World in Ripeness* by H. E. Bates – Michael Joseph 1972, (and to Laurence Pollinger Ltd and the Estate of H. E. Bates); Faber and Faber for permission to cite Sir Geoffrey Faber's article which apppeared in London Mercury in 1937. Century Hutchinson for permission to quote extracts from *Short Story Writing for Profit, Journalism for Profit, The Commercial Side of Literature* and to reproduce their contemporary advertisements. Bernard Shaw's card is illustrated by kind permission of The Society of Authors acting on behalf of the Estate of Bernard Shaw. The frontispiece illustration courtesy of Topham Picture Library

Index

Index

The Joseph Family Tree
Condensed

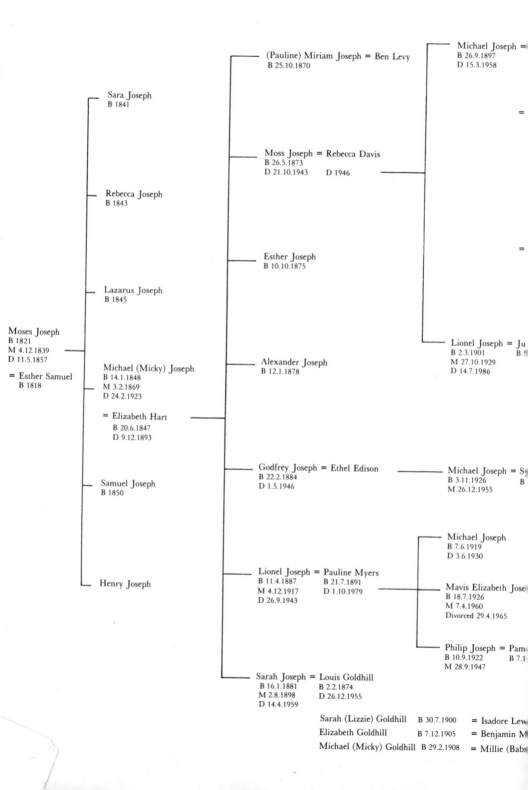

Moses Joseph
B 1821
M 4.12.1839
D 11.5.1857

= Esther Samuel
B 1818

Sara Joseph
B 1841

Rebecca Joseph
B 1843

Lazarus Joseph
B 1845

Michael (Micky) Joseph
B 14.1.1848
M 3.2.1869
D 24.2.1923

= Elizabeth Hart
B 20.6.1847
D 9.12.1893

Samuel Joseph
B 1850

Henry Joseph

(Pauline) Miriam Joseph = Ben Levy
B 25.10.1870

Moss Joseph = Rebecca Davis
B 26.5.1873
D 21.10.1943   D 1946

Esther Joseph
B 10.10.1875

Alexander Joseph
B 12.1.1878

Godfrey Joseph = Ethel Edison
B 22.2.1884
D 1.5.1946

Lionel Joseph = Pauline Myers
B 11.4.1887   B 21.7.1891
M 4.12.1917   D 1.10.1979
D 26.9.1943

Sarah Joseph = Louis Goldhill
B 16.1.1881   B 2.2.1874
M 2.8.1898   D 26.12.1955
D 14.4.1959

Michael Joseph =
B 26.9.1897
D 15.3.1958

=

=

Lionel Joseph = Ju
B 2.3.1901   B 9
M 27.10.1929
D 14.7.1986

Michael Joseph = S
B 3.11.1926   B
M 26.12.1955

Michael Joseph
B 7.6.1919
D 3.6.1930

Mavis Elizabeth Jose
B 18.7.1926
M 7.4.1960
Divorced 29.4.1965

Philip Joseph = Pam
B 10.9.1922   B 7.1
M 28.9.1947

Sarah (Lizzie) Goldhill   B 30.7.1900   = Isadore Lew
Elizabeth Goldhill   B 7.12.1905   = Benjamin M
Michael (Micky) Goldhill B 29.2.1908   = Millie (Babs